Psychiatric Disorders

To the children and families who persevere and thrive despite battling the medical conditions described in this volume.

And to our families.

P.C.M. & S.R.S.

Psychiatric Disorders

Paul C. McCabe
Steven R. Shaw

Current
Topics
and
Interventions
for
Educators

A JOINT PUBLICATION

NASP

CORWIN
A SAGE Company

For information:

Corwin
A SAGE Company
2455 Teller Road
Thousand Oaks, California 91320
(800) 233-9936
Fax: (800) 417-2466
www.corwin.com

SAGE Ltd.
1 Oliver's Yard
55 City Road
London EC1Y 1SP
United Kingdom

SAGE India Pvt. Ltd.
B 1/I 1 Mohan Cooperative
   Industrial Area
Mathura Road, New Delhi 110 044
India

SAGE Asia-Pacific Pte. Ltd.
33 Pekin Street #02-01
Far East Square
Singapore 048763

Printed in the United States of America

Library of Congress Cataloging-in-Publication Data

Psychiatric disorders : current topics and interventions for educators/[editors] Paul C. McCabe, Steven R. Shaw;
"A joint publication with the National Association of School Psychologists."
     p. cm.
Includes bibliographical references and index.
ISBN 978-1-4129-6875-1 (cloth)
ISBN 978-1-4129-6876-8 (pbk.)

   1. Educational psychology. 2. School health services. 3. Children—Mental health services. 4. Behavior disorders in children. 5. Children—Diseases—Treatment. 6. Pediatrics. I. McCabe, Paul C. II. Shaw, Steven R. III. Title.

LB1051.P7287 2010
371.7'13—dc22   2009047383

This book is printed on acid-free paper.

10   11   12   13   14   10   9   8   7   6   5   4   3   2 1

Acquisitions Editor:	Jessica Allan
Associate Editor:	Joanna Coelho
Production Editor:	Libby Larson
Copy Editor:	Paula L. Fleming
Typesetter:	C&M Digitals (P) Ltd.
Proofreader:	Theresa Kay
Indexer:	Jean Casalegno
Cover Designer:	Rose Storey

Contents

SECTION II: Psychopharmacology

Preface

This book exists for two primary reasons: (1) the incredible pressures on educators to address children's medical issues in school settings and (2) the rapid pace of news and information delivery, which often occurs despite safeguards that try to ensure credibility and verifiability. Educators are charged with making policies; differentiating instruction; providing educational accommodations; managing the physical plant; providing special education services' collaborating with families; and working with the community in response to children's medical, physical, and psychological issues. However, educators often have little training, support, or information to address these important issues. When faced with a medical question, many people (including us) turn to the Internet. Although much information from the Internet is high quality, much is not. Peer-reviewed scientific papers of high quality are often given the same weight in search engine results as advertisements for the latest snake oil. Information about medical issues is presented (1) in esoteric medical science journals with little relevance to schooling, (2) as part of encyclopedic but cursory overviews of many topics, and (3) in summarized and simplified form on Web sites with questionable accuracy and oversight. We developed this book to give support and information to educators based on a critical review of scientific research that is credible, in depth, and practical.

Psychiatric Disorders is the third book in a three-volume series titled Current Topics and Interventions for Educators. This series presents detailed reviews of recent scientific research on a variety of topics in pediatrics that are most relevant to schools today. Current Topics and Interventions for Educators is intended to provide not only detailed scientific information on pediatric issues but also glossaries of key medical terms, educational strategies, case studies, handouts for teachers and parents, and discussion questions. Readers are presented with critical reviews of scientific medical research, including discussion of controversial issues. The authors of each chapter have completed scholarly reviews of the extant research and carefully considered the quality of research design, methodology, and sampling in determining what can be considered empirically valid conclusions versus conclusions based on hyperbole, conjecture, or myth. We believe that this information will help educators address the pediatric issues that affect schoolchildren and better equip educators to discuss these issues with parents, staff, and medical teams.

This book has its origins in a regular feature in the National Association of School Psychologists (NASP) publication *Communiqué* called "Pediatric

School Psychology." We edited and published many detailed research articles that provided depth of information and critical evaluation of research to keep school psychologists current on medical knowledge that could impact their practice in the schools. We found that school psychologists shared this information with policy makers, administrators, social workers, teachers, therapists, and families. This feedback told us that there is wider audience for this information.

Educators, students, school nurses, administrators, policy makers, and school psychologists can use this book in a variety of ways. It can serve as a reference tool, textbook for a course, or a basis for continuing education activities in schools. The literature reviews are critical, challenge popular understanding, and often present controversial information. We would also like the information in this book to serve as grist for discussion and debate. More than ever, educators are charged by law, regulation, or circumstance to address medical issues despite lacking medical training. Therefore, consultation, reasoned discussion, debate, and consensus building can lead to improved educational services for children with medical and psychiatric issues.

Psychiatric Disorders is a 13-chapter volume divided into three sections: (1) neuropsychiatric conditions affecting schoolchildren, (2) psychopharmacology, and (3) dietary control and supplement use. Section I on neuropsychiatric issues affecting schoolchildren includes some of the psychiatric issues receiving the most media coverage and affecting the most children and addresses the questions about psychiatric issues that educators often hear. These conditions include Tourette syndrome, bipolar/mood disorders, and separation anxiety disorder. Section II on psychopharmacology discusses the use of atypical antipsychotics and autism, treating tardive dyskinesia in children, medical management of attention deficit/ hyperactivity disorder (ADHD), polypharmacy prescription practice, and side effects of common health medications. Section III on dietary control and supplement use includes dietary treatments for autism, identification and treatment of eating disorders, and use of steroids in adolescence. Although not inclusive, this volume covers topics that are among the most urgent and current in pediatrics in the schools.

—Paul C. McCabe and Steven R. Shaw, Editors

Acknowledgments

A large-scale project like this cannot take place without the assistance of many people. Jennifer Bruce and Sarita Gober provided many hours of editorial assistance in this project. Their support, skill, and good humor made this project possible. In addition, external reviewers read chapters and provided valuable comments. All chapters were improved because of the efforts of these students, educators, and scholars. The reviewers are Tiffany Chiu, Ray Christner, Jason Collins, Janine Fisher, Sarah Glaser, Sarita Gober, Terry Goldman, Michelle Harvie, Tom Huberty, Susan Jones, Robin Martin, Tawnya Meadows, Tia Ouimet, Mark Posey, Sara Quirke, Amira Rahman, Shohreh Rezazadeh, Jennifer Saracino, Christopher Scharf, Khing Sulin, and Jessica Carfolite Williams. Of course, the authors deserve the lion's share of appreciation, because their expertise, hard work, talent, and timeliness made this work possible. Many thanks for their expertise and generosity.

We would also like to thank the NASP publishing board and the editorial staff of NASP and Corwin for their encouragement and expertise in improving the content of this book and believing in the project, and we would like to acknowledge Andrea Canter, former editor of *Communiqué*, who supported the "Pediatric School Psychology" column from its inception and encouraged the dissemination of this work.

Paul McCabe would like to thank his colleagues at Brooklyn College of the City University of New York for their logistical support and encouragement of this project. He would also like to thank the many talented, hard-working graduate students who have worked with him over the years to contribute to the "Pediatric School Psychology" column and this project. Finally, he would like to offer grateful thanks to friends and family for their love and encouragement, especially to Dan.

Steven Shaw would like to thank the physicians from the Greenville Hospital System, South Carolina, who shaped his views of how education and pediatrics interact. Most notable of these physicians are Desmond Kelly, Nancy Powers, Mark Clayton, Lynn Hornsby, Curtis Rogers, and William Schmidt. And, of course, thanks to Isabel, Zoe, and Joyce for their love, support, and patience.

About the Editors

 **Paul C. McCabe, PhD, NCSP,** is an Associate Professor of School Psychology in the School Psychologist Graduate Program at Brooklyn College of the City University of New York. Dr. McCabe received his PhD in Clinical and School Psychology from Hofstra University. He holds undergraduate degrees from University of Rochester and Cazenovia College. Dr. McCabe is a New York State–certified school psychologist, New York State–licensed psychologist, and a Nationally Certified School Psychologist (NCSP). Dr. McCabe serves on the editorial boards of several publications in school psychology and developmental psychology and has consulted at state and national levels on issues of early childhood assessment and best practices, pediatric issues in schools, and training in school psychology. Dr. McCabe conducts and publishes research in (1) early childhood social, behavioral, and language development and concomitant problems; (2) pediatric school psychology and health issues addressed by schools; and (3) social justice issues in training, especially training educators to advocate for gay, lesbian, bisexual, and transgendered youth.

 **Steven R. Shaw, PhD, NCSP,** is an Assistant Professor in the Department of Educational and Counselling Psychology at McGill University in Montreal, Quebec. Dr. Shaw received a PhD in school psychology from the University of Florida. He has been a school psychologist since 1988 with clinical and administrative experience in schools, hospitals, and independent practice. He is editor-elect of *School Psychology Forum* and serves on the editorial board of several professional journals. He has conducted workshops and consulted with educational policy makers to address the needs of children with borderline intellectual functioning in the United States, Canada, Pakistan, Moldova, Poland, India, and Egypt. Dr. Shaw conducts and publishes research in (1) the behavior and language development of children with rare genetic disorders; (2) resilience factors for children with risk factors for school failure, especially borderline intellectual functioning; and (3) pediatric school psychology and health issues addressed by schools.

About the Contributors

Larry M. Bolen, EdD, is a Professor of Psychology and Associate Dean of Planning in the Department of Psychology at East Carolina University. He received his doctorate from the University of Georgia and completed his BA and MA at West Georgia College. His research interests include psychometric properties of intelligence tests, CHC (fluid-crystallized) intelligence theory, acute and chronic health conditions affecting school learning, and visual-motor functioning.

Tara Brinkman is a graduate student in the School Psychology Program at Michigan State University. Her interests include research and clinical issues in assessment and psychological issues of children with ADHD.

Michael B. Brown, PhD, is a Professor of Psychology at East Carolina University. He completed his graduate and undergraduate work at Virginia Polytechnic Institute. His research interests include (1) pediatric school psychology, including educational and behavioral issues from chronic disorders with a special interest in mucopolysaccharide disorders (Hurler, Schaie, Hurler-Schaie, Hunter, San Fillipo, and Morquio syndromes), childhood cancer, and school-based health centers; (2) professional issues in school psychology; and (3) diverse issues affecting children and schools.

John S. Carlson, PhD, NCSP, is an Associate Professor and Director of Clinical Training in the School Psychology Program at Michigan State University in East Lansing. Dr. Carlson received his PhD in School Psychology from the University of Wisconsin–Madison. He is a licensed psychologist in Michigan and has a private practice called Child and Adolescent Psychological Services, PLC. Dr. Carlson is on the editorial boards of several publications representing a diverse array of fields, including the *Journal of School Psychology, Journal of Child and Adolescent Psychiatric Nursing,* and *Training and Education in Professional Psychology.* Dr. Carlson publishes and conducts research on school psychopharmacology, treatment of selective mutism, dissemination and implementation of evidence-based interventions, early identification of behavioral problems in Head Start children, and issues associated with the prevention of preschool expulsion.

Jason Collins, MS, CAS, NCSP, is a school psychologist working for the Newark Public Schools in Newark, New Jersey. Mr. Collins received his MS and CAS in School Psychology from the Rochester Institute of Technology with a focus on working with children who are deaf and hard of hearing. He holds an undergraduate degree in Psychology from St. John Fisher College in Rochester, New York. Mr. Collins is a New Jersey State–certified school psychologist and a Nationally Certified School Psychologist (NCSP). Mr. Collins serves on the School Leadership Council at Bruce Street School for the Deaf and consults at a district level on developing educational programs for students who are deaf and hard of hearing.

Catherine Cook-Cottone, PhD, a Licensed Psychologist and Certified School Psychologist, is an Associate Professor in the Department of Counseling, School, and Educational Psychology at State University of New York at Buffalo and Director or the School Psychology MA/AC program. She teaches classes in counseling with children and adolescents, infant and preschool assessment, reading diagnostics, and the history of psychology. She also maintains a private practice with the East Amherst Psychology Group. Working with adults, adolescents, and children, she specializes in the assessment and treatment of anxiety-based disorders (e.g., post-traumatic stress disorder and generalized anxiety disorder), eating disorders (including other disorders of self-care), development of emotional regulation skills, and academic/reading difficulties. Her therapeutic approach includes constructivist therapies that facilitate neurological, emotional, and dialectic integration, including narrative, bibliotherapeutic, and creative approaches. Catherine's research has a neuropsychological focus and addresses two areas: (1) intervention for psychosocial disorders and (2) the development of reading.

Tamara Dawkins, MA, OPQ, is a PhD student in the School/Applied Child Psychology Program and course lecturer in the Department of Educational and Counselling Psychology at McGill University in Montreal, Quebec. Ms. Dawkins completed her MA in Educational Psychology at McGill University and holds a BA from the same institution. She is a licensed school psychologist in the province of Quebec. Ms. Dawkins conducts research within a developmental psychopathology framework investigating visual attention skills in children with typical development, autism, and Down syndrome.

Caryn R. DePinna, MSEd, received her graduate degree from the School Psychologist Graduate Program at Brooklyn College of the City University of New York and is currently a doctoral candidate in School-Community Psychology at Hofstra University. She holds an undergraduate degree in psychology from State University of New York at Geneseo. Caryn has published research on alternative treatments for autism and has several years of work experience with the autistic population. Caryn's other interests lie in treatments for childhood mental illness and classroom strategies to address children with ADHD.

Daniel Farrell, MS, CAS, is a certified school psychologist in Peoria, Arizona. Daniel received his master's degree and Certificate of Advanced Graduate Study in School Psychology from Rochester Institute of Technology. He holds an undergraduate degree from St. Lawrence University.

Janine Fischer, EdS, is a school psychologist in the Peoria Unified School District, Peoria, Arizona. She received her master's and educational specialist degrees from the College of William and Mary and undergraduate degree from Virginia Commonwealth University. Ms. Fischer is an Arizona State–certified school psychologist. Her interests lie in the area of response to intervention and mental health disorders in the school system.

Sarita Gober, MSEd, is a certified school psychologist who recently graduated from Brooklyn College of the City University of New York's School Psychologist Graduate Program. She is currently a doctoral candidate in School Psychology at Rutgers University. She holds a BA in Psychology from Yeshiva University's Stern College for Women. Sarita is currently working at Brooklyn Children's Center, an inpatient children's psychiatric state hospital. Sarita has published numerous research articles and presented in research forums on adolescent motivations to take anabolic steroids. Ms. Gober's other research interests include (1) children's school readiness skills (i.e., early literacy skills) and (2) attachment relationships and interactions between mothers and children.

Betsy Chesno Grier, PhD, is a pediatric psychologist with the University of South Carolina Medical School. She is a South Carolina State–licensed school psychologist. Her clinical and research interests involve pediatric bipolar disorder and other mental health issues.

Elizabeth H. Jeffords, MD, is a pediatric psychiatrist with the University of South Carolina School of Medicine. Her research interests include autism, pediatric bipolar disorder, and issues in intellectual disabilities.

Erika E. Levavi, MSEd, is a Bilingual School Psychologist intern in the New York area. She received her MSEd in School Psychology and an undergraduate degree in psychology and philosophy from Brooklyn College of the City University of New York. Mrs. Levavi was a school psychologist trainee at a New York City Department of Education public school. Her professional interests lie in atypical childhood development and multicultural issues in school psychology.

Angela Maupin is a graduate student in the School Psychology Program at Michigan State University. Her interests include research and clinical issues in assessment and psychological issues of children with ADHD.

Sara Pollak-Kagan, BS, is a student in the School Psychologist Graduate Program at Brooklyn College of the City University of New York. She received her bachelor's degree in Graphic Design and Judaic Studies from Touro College in New York. Ms. Pollak-Kagan currently teaches art history at Manhattan High School for Girls and is interested in conducting research in art and creativity and how it relates to childhood development.

Florence J. Schneider, PhD, is an Assistant Professor in the Behavioral Sciences and Human Services Department at Kingsborough Community College of the City University of New York. Dr. Schneider received her PhD in Education from Capella University. She received her MA degree in Educational Psychology from New York University and has an undergraduate degree in Psychology and Special Education from Brooklyn College of the City University of New York. Dr. Schneider holds New York State certifications and New York City licenses as a Teacher of Special Education and Teacher of Elementary Education. She has been a teacher of individuals with special needs for 20 years and, in her current position, has educated future teachers for 13 years. Dr. Schneider's research interests and publications are in the area of teacher education, especially preparation for the inclusive education of students with special needs.

Megan L. Wilkins, PhD, is a pediatric psychologist with the University of South Carolina Medical School. Her clinical and research interests involve autism, developmental disabilities, and adjustment of children with medical issues.

SECTION I

Neuropsychiatric Conditions Affecting Children

1

Developments in Neuropsychiatric Treatment

New Challenges and Old Problems

Paul C. McCabe and Steven R. Shaw

INTRODUCTION

Advances in medical science have enabled researchers to study brain-behavior connections with greater specificity than ever before. While there has always been a presumed connection between biological mechanisms and behavior, affect, and personality, limitations in medical science restricted this association to the hypothetical at best. However, new technologies employed to study the ways that neural mechanisms interrelate, and new understandings about the neurochemical patterns leading to disordered behavior, have helped to advance diagnostic and treatment accuracy of psychiatric conditions. For example, advances in research focused on neuronal integration, which is the coordination and adjustment of neural activity across multiple brain regions, have helped develop models that explain how complex behavior, such as emotion and cognition, occur (Northoff, 2008). These advances have helped elucidate the neuropsychiatric foundations of behavior, emotion, personality, as well as the origin and prolongation of disordered behavior.

Despite these advances, there remain challenges in the treatment of psychiatric conditions. Our understanding of the structure and function of neuronal integrated networks is increasingly advanced, but there remain questions with regard to mechanisms of interneuronal communication. The precise nature of how neurotransmitters are fitted to adjoining neurons either to facilitate or block a transmission is not entirely understood. Yet psychopharmacological medications are manufactured with the intention of facilitating or impeding this interneuronal exchange. Newer medications can increasingly target precise neural systems through enhanced specificity, but side effects remain a problem and impact treatment adherence. Although science has facilitated a greater understanding of the neurological bases of psychiatric disorders, most medications designed to ameliorate these disorders cannot be solely used as a panacea. Rather, most neuropsychiatric conditions require a balance of psychopharmacology and psychotherapeutic intervention for optimal results. Educators are cautioned that while advances in neuropsychiatric science are encouraging, a multipronged multidisciplinary approach is likely the best strategy to identify and treat psychiatric conditions.

LINKING NEUROTRANSMITTERS TO BEHAVIOR

Recent research has identified specific neurotransmitters and receptor sites implicated in a variety of functions associated with cognition, emotion, and behavior. For example, while research has confirmed the role of the neurotransmitter serotonin as participatory in cognitive tasks, more recent research has identified serotonin subtypes responsible for supporting specific higher-order functions. The serotonin subtype $5\text{-}HT_{1A}$ has been identified as having a primary role in coordinating memory consolidation, and stimulation of $5\text{-}HT_{1A}$ receptors in rats has lead to learning impairments by inhibiting memory-encoding mechanisms (Ögren et al., 2008). The receptor has also been implicated in the retrieval of aversive or emotional memories, suggesting a primary role in memory consolidation tasks (Ögren et al.). In addition, $5\text{-}HT_{1A}$ has been associated with a number of psychiatric disorders, including depression, panic disorder, and neurosis—all of which have symptoms that include or are triggered by emotionally laden memories. Furthermore, specific alleles located on the $5\text{-}HT_{1A}$ gene [e.g., C(-1019)] have been identified as playing a functional role in $5\text{-}HT_{1A}$ receptor irregularities and predisposition to mental illness (François, Czesak, Steubl, & Albert, 2008).

Similarly, recent research has identified multiple receptor sites for the neurotransmitter dopamine, which is implicated in dopaminergic functions. Dopamine plays a role in a variety of behaviors and cognitive functions, including attention, arousal, mood, learning, and more. It has also been associated with operation of the reward and motivation centers of the brain. The interrelationships among neurotransmitters is complex. For example, dopamine is a precursor for other neurotransmitters, including norepinephrine and epinephrine, and dopamine has a complementary or reciprocal relationship with neurotransmitters such as glutamate and GABA. Researchers are continuing to investigate these complex relationships in facilitating or inhibiting a variety of neural functions.

INCREASING SPECIFICITY OF MEDICATIONS

Medications that bind to specific receptors rather than impacting multiple neurotransmitter systems have greatly improved the efficacy of psychopharmacological interventions while reducing side effects. For example, older classes of antipsychotic medications affect multiple dopaminergic receptors by reducing the amount of available dopamine at the synapse, thus blocking dopamine transmissions and consequently reducing psychotic symptoms. However, other behavioral systems are also interrupted in the process, such as physical motor coordination, which can lead to Parkinsonian-like motor responses. As noted above, reducing the amount of available dopamine would also reduce the amount of successor neurotransmitters such as norepinephrine, which has an important role in modulating emotions, stress, and attention.

However, medications that target specific dopamine receptors (e.g., dopamine 2, or D2), such as partial dopamine agonists used in treating symptoms of schizophrenia, have been helpful in reducing powerful side effects that affect arousal, attention, motor functions, and so on. These newer classes of partial dopamine antagonists have shown promise with children and adolescents with schizophrenia by reducing positive and negative symptoms of the disorder (Findling et al., 2008). Other researchers pursuing competing neural pathways, such as regulating and inhibiting the neurotransmitter glutamate as a means to reduce psychotic symptoms, are finding promising results (Paz, Tardito, Atzori, & Tseng, 2008). This is important, as new evidence is suggesting that prolonged exposure to anti-dopaminergic medications, including those specifically targeting D2 subtype receptors, may lead to cortical atrophy (Paz et al.) and inhibit the growth of new synaptic connections within the dopamine system (Fasano, DesGroseillers, & Trudeau, 2008).

Increasing specificity of medications and the invention of medications affecting differing neurotransmitter systems is helping medical professionals tailor interventions to the precise symptoms associated with a particular psychopathology. For example, treatments for depression now include a variety of medications that target different neurotransmitter systems. This newer class of medications includes selective serotonin reuptake inhibitors (SSRIs), serotonin and norepinephrine reuptake inhibitors (SNRIs), norepinephrine and dopamine reuptake inhibitors (NDRIs), and noradrenergic and specific serotonergic antidepressants (NaSSAs). There are more in development, including a triple-action serotonin-noradrenaline-dopamine reuptake inhibitor (SNDRI) that is showing early promise as an antidepressant (Breuer et al., 2008) as well as an anti-obesity agent (Tizzano et al., 2008). These medications have the potential to target multiple problems associated with complex psychiatric conditions.

MEDICATION SIDE EFFECTS

Despite advances in medication therapies, side effects caused by treatment regimens remain significant obstacles. The greater the medication side effects, the more likely treatment adherence will be affected. However, when medication specificity increases affinity to target receptor subtypes (rather than global receptor systems) and lowers affinity to undesired receptor subtypes, the result is a diminution of the pervasiveness and intensity of unwanted side effects (Tallman & Dahl, 2002).

Common side effects for the newer classes of antidepressant medications include insomnia, restlessness, anxiety, nausea, weight gain or loss, sweating, dry mouth, drowsiness, diarrhea, and headaches. These effects can range from mild to severe in intensity and frequency. The newer antipsychotic medications include side effects such as drowsiness, tachycardia (increased heart rate), dizziness, weight gain, reduced sexual arousal or interest, rash, tremor, problems with menstrual cycle, and extrapyramidal motor effects (National Institute of Mental Health, 2008). The degree to which children and adolescents can cope with medication effects and understand how the medications are helping them will determine whether or not they will adhere to the regimen.

Most psychopharmacological drugs, including newer medications, generate unwanted side effects. However, the newer medications generally produce fewer and less intense effects that are more easily tolerated. Children and adolescents are particularly susceptible to any medication effects that make them feel or appear abnormal or cause significant physical distress. It is important that physicians, parents, and the school multi-disciplinary team work with students to help them understand the purpose of the medications and any anticipated side effects.

(DE-)EMPHASIS ON TALK THERAPIES

The changing landscape of medical insurance provision has been cited as one of the primary reasons behind the increased prescription of psychopharmacological drugs and concomitant decrease in psychotherapies used to treat neuropsychiatric conditions. Between 1996 and 2005, the number of office visits to psychiatrists decreased from 44.4% to 28.9%, and the percentage of psychiatrists who provide psychotherapy to their patients dropped from 19.1% to 10.8% (Mojtabai & Olfson, 2008). Meanwhile, the prescription rates for psychopharmacological prescriptions increased during the same period. This trend can be attributed to growth and advancement of psychopharmacological treatments, but it is also likely a by-product of financial incentives brought about by changes in reimbursement through managed care (Mojtabai & Olfson).

Despite this trend, research on most forms of psychopathology indicates that psychotherapeutic interventions contribute significantly to treatment gains and, in some cases, are superior to psychopharmacology. A meta-analysis of treatments for depression indicated that both psychotherapy and medication are effective treatments; however, psychotherapy provides a prophylactic effect that medication does not (Imel, Malterer, McKay, & Wampold, 2008), and this positive effect is evident up to 6 months later (David, Szentagotai, Lupu, & Cosman, 2008). For many disorders, a combined approach of psychopharmacological intervention plus cognitive-behavioral therapy demonstrates the most favorable outcome; these include body dysmorphic disorder (Ipser, Sander, & Stein, 2009), obsessive-compulsive disorder (Flament, Geller, Irak, & Blier, 2007), and attention deficit/hyperactivity disorder (ADHD; Bachmann, Bachmann, Rief, & Mattejat, 2008). The superiority of psychotherapy over psychopharmacology for treatment efficacy has been well demonstrated in meta-analytic studies of child and adolescent conduct disorder, depressive disorders, and anxiety disorders (Bachmann et al.).

Furthermore, recent studies are questioning whether some psychopharmacological treatments are even effective beyond the placebo effect. Kirsch et al. (2008) evaluated the adult medication trials for four SSRI antidepressants (fluoxetine [e.g., Prozac], venlafaxine [e.g., Effexor], nefazodone [e.g., Serzone], and paroxetine [e.g., Paxil]) that were submitted to the Food and Drug Administration between 1987 and 1999. They found that the greater the symptom severity, the more likely the medications demonstrated efficacy; however, treatment effect sizes were relatively small even for severely depressed patients (Kirsch et al.). Similar results have been found in reviews of research on children and adolescents treated with antidepressants. In one review, the authors concluded that "in general, nine depressed youth must be treated with an antidepressant to obtain one clinical response above that achieved with placebo" (Boylan, Romero, & Birmaher, 2007, p. 27). They further reported that between 1 and 3 children out of 100 taking antidepressants showed onset or worsening of suicidality and, therefore, recommended the use of antidepressants in only the most severe cases.

FUTURE DIRECTIONS

Despite advances in neuropsychiatric science and psychopharmacological specificity, significant challenges remain regarding the use of these treatments with children and adolescents. There is a significant paucity of clinical trials of most psychopharmacological medications with these age groups. Therefore, an insufficient database exists regarding efficacy, safety, adverse events, and long-term outcomes for children and adolescents (Koelch, Schnoor, & Fegert, 2008), and this information cannot be reliably extrapolated from adult trials (Vitiello, 2003). Clearly, one must consider ethical concerns when organizing clinical trials of psychopharmacological medications with children and adolescents. Scholars have advocated for integration of research ethics into the research development and design as opposed to applying research ethics from an oversight perspective (Tan & Koelch, 2008). Much additional research on the efficacy and safety of child and adolescent psychopharmacology still needs to be done.

In the meantime, we already know that many psychotherapy protocols have been empirically validated with a range of psychiatric conditions and can be successfully implicated without concern for adverse effects. Research has unequivocally demonstrated that the use of psychopharmacological agents alone as the sole means of treatment is rarely effective and that it fails to inoculate the individual against future occurrences (thus promoting dependence on the medication). Psychological and psychosocial interventions addressing children's emotional and behavioral issues within the family and school contexts are also needed (Scharf & Williams, 2006).

This means that school psychologists, educators, and family members have an important role to play in the therapeutic intervention for children and adolescents with neuropsychiatric conditions. Children and adolescents with psychiatric conditions require support in managing and attenuating their symptoms in addition to addressing academic and social pressures. Parents can help ensure a proper treatment regimen by providing a family history of psychiatric illness and family members' responsiveness to certain psychotropic medications (Scharf & Williams, 2006). Parents can also help decide when medications should begin or change depending on events in the child's life, as well as monitor the child's or adolescent's adherence to the prescribed regimen (Scharf & Williams). Parents can also advocate for psychotherapy for their child, even as a first step before medication trials are initiated. Educators can assist parents by sending home daily or weekly reports of the child's behavior and/or symptoms, working closely with the child to ascertain if his or her symptoms are manageable, and working with the school multidisciplinary team to develop accommodations as necessary. Interventions using a multipronged approach, including psychosocial therapy, family supports, educational accommodation, and psychopharmacology (as needed), are likely to lead to more favorable outcomes for the individual than any single approach.

2

Neurochemical Bases of Tourette Syndrome and Implications for Educators*

Jason Collins and Paul C. McCabe

Nick, an 8-year-old third grader, was sent to the principal's office after being involved in a fight. "Shaun called me a freak," Nick explained to Ms. Ragucci, the principal. "He saw me making faces and shrugging my shoulders, but I didn't do it on purpose. It just happens sometimes and I can't help it."

As Nick continued to explain his side of the story, Ms. Ragucci noticed some of the movements Nick was describing. He also cleared his throat frequently. Ms. Ragucci sent Nick back to class, deciding to meet with his teacher before making any decisions. Mr. Lester, his teacher, reported that he had observed Nick's movements all year and confirmed that he was continuously clearing his throat. Ms. Ragucci also reviewed Nick's file, discovering comments on previous report cards that suggested Nick had been struggling with these behaviors since first grade.

Ms. Ragucci decided to ask Nick's parents to come for a meeting with his teacher and the school psychologist. When his parents were asked if they had similar concerns, they indicated that Nick had been making unusual noises and

*Adapted from Collins, J., & McCabe, P. C. (2004). Neurochemical bases of Tourette's disorder and implications for school psychologists. *Communiqué, 33*(3), 5–6. Copyright by the National Association of School Psychologists, Bethesda, MD. Use is by permission of the publisher. www.nasponline.org

movements at home and getting into trouble at school and they had been receiving notes from his teacher warning that his grades were falling.

Ms. Martin, the school psychologist, listened to the description of Nick's symptoms and suggested that these mannerisms and behaviors could be part of a neurological disorder. She advised Nick's parents to consult with their primary care practitioner, who would likely make a referral to a pediatric neurologist, child psychiatrist, or developmental pediatrician.

When Nick's parents returned to the school the following month, they reported that Nick had been diagnosed with Tourette syndrome. The developmental pediatrician had prescribed a low-dose trial of clonidine and recommended they ask the school about what accommodations could be made for Nick.

INTRODUCTION

According to the *Diagnostic and Statistical Manual of Mental Disorders* (4th ed., text revision, American Psychiatric Association [APA], 2000), Tourette syndrome (TS) is a neuropsychiatric disorder that is characterized by the occurrence of multiple motor tics and one or more phonic tics. George Gilles de la Tourette first described TS in 1885. Research has since evolved from an earlier emphasis on psychodynamic causes to a greater emphasis on the genetic etiology of TS and its neurobiological bases (Leckman, 2002). Much of the prevailing research on TS has suggested an involvement and dysfunction of neurochemical systems, particularly the dopamine system, in the emergence of the disorder (Albin, 2006). The resulting manifestations have significant implications for educators working with children and adolescents with TS.

BACKGROUND

Prevalence and Epidemiology

A generally accepted prevalence for TS is 5 cases per 10,000 (*DSM-IV-TR*). However, this number varies depending on the population studied and methodologies used. Hospitalized and treatment populations, which include patients with the most severe symptoms and with varying ages, show a prevalence of 0.5 to 49.5 cases per 10,000 (Stefanoff & Mazurek, 2003). These studies are more representative of what might be expected in a clinical setting as opposed to the general school population. Large-scale screening studies suggest estimates ranging from 4.3 to 10 per 10,000, which may be more representative of the general population (Stefanoff & Mazurek, 2003).

Although there is no consensus regarding the prevalence of TS, a review of the prevailing literature does suggest that TS is more common than previous estimates indicated and is more common in children, supporting the need for vigilance when working with school-age children in primary care and educational settings. TS is found in all countries and in all racial and socioeconomic groups (Freeman et al., 2000). TS does, however, tend to occur in males three to four times more often than females (Robertson, 1994).

Clinical Phenomenology

Typically, TS begins with brief bouts of a simple motor tic, such as eye blinking or nose twitching. Research suggests a median onset of simple motor tics of 5 or 6 years (Leckman et al., 1998). Phonic (vocal) tics, which are one of the diagnostic differences between TS and tic disorders, involve words or sounds (clicks, grunts, yelps, barks, sniffs, snorts, etc.). On average, phonic tics begin 1 to 2 years after the onset of motor symptoms. The term *phonic tic* is used rather than *vocal tic*, as not all abnormal sounds and noises in TS are produced by the vocal cords.

A waxing and waning of both multiple motor tics and at least one phonic tic characterize the course of this lifelong syndrome. After onset, there is typically a progressive pattern of tic worsening, with the most severe symptoms generally occurring between the ages of 8 and 12 (Bloch et al., 2006; Leckman et al., 1998). The number, frequency, location, and complexity of tics typically change during the course of TS. Tics can also vary from being virtually continuous to occurring only a few minutes a day. Moderating this may be the fact that TS is a stress-sensitive syndrome. Feelings of stress, anxiety, fatigue, and excitement aggravate tics (Leckman, 2002).

Late adolescent or early adulthood follow-up studies have demonstrated subsequent improvements in the frequency and severity of tics (Bloch et al., 2006; Pappert, Goetz, Louis, Blasucci, & Leurgans, 2003). Robertson (1994) reported that in as many as 30% to 40% of cases, tic symptoms remit completely. The decrease in tic symptoms over the course of adolescence is consistent with available epidemiological data showing a lower prevalence of TS among adults compared with children.

One of the most widely known symptoms of TS is coprolalia. This symptom involves involuntary outbursts of obscene words or socially inappropriate and derogatory remarks. Despite being well known, it is one of the rarest symptoms of TS, occurring in less than 15% of patients (Freeman et al., 2000; Tourette Syndrome Association, 2009). The development of this symptom is often related to the presence of co-occurring disorders and should be an indicator to school professionals that additional disorders may be impacting the child. Although coprolalia is rare, it can be one of the most disabling symptoms of TS, as it affects the child's safety, ability to stay in school, and socialization.

As many as 80% of patients report premonitory urges, described as a generalized inner tension, before a tic occurs (Fonagy, Target, Cottrell, Phillips, & Kurtz, 2002; Leckman, 2002). This sensation occurs in the muscle groups expressing the tic and is described as a tension that is relieved by performing the tic. Some individuals have been able to suppress these urges to tic for short durations (Fonagy et al.). Longer duration of tic suppression, however, is associated with increasing levels of tension and prolonged, intensified tics once expressed. Tic suppression has led to one of the biggest misperceptions about children with TS. Many parents and educators believe that since tics can be partially controlled at times, their occurrence in the classroom or at inappropriate times must be purposeful attempts to distract others and break the rules. There are two important facts to be considered. First, not every person with TS can exert control over when they tic. This is especially true of children. Secondly, even though individuals with TS might have limited control over when they tic under the best of circumstances, this control comes at a great cost.

TS does not directly affect intelligence, as many individuals have average to above average IQs (Prestin, 2003). One cognitive area that is affected is visual-motor integration. On tests of visual-motor integration, children with TS generally score lower than children without TS (Schultz et al., 1998).

Comorbidity

Tics are not the only problems facing people with TS. Comorbid disorders create unique difficulties for a majority of children with TS. The range of these difficulties is broad and includes problems with attention and learning, impulse control, obsessive-compulsive behaviors, anxiety and mood disorders, as well as difficulties with living and adaptation. Although the estimates vary, children and adolescents with TS are more likely to have a comorbid psychiatric disorder than those without TS (Gaze, Kepley, & Walkup, 2006). Robertson (2006) reported that the occurrence reaches as high as 90%; however, such high prevalence estimates might not accurately reflect prevalence rates in all settings. Clinical populations typically have higher rates of comorbidity than the general population.

The most common comorbid disorder reported in the literature is attention deficit/hyperactivity disorder (ADHD; Fonagy et al., 2002). Freeman (2007) examined data from a worldwide clinical data set of individuals with tics and found that the reported prevalence of ADHD in TS was 55%. Obsessive-compulsive disorder (OCD) is another disorder often associated with TS. Clinical studies have shown that approximately one third of TS patients also have OCD and at least 50% present with obsessive-compulsive symptoms (Hounie et al., 2006).

Behavioral and affective disorders, mood disorders, and anxiety disorders are also more prevalent among clinical TS patients than among the general population (Coffey & Biederman, 2000; Robertson, Banerjee, Hiley, & Tannock, 1997; Robertson & Orth, 2006). Much of this research has focused on clinical (i.e., severe) populations, however, and may not generalize to those individuals with mild to moderate symptoms who are more commonly seen in the schools. Nevertheless, school professionals should consider these comorbid disorders in their assessments, as the existence of these disorders will have implications for intervening in the educational environment.

Neurochemical Bases

Clinical pharmacology has provided some of the most significant clues to understanding TS and its neurochemical bases. Clinical trials with various drugs demonstrate that tics are most reliably suppressed by dopamine antagonists and that dopamine agonists can exacerbate tics, implicating involvement of the central nervous system (CNS) and the dopaminergic system (Leckman, 2002). Interruptions in the transmission of messages facilitated by dopamine play an important role in controlling tics in TS (Albin, 2006). Neuroimaging studies have also supported involvement of the dopamine system and are attempting to pinpoint the neuroanatomic localization of TS. This research is increasingly implicating the involvement of the basal ganglia (Albin).

The basal ganglia are a group of interconnected nuclei in the brain believed to be involved in the modification of motor control. The basal ganglia receive input primarily from the cortex, as well as other areas of the brain, and subsequently exert influence back on those areas. One of the basal ganglia's primary roles in these interactions is to control voluntary movements through a process known as disinhibition (Chevalier & Deniau, 1990). In this process, the basal ganglia exert constant inhibitory control over regions of the brain that produce movements until a signal from the cerebral cortex disrupts that inhibition, effectively disinhibiting the target area of the brain, resulting in desired movements. One of the most important neurotransmitters responsible for transmitting these signals is dopamine.

Dopamine is implicated in the regulation of different physiological functions in the central nervous system, and its importance in the control of movement has been demonstrated in Parkinson's disease research. Clinical pharmacological trials have shown that the introduction of dopamine agonists increases motor activity in subjects and the introduction of dopamine antagonists decreases motor activity (Kienast & Heinz, 2006). The dopamine hypothesis in TS purports that abnormalities in the neurotransmission of messages facilitated by dopamine create disturbances in the disinhibition process, resulting in tics.

IMPLICATIONS FOR EDUCATORS

Individuals with TS are a heterogeneous group. Symptoms manifested by some children are very mild and require few, if any, accommodations. Other children with TS outgrow it or see a substantial reduction in their symptoms by early adulthood (Hendren, 2002). However, approximately one third of the children diagnosed with TS exhibit major symptoms throughout their lives (*DSM-IV-TR*). Although most students with TS have normal to near normal intelligence, approximately 40% also have a learning disability (Prestin, 2003). In addition, social-emotional functioning tends to be an area of difficulty, as students with TS (especially those with more severe symptoms and comorbid disorders) tend to have problems interacting with and being accepted by peers. School difficulties also include attention problems, low perseverance, and organizational difficulties (Leckman, 2002). The role of educators in the identification, assessment, and management of students with TS is critical when considering all of the immediate symptoms and secondary problems these students face.

Identification is an important role for educators. Being familiar with the phenomenology of TS, as well as the typical course, is important for all professionals working in the educational setting. Accurate historical records can help educators to make quicker and more accurate identifications. For example, a student's simple vocal tic in first grade may be dismissed by the teacher as nervousness if not for information from a previous teacher who observed and documented excessive blinking for a period of 2 months. The cumulative story told by this information might lead to a referral that otherwise would have been delayed until more severe symptoms presented.

Another domain, particularly important to school psychologists, is that of assessment. The clinician, family, child, and others involved with the child should collaborate to ensure an accurate and complete history. This is important because there is no lab test to confirm TS. Also, because other disorders such as ADHD and OCD frequently co-occur with TS, it is critical to provide medical professionals with accurate and specific information that will help them make appropriate diagnoses and save valuable time when developing a treatment plan. Therefore, assessment should focus on onset, progression, waxing and waning, factors that have worsened or ameliorated tic status, and present functioning (Leckman, 2002). All of these considerations will help to determine the diagnosis of TS as opposed to another tic disorder and will help to identify comorbid disorders. The assessment will also be critical in developing interventions and management strategies that will be effective. This information should be obtained using multiple methods as well as multiple sources. Direct observations, standardized rating forms, and self-report are three methods that are useful in obtaining accurate and useful information. Informants should include parents, teachers, and the individual, if old enough, and could also include related service providers, the school nurse, and any other school professional that may be working directly with the child.

A third focus of educators is in effectively managing the symptoms of TS and secondary problems that might arise. A thorough and accurate assessment of the student should lead to recommendations for accommodating a student's needs in accessing and progressing in the general education curriculum. The level of supports needed to do this will likely play a role in whether the student qualifies for services under Section 504 of the Rehabilitation Act of 1973 or the Individuals with Disabilities Education Improvement Act (IDEIA, 2004). With the reauthorization of IDEIA, TS has been specifically listed as a disability under Other Health Impaired (OHI). Educational interventions to manage the symptoms of TS and secondary problems should focus on direct interventions, classroom accommodations and modifications, and educating staff and students.

Direct interventions focus on reducing the psychological burden on students and their families. Murray (1997) suggested explaining the scope of TS and describing the symptoms to a degree that is developmentally appropriate for the child so that he or she knows what to expect. In addition, describing the circumstances that affect severity, such as stress, excitement, and fatigue, is important to develop self-monitoring skills in students with TS. Counseling may be necessary to assist a child with TS learn how to cope with the emotional stress of a disability; improve social skills; and manage stress, excitement, and fatigue.

Classroom accommodations and modifications will be an important part of any intervention plan for students with TS. Whenever developmentally appropriate, it is beneficial to include the student in choosing classroom strategies for managing tics, as well as how to respond when a bout of tics occurs. It is also important to keep in mind that tics wax and wane in intensity and frequency and they can change over time, so any intervention plan should be flexible and the team should be prepared to make adjustments as necessary.

Educating peers and staff members working directly with the student is another way to help manage the impact of TS. Children with TS are often perceived as being more withdrawn and less popular than their peers and are more likely to be teased by both peers and teachers. Educators generally rate students with TS as more withdrawn and aggressive than students without TS. Educating students and teachers has been shown to prevent the formation of these negative impressions and to reduce social rejection (Marcks, Berlin, Woods, & Davies, 2007). In addition, enlisting the collaboration of the student, parents, and treating professionals can help to ensure a collaborative approach to education and best practices in managing the TS symptoms. Issues of confidentiality and the importance of collaboration with the student and his or her parents are key here. Prior to disclosing TS, obtain permission from both the student and his or her parents.

Treatment of TS with a dopamine antagonist medication is common (Fonagy et al., 2002). While prescribing these interventions is outside the scope and practice of most professionals working in the educational setting, monitoring the effectiveness of pharmacological interventions is an essential role for educators. This is especially important, since many of the medications simply reduce the severity of the symptoms and some medications produce notable side effects. Educators can play a key role in monitoring and documenting these side effects to assist medical professionals in finding the appropriate pharmacological treatment and dosage. School psychologists in particular have training in behavioral monitoring and observational techniques that can meet this need.

EDUCATIONAL STRATEGIES

- Provide extended time for reading and writing assignments and for tests.
- Some students may need to take tests in a separate location.
- If a student has phonic (vocal) tics, then consult with that student privately before calling on him or her to read aloud in class or answer questions out loud.
- Consider accommodations for written work, such as providing a note taker, copies of class notes, shortened assignments, and the opportunity to make oral rather than written reports. Also, consider allowing alternative means of production, such as keyboarding, tape recording, or use of voice dictation software, for older students.
- Publicly, it is best to ignore tics. Pointing out the student's tics or commenting on them increases stress and anxiety, potentially worsening the tics.
- Model acceptance. The teacher sets the tone in the classroom and can impact how the other students treat the student with TS through modeling.
- Provide the student with a permanent pass to leave the classroom at his or her own discretion to "get the tics out" in private or if the tics are becoming overwhelming.
- Let the student leave class early to be in the hallway before everyone else.
- Avoid ordering the student to leave. That is essentially punishing the student for tics and can make tics worse and/or lead to emotional or behavioral reactions.
- Recognize that tics tend to worsen later in the day.

DISCUSSION QUESTIONS

1. What recommendations could the school make in terms of accommodations for a child with TS? Would special education or a 504 accommodation be appropriate? Why?

2. What should the teacher tell the class about TS? Should she or he say anything at all?

3. What information could the school provide to parents and the physician of a child with TS that would be helpful in monitoring the outcomes of a medication trial? How would this information be obtained, and who would be responsible for maintaining it?

4. What changes could the school implement to help identify students with TS sooner?

5. Some tics are very subtle, perhaps no more than an eye blink, head nod, grimace, or vocal tone or hum. What do educators need to know to identify students with TS and tic disorders, especially those with more subtle symptoms?

RESEARCH SUMMARY

- The prevalence of TS is commonly thought to be 5 per 10,000 individuals. However, more recent research suggests the numbers, particularly in school-age children, may be even higher, with estimates ranging from 10 to 115 per 10,000. Occurrence in males is three to four times more frequent than in females.
- Despite being well known, coprolalia (tics that involve obscenities) is one of the rarest symptoms of TS, occurring in less than 15% of individuals with TS.
- TS often occurs with other comorbid disorders in children. ADHD (occurring in approximately one half of individuals with TS) and OCD (occurring in approximately one third of individuals with TS) are two of the most common co-occurring disorders.
- Although tics can sometimes be suppressed, not everyone can suppress the urge to tic (especially children). Furthermore, research has shown that when tics are suppressed, they later manifest with longer duration and greater intensity.
- Tics are most reliably suppressed by dopamine antagonists and exacerbated by dopamine agonists, implicating involvement of the CNS and the dopamine system. Medications that serve as dopamine antagonists are typically prescribed for symptom control.

RESOURCES

National Tourette Syndrome Association (TSA): www.tsa-usa.org/ index.html. The TSA offers access to research, facts, newsletters, support groups, doctors, and related links.

Growing Up With Tourette Syndrome: Information for Kids: http:// tskids4.tripod.com/index.htm. This Web site provides kid-friendly information about TS, with two sections containing content and language specifically for children ages 5 to 8 and ages 9 to 13. Also includes a parent page with links to informational sites written for adults.

HANDOUT

TOURETTE SYNDROME

Tourette syndrome (TS) is a genetic, neurological disorder characterized by tics. Tics are involuntary, rapid, sudden movements (motor tics) or vocalizations (phonic tics) that occur repeatedly. For someone to be diagnosed with TS, both types of tics must occur, although not necessarily at the same time. Tics can vary in severity, duration, and frequency and are often made worse by stress, anxiety, excitement, and fatigue. The tics must occur for at least 1 year and begin prior to age 18. Symptoms usually begin at the age of 5 or 6 and reach their peak severity between the ages of 10 and 12. There is no known cure for TS; however, some medications can effectively treat its symptoms.

Common Misperceptions About TS and Related Facts:

- **Misperception:** Everyone with TS uses obscene language. **The truth is** that coprolalia (tics that involve obscene language or socially inappropriate phrases) is one of the rarest symptoms of TS, seen in less than 15% of those with TS.
- **Misperception:** The behaviors seen in individuals with TS (tics) are purposeful and intentionally disruptive. **The truth is** that tics are involuntary symptoms of this neurological syndrome. While research shows that tics can sometimes be suppressed, it is at the cost of a rebound effect, causing explosive and severe tics after the suppression period.
- **Misperception:** The presence of tics warrants the use of medications. **The truth is** that not all children with TS need medication. The tics must be disturbing enough to the child physically or socially to warrant this type of intervention.
- **Misperception:** Tics are the only manifestations of TS that need to be considered when planning treatment for my child. **The truth is** that some children with TS suffer from other disorders as well, known as comorbid conditions. While not all children with TS will have a comorbid condition, it is important to be aware of the possibility and what to look for. Some of the most common comorbid disorders are attention deficit/hyperactivity disorder (ADHD), obsessive-compulsive disorder (OCD), and learning disabilities. Many children also will need assistance with learning how to cope with TS emotionally and socially.
- **Misperception:** TS is a lifelong condition with a poor prognosis. **The truth is** that while TS is still considered to be a lifelong condition, the prognosis for improvement is good. Many (but not all) people with TS see their symptoms improve by the end of the second decade of life, and in some cases, symptoms even disappear completely by adulthood.
- **Misperception:** TS is so rare that no one really understands it. **The truth is** that TS is much more common than originally thought. Although there is no consensus as to its prevalence, recent literature estimates it to be between 1 and 10 per 1,000 people.

Most important, the child with TS needs your reassurance and your support. Learning more will help to understand this syndrome and how it is impacting your child's life.

3

Diagnosis and Treatment of Pediatric Bipolar Disorder*

Betsy Chesno Grier, Megan L. Wilkins,
and Elizabeth H. Jeffords

Andy is 5-year-old kindergartner who recently was expelled from school for hitting and kicking his teacher. Once separated from his teacher, Andy continued to appear agitated and aggressive toward other adults. Andy's parents report that he was hyperactive and aggressive for 2 days after this incident. He did not sleep at all that night. The following day, he reportedly was sad and apologized for his behavior. He slept for 16 hours that night.

Andy had been sent home on two previous occasions for hitting other children and is frequently inattentive and overactive in the classroom. His teachers and parents are confused because there is never an identifiable reason for his aggression; angry and aggressive outbursts appear unprovoked. Andy's family physician suspected ADHD but referred Andy to a child and adolescent psychiatrist. Andy sometimes demonstrated signs of mania, including grandiose ideas (beyond normal childhood fantasy), overactivity, limited need for sleep, racing thoughts, hyperactivity, problems with impulse control, and aggression.

(Continued)

*Adapted from Grier, E. C., Wilkins, M. L., & Szadek, L. (2005). Bipolar disorder in children: Treatment and intervention, Part II. *Communiqué, 34*(3), 38–41, and Grier, E. C., Wilkins, M. L., & Szadek, L. (2005). Bipolar disorder in children: Identification and diagnosis, Part I. *Communiqué, 34*(2), 28–32. Copyright by the National Association of School Psychologists, Bethesda, MD. Use is by permission of the publisher. www.nasponline.org

(Continued)

On other days, Andy was completely different: He slept more than 12 hours daily, was irritable, was tearful for no apparent reason, and was lethargic. These behaviors swung from one extreme to another from day to day and sometimes within the course of a single day. Andy's mother said, "I would like to say that he is extremely moody, but that does not scratch the surface."

The child and adolescent psychiatrist diagnosed Andy with early-onset bipolar disorder. He started Andy on a dose of valproic acid (i.e., Depakote) and recommended Andy's family receive counseling to address how Andy's behavior affected the entire family, to help them develop home-based interventions to manage his behavior, and to work with his educators to support him in school.

Following the implementation of medical and therapeutic interventions, Andy gradually showed less extreme mood and behavior changes over time. Most importantly, his aggression waned. He was able to re-enter his original school. Andy's teacher now considers him inattentive and mildly moody, but there is no evidence of physical aggression or out-of-control behaviors.

INTRODUCTION

According to the *Diagnostic and Statistical Manual of Mental Disorders* (4th ed., text revision, American Psychiatric Association [APA], 2000), bipolar disorder is a neurobiological disorder that is characterized by distinct periods of manic and depressive episodes leading to severe impairment in functioning Although bipolar disorder is well researched and is an established diagnostic category in adults, the existence of bipolar disorder in children continues to be controversial. For children, bipolar disorder is a continuous, nonepisodic, and rapid cycling disorder affecting mood, behavior, energy, and sleep with poor prognosis (Biederman, Mick, & Faraone, 2004; Kowatch et al., 2005). Bipolar disorder is highly heritable, and prevalence rates range from 1% to 2% (*DSM-IV-TR*) to 3% to 6% in the adolescent and adult populations (Lewinsohn, Seeley, & Klein, 2003). The occurrence of bipolar disorder in children is largely unknown given the debate about the criteria for diagnosis. Research efforts pertaining to pediatric bipolar disorder are underway to increase understanding of the diagnosis and implications on children's functioning. However, there continue to be uncertainties about the diagnostic criteria, clinical presentation, and appropriate treatment approaches for children. Recent literature has called for clarification of diagnostic criteria and proposed changes to improve their diagnosis and treatment (Post & Kowatch, 2006; Smith, 2007), although some literature continues to assert that bipolar disorder cannot be diagnosed until adolescence (Duffy, 2007).

BACKGROUND

Symptoms of Bipolar Disorder

The *DSM-IV-TR* recognizes that children can have depressive episodes but not manic and mixed episodes. The current diagnostic criteria of mania based on adult patterns are difficult to apply to children, as children manifest symptoms differently than adults (Tillman & Geller, 2003), often showing severe irritability, lack of clear episodes, a mixed presentation, chronic course, and coexisting disorders (Biederman, Farone, et al., 2004; Kowatch et al., 2005). Although research is limited, the progression of bipolar disorder in children may not result in adult bipolar disorder. Most research supports the notion that children present with rapid or ultra-rapid cycles of mixed states (Kowatch et al.) occurring several times each week, day, and hour with no clear onset of cycles.

Depressive, manic, and mixed episodes must be distinguished from typical child development, and the episodes must significantly impair a child's normal functioning with regard to self-care, getting along with others, and/or learning. To meet diagnostic criteria, a major depressive episode requires five or more symptoms during a 2-week period that represent a change from previous behavior (*DSM-IV-TR*). In addition to core symptoms of depressed mood or loss of interest in activities, a child also must meet four of seven depressive characteristics as described in the *DSM-IV-TR*, including weight loss/gain, insomnia/hypersomnia, psychomotor agitation/retardation, fatigue/loss of energy, feelings of worthlessness/inappropriate guilt, diminished ability to concentrate, and/or recurrent thoughts of death or suicidal ideation/attempt. An educator may observe a depressed mood in a child as being sad, irritable, anxious, argumentative, aggressive, and/or whiny to an excessive degree. A child exhibits loss of interest by being unmotivated to play, showing little to no pleasure in play, and displaying a lack of curiosity.

A manic episode consists of a distinct period of abnormally and persistently elevated, expansive, or irritable mood lasting at least 1 week that represents a change from previous functioning (*DSM-IV-TR*). A hypomanic episode consists of the same symptoms but differs in duration (i.e., at least 4 days) and severity. In contrast to the episodic presentation of mania in adults, mania in children presents with a lack of clear onset (Kowatch et al., 2005). The *DSM-IV-TR* requires that three or more (four or more if mood is only irritable) manic symptoms be present. These include inflated self-esteem/grandiosity, decreased need for sleep, being more talkative than usual, flight of ideas/racing thoughts, distractibility, psychomotor agitation, and excess involvement in pleasurable activities that have high potential for painful consequences. Educators may observe a child with an elevated or euphoric mood as being unusually happy, silly, or giddy out of context to a problematic degree.

An excessively irritable mood also may be indicative of mania in a child. The irritable child may be observed as being short-tempered, having frequent hostile outbursts, and showing excessive frustration when told no. However, there is debate about the validity of using an irritable mood as a defining characteristic of mania in children. Some longitudinal research suggests that irritable mood, not euphoria, is predominately observed in children with bipolar disorder (Biederman, Faraone, et al., 2004). The term *affective storm* is commonly used to describe this period of irritability due to the "prolonged and aggressive temper outbursts" (Biederman, Faraone, et al., p. S46) resulting in out-of-control behavior that lasts for hours at a time. In contrast, other researchers (e.g., Geller & DelBello, 2003) reason that an irritable mood is a characteristic associated with most childhood disorders (e.g., ADHD, conduct disorder, anxiety disorders, pervasive developmental disorders), environmental stress, and the effects of medication and that the presence of irritability alone does not indicate a diagnosis of bipolar disorder.

Differential Diagnosis

There is a strong link between ADHD and bipolar disorder in children. Several potential symptoms of mania (e.g., talkativeness, distractibility, and psychomotor agitation) also are cardinal symptoms of ADHD. According to the *DSM-IV-TR*, a child could meet criteria for a manic episode if he or she has a euphoric mood and these three shared symptoms. Geller and DelBello (2003) suggested a child can meet the criteria for a manic episode if he or she manifests three to four symptoms not including those that overlap with ADHD. The most manic-specific symptoms have been found to include elated mood, grandiosity, flight of ideas, decreased need for sleep, hypersexuality, acting out daredevil behaviors, inappropriate silliness, and uninhibited social interaction. Children with ADHD do not present with common patterns found in bipolar disorder, including excessive mood lability, extended tantrums and rage, intentional aggression, suicidality, hypersexuality, and grandiosity.

In most studies, the majority of children diagnosed with bipolar disorder had coexisting ADHD, yet a much smaller percentage of children with ADHD met the criteria for mania. Biederman, Mick, and colleague (2004) reported 87% of children with bipolar disorder also had ADHD, while only 20% of children with ADHD met criteria for bipolar disorder. If a child with bipolar disorder presents with coexisting ADHD, the impairment is more severe with higher probability of psychotic symptoms (Wolf & Wagner, 2003). The increased impulsivity associated with ADHD contributes to the severity of mixed mania and potential to act in lethal ways (e.g., suicide; Biederman, Mick, et al.).

Learning disabilities also are common in children with bipolar disorder, especially if there is a coexisting diagnosis of ADHD (McClure et al., 2005). Further, up to half of children who experience depression ultimately develop bipolar disorder (Geller et al., 2002). Anxiety disorders are commonly associated with bipolar disorder, with obsessive-compulsive disorder showing the highest comorbidity (Masi et al., 2004). Research suggests that coexisting panic disorder and bipolar disorder results in higher levels of psychosis and suicidal ideation (Weller, Calvert, & Weller, 2003). Considering that some children with bipolar disorder can be volatile, short-tempered, willful, and generally difficult to manage, it is understandable that there also is strong comorbidity with oppositional defiant disorder (Papolos, 2003). Violent, aggressive, and malicious themes are evident in conduct disorder, which also can co-occur with bipolar disorder (Weller et al., 2003). Another common comorbid diagnosis reported in the literature is pervasive developmental disorder (e.g., autism spectrum disorders and Asperger disorder; Geller & DelBello, 2008). Differentiating symptoms to determine the primary diagnosis and/or the presence of coexisting disorders is complicated. Bipolar disorder in children may be understood as a spectrum disorder due to its strong symptom overlap and comorbidity with many other childhood disorders. Research is underway to determine if there are identifiable subtypes of bipolar disorder in children (Papolos).

Interventions for Pediatric Bipolar Disorder

Medical Management. Treatment of bipolar disorder in children often involves the prescription of psychotropic medications. The most commonly prescribed classes of medication are mood stabilizers and antipsychotics (Kowatch et al., 2005). Research regarding the use of these medications in children is limited, and treatment guidelines for children with bipolar disorder are largely based on research completed in adults. Nonetheless, the severity of symptoms exhibited by children with bipolar disorder necessitates the use of medication as part of treatment with goals of reducing symptoms associated with bipolar disorder, preventing reoccurrence, treating coexisting disorders, and improving the child's ability to function.

Mood stabilizers are used to alleviate symptoms of mania or depression and to control mood cycling (Fristad & Goldberg-Arnold, 2004). Mood stabilizers, which may take a few weeks to demonstrate effectiveness, include lithium, divalproex, and carbamazepine, but the Food and Drug Administration (FDA) has approved lithium for use only in children older than 12 years of age (Giedd, 2000).

Divalproex (i.e., valproic acid, Depakene, Depakote, Depakote XR) is an anticonvulsant medication used to treat seizures, to prevent migraines, and to manage mood cycling. In adults, divalproex has been effective in treating mixed episodes and rapid cycling (Geller & DelBello, 2003). Carbamazapine (i.e., Tegretol) is an anticonvulsant medication also used to treat bipolar disorder, showing efficacy in adults with both euphoric and mixed manic episodes.

Antipsychotic medications are used to control psychotic symptoms (e.g., delusions and hallucinations), to stabilize mood, and to decrease agitation (Fristad & Goldberg-Arnold, 2004). New atypical antipsychotics have better side effect profiles than typical antipsychotics. They include risperidone (i.e., Risperdal), olanzapine (i.e., Zyprexa), quetiapine (i.e., Seroquel), clozapine (i.e., Clozaril), aripiprazole (i.e., Abilify), and ziprasidone (i.e., Geodon). They also may be used in combination with mood stabilizers to aid in controlling the aggression often exhibited by children with bipolar disorder (Pavuluri, Naylor, & Janicak, 2002). Risperidone and Abilify recently were approved by the FDA to manage mania in youth.

Selective serotonin reuptake inhibitors (SSRIs) have been effective in reducing depressive symptoms in patients with bipolar disorder after mood stabilization (Biederman, Mick, Spencer, Wilens, & Faraone, 2000). SSRIs also have been effective in treating anxiety disorders that may coexist with bipolar disorder. Health care providers must proceed with caution when using SSRIs, as they can cause increased energy and activity level that may be misinterpreted as a mania and/or ADHD.

Stimulants are the main class of medications used to treat ADHD in children. They include medications such as Ritalin, Ritalin LA, Adderall, Adderall XR, Vyvanse, Concerta, Focalin, Focalin XR, and Methylin. Extensive research has supported their safety and efficacy in treating ADHD. Some scholars believe that stimulants are ineffective in the treatment of bipolar disorder and may actually induce mania in some children (Giedd, 2000; Schapiro, 2005). However, if ADHD coexists with bipolar disorder, the addition of a stimulant as adjunct therapy can be useful after mood stabilization has occurred (Pavuluri et al., 2002).

Psychopharmacological treatment of bipolar disorder in children can be challenging given the limited amount of research and the complexity surrounding diagnosis. Of those studies that exist, only short-term results have been reported; long-term use in children has not been investigated thoroughly. Before initiating medication, the target symptoms in a child should be described via comprehensive assessment to assist in determining the mode of psychopharmacological treatment. Diligent follow-up is imperative when managing medication in children with bipolar disorder due to potential side effects.

Psychosocial Interventions. Psychotropic medications often are used as the first mode of treatment prior to psychosocial intervention efforts due to the extreme mood lability frequently present in children with bipolar disorder. To date, well-established psychosocial treatment has not been substantiated for intervening with children with bipolar disorder. Although guidelines exist that outline treatment approaches with individuals, groups, and families (Young & Fristad, 2007), these recommendations are based on single-site studies and/or clinical experience and have yet to be empirically validated.

Initial research has suggested that cognitive-behavioral therapeutic strategies and family psychoeducational approaches may be effective in the treatment of bipolar disorder in children (Kowatch et al., 2005). Danielson, Feeny, Findling, and Youngstrom (2004) proposed a model for cognitive-behavioral treatment of children with bipolar disorder consisting of 12 therapeutic sessions with potential follow-up treatment if needed, including a focus on medication adherence, mood monitoring, anticipation of stressors and use of problem-solving to address them, identification and modification of unhelpful thinking, sleep regulation, use of relaxation, and family communication. Pavuluri and colleagues (2004) demonstrated promising results for the use of combined cognitive-behavioral and family-focused strategies (e.g., problem-solving techniques for the family and behavioral management techniques to establish routine and consistency) with psychopharmacological treatment, showing overall improvements in global functioning in the child with bipolar disorder based on therapist ratings. Fristad and Goldberg-Arnold (2003) found increases in positive family ratings, perceptions of parental support by children, and knowledge regarding bipolar disorder for children receiving group family psychoeducation. Fristad (2006) also has extended this treatment to individual families in recent research. Miklowitz and colleagues (2004) found involving families via psychoeducation in the treatment of bipolar disorder in children decreased both depressive and manic symptoms and improved overall behavior at 1 year posttreatment.

Although future research is needed to establish efficacy, utilizing cognitive-behavioral strategies and involving families in treatment is an increasing trend in treatment of mood disorders. When paired with psychopharmacologic treatment, these psychosocial interventions seem to offer hope of decreasing the severity of some of the symptoms that are prevalent with bipolar disorder in children.

Conclusion

Bipolar disorder exists in children, but its expression is atypical from the classic adult illness. Research continues to elucidate the biology, onset, diagnostic profile, course, and outcome of bipolar disorder in children. It is recognized to be a rapid-cycling, nonepisodic, and debilitating disorder resulting in chronic and severe mood, energy, sleep, and behavior fluctuations. This leads to an assortment of unpredictable behaviors, which create instability in the life of the child and necessitate intervention. Intervention typically takes the form of a combination of psychotropic medication, family intervention, and school supports for the child. Educational professionals are in a unique position to support other professionals in the diagnosis and treatment of this disorder and should stay abreast of the developing literature.

IMPLICATIONS FOR EDUCATORS

Several avenues of school-based intervention are available for the child with bipolar disorder. Children diagnosed with bipolar disorder can be served by general education, special education, or a combination of these services. A formal plan can be developed under Section 504 of the Rehabilitation Act if the disorder *substantially* limits the child's education. Generally, this type of plan is implemented through accommodations in the general education classroom and/or within the school environment, but it can also include behavior plans and school-based counseling. Under IDEA, an Individual Education Plan (IEP) can be created under the "Emotional Disability" or "Other Health Impaired" categories if the disorder adversely affects the child's learning. The Child and Adolescent Bipolar Foundation has advocated for children with bipolar disorder to be identified as "Other Health Impaired" due to the biological component of the illness.

Classroom teachers are vital in supporting the child with pediatric bipolar disorder in school. They are in charge of instruction as well as the implementation of individualized behavioral interventions. Teachers can modify the child's academic schedule to help with disrupted sleep-wake cycles, create a safe area in the room as a place to calm down, and allow typed schoolwork to bypass any perfectionistic tendencies hindering the child in class. As mentioned, the child with bipolar disorder likely has coexisting attention problems and ADHD, so preferential seating, frequent breaks, and organizational aids (e.g., planners) would be helpful accommodations to support the child in the classroom. Teachers must be aware of the child's individual issues (e.g., types of medications and nature of diagnostic pattern) so that they can describe behaviors associated with school performance, energy level, mood, and social interactions to support treatment. Teachers who have knowledge about the child's individual situation can be sensitive to the child's needs and encourage the child in the classroom in a way that accommodates the child's disorder(s) yet capitalizes on his or her strengths.

EDUCATIONAL STRATEGIES

- Know that each child with pediatric bipolar disorder is different and will require differing levels of support in the school system.
- Foster communication and collaboration among educators and mental health professionals to support medical treatment and educational success of the child.
- Be aware of the wide variety of services available in the public schools to support a child with pediatric bipolar disorder, including general education with minimal supports, general education with Section 504 accommodations to be implemented in the classroom and school setting, and special education with the development of an IEP.
- An IEP can be developed to support the child with pediatric bipolar disorder ("Emotional Disability" or "Other Health Impaired") if the disorder adversely affects the child's learning.
- Understand that creating and implementing Section 504 plans, IEPs, and other support plans in the school necessitates a comprehensive, and sometimes lengthy, process involving a multidisciplinary team—including the parents and/or caregivers.
- Involve school psychologists and counselors for services such as individual counseling, social skills training, and/or classwide intervention to support the student's success.
- Involve the school nurse to address medical issues with the school team, monitor the child in school, support adherence to the child's medication regimen, and help communicate with medical providers outside of school.

DISCUSSION QUESTIONS

1. How does bipolar disorder differ in children when compared to the adult presentation?

2. How do you differentiate bipolar disorder in children with coexisting disorders?

3. How might bipolar disorder impact the educational progress of a child?

4. Describe treatment options for bipolar disorder in children.

5. What is the role of the teacher or school psychologist in supporting a student with bipolar disorder in the school setting? What types of accommodations, if any, might be necessary?

RESEARCH SUMMARY

- Bipolar disorder exists in children, but it appears differently than in adults.
- Bipolar disorder is highly heritable. Its prevalence rates range from 1% to 6% in the adolescent and adult populations. Prevalence rates

in childhood are more difficult to ascertain due to debate among scholars about diagnosis.

- Bipolar disorder in children is a rapid-cycling, nonepisodic, and debilitating disorder resulting in chronic and severe instability in mood, energy, sleep, and behavior that affects daily living at home, school performance, and socialization.
- Research is underway to clarify the biology, onset, diagnostic profile, course, and outcome of bipolar disorder in children, which remains a controversial subject.
- Childhood bipolar disorder is often comorbid with ADHD and learning disabilities. Other comorbid disorders include depression, anxiety (especially obsessive-compulsive disorder), panic disorder, oppositional defiant and conduct disorders, and pervasive developmental disorders.
- Effective intervention involves medication treatment, family intervention, and school supports, as well as collaborative communication among all involved with the child with pediatric bipolar disorder.

RESOURCES

Web Sites

Child & Adolescent Bipolar Foundation: www.bpkids.org

Georgia Childhood Bipolar Foundation: www.gcbf.org/resources/moodcharts.html

Juvenile Bipolar Research Foundation: www.bpchildresearch.org

National Institute of Mental Health (NIMH), *Bipolar disorder in children and teens: A parent's guide* (NIH Publication No. 08-6380): www.nimh.nih.gov/health/publications/bipolar-disorder-in-children-and-teens-a-parents-guide/index.shtml. This 2008 booklet is also available in a shorter, "easy-to-read" version.

Helpful Books for Parents

Fristad, M. A., & Goldberg-Arnold, J. S. (2004). *Raising a moody child: How to cope with depression and bipolar disorder.* New York: Guilford Press.

Papolos, D., & Papolos, J. (2006). *The bipolar child: The definitive and reassuring guide to childhood's most misunderstood disorder* (3rd ed.). New York: Broadway Books.

Pavuluri, M. (2008). *What works for bipolar kids: Help and hope for parents.* New York: Guilford Press.

Helpful Books for Children

Anglada, T. (2004). *Brandon and the bipolar bear: A story for children with bipolar disorder.* Murdock, FL: BPChildren.

McGee, C. C., & Hall, N. C. (2002). *Matt the moody hermit crab.* Nashville, TN: Soulwave. This book is available from the author at http://www.mattthemoodyhermitcrab.com.

HANDOUT

PEDIATRIC BIPOLAR DISORDER

Bipolar disorder is a highly heritable, neurobiological disorder that causes severe disturbance in mood, behavior, energy, and sleep. For children, bipolar disorder is a continuous, nonepisodic, and rapid-cycling disorder. Children with early-onset bipolar disorder experience a wide spectrum of symptoms that range from mild to extreme and affect everyday activities.

Common Challenges at Home

- Shows a wide range of behaviors and appears tired, bored, lethargic, irritable, explosive, distractible, impulsive, overly talkative, energetic, and giddy all in a short period of time or in alternating periods throughout the day.
- Has trouble getting up in the morning.
- Complains about health in and out of school.
- Has difficulty expressing feelings and frustrations.
- Has negative thoughts and feels hopelessness.
- Has feelings of failure if unable to do things others might consider simple.
- Does not use good stress-management techniques.
- May be self-aggressive and talk of suicide.
- May be self-absorbed in grandiose thoughts.
- Has poor concentration and ability to attend.
- Has difficulty establishing friendships.
- Shows poor judgment and poor decision-making and problem-solving skills.

Home-Based Intervention Strategies

- Provide positive praise and understanding to boost the child's self-esteem.
- Structure activities throughout child's day to promote routine.
- Support the development of friendships.
- Implement consistent behavior management strategies.
- Inform educators about bipolar disorder in children and your child's specific needs.
- Work with educators to be consistent at home and school.

School-Based Intervention Strategies

- Advocate for a comprehensive psychological assessment to guide intervention and educational supports for children who also have learning difficulties.
- Request development of an Individual Education Plan (IEP) via "Other Health Impaired" category or an accommodation plan via Section 504 to support classroom learning and behavior. Request a Functional Behavior Assessment (FBA) as needed for difficult-to-manage behaviors and to support academic learning.
- Request that the most difficult subjects be taken at the time of the day when the child's mood is best, if possible.
- Collaborate with the school to establish a crisis intervention plan for potential behavior outbursts (e.g., "safe place").
- Request that an aide be placed with child in the classroom as needed for safety purposes.

Psychosocial Treatments to Support Mood and Behavior

- Family therapy
- Individual therapy
- Group therapy
- School-based therapy

4

Parental Control and Separation Anxiety Disorder

Erika E. Levavi, Florence J. Schneider, and Paul C. McCabe

Juliana enters second grade holding her mother's hand. Her mother repeatedly hugs and kisses her as she states that she is leaving. Instead of leaving, her mother performs Juliana's tasks, such as hanging up her jacket. As Juliana clings to her mother, her mother utters that she will be back and promises not to be late. Juliana's mother moves toward the door several times, and each time, Juliana shouts and cries. The teacher asks the mother to leave and tells Juliana that she can sit near her as long as she needs but she must take a seat. She shuffles over to sit down with a lowered head. She remains silent for most of the day and does not engage in any work or interaction with others but rather glances at the door. When asked if she would like to join in, Juliana complains of a stomachache. On the second day, her mother reports that Juliana had nightmares about school. On the third morning, Juliana and her mother arrive late, and the mother describes Juliana's strong reluctance to attend school.

The teacher decides to plan a meeting with Juliana's mother and the school psychologist. At the meeting, several suggestions are made. Beginning on Monday, Juliana and her mother will be met at the entrance to the school by a school aide whom Juliana knows from first grade. The aide will escort Juliana to her class and announce that mothers can no longer walk to the room. The mother is directed to complete a good-bye ritual in 1 minute and wish Juliana a pleasant day, and she is instructed not to mention her return. When Juliana arrives in the room, the teacher will keep her near her for the first 15 minutes of class and prepare special tasks in which Juliana can be helpful. If Juliana appears sad, the teacher may ask if anything is bothering her. If she mentions home or her mother in any way, the teacher plans to express empathy while supplying emotion words such as *scary* and *lonely*. The teacher will reassure Juliana that she is safe in this class and everyone wants to be her friend. As the class writes in their journals, the teacher may suggest that Juliana write and draw about her feelings. Juliana's mother has been asked to speak with the school psychologist to discuss issues of parental control and alternative forms of expressing her love for Juliana.

INTRODUCTION

Separation anxiety disorder (SAD) is the most prevalent anxiety disorder in children. SAD accounts for almost one half of anxiety disorders in children and is diagnosed in about 10% of the general childhood population with the earliest age of onset (Pincus, Eyberg, & Choate, 2005). According to the *Diagnostic and Statistical Manual of Mental Disorders* (4th ed., text revision, American Psychiatric Association [APA], 2000), children with SAD experience developmentally inappropriate anxiety when confronted with separation from a caregiver that causes significant impairment in their daily functioning. Anxiety due to separation is considered typical and healthy for young children. However, it becomes a disorder when anxiety becomes excessive, intense, frequent, or beyond what is considered developmentally appropriate for children 6 to 18 years old.

Anxiety disorders tend to run in families. Children whose mothers suffer from anxiety are seven times more likely to develop anxiety when compared with other children (Turner, Biedel, & Epstein, 1991). Similarly, parents of children with an anxiety disorder are more likely to experience anxiety symptoms themselves. On the other hand, family and twin studies indicate that only 30% to 40% of the variance in anxiety disorders in children is due to heritability (Ballash, Leyfer, Buckley, & Woodruff-Borden, 2006). Research has revealed that parent-child interactions play a significant role in the development and maintenance of SAD (Wood, 2006). Furthermore, research suggests that parental characteristics related specifically to control are a major predictor of anxiety symptoms and SAD in children.

BACKGROUND

Specific patterns of family interactions have been identified as factors in the development and maintenance of SAD. One such family characteristic is the construct of parental control. According to Chorpita and Barlow's (1998) model of anxiety development, anxiety disorders stem from feelings of having little control over one's life circumstances. Parents of anxious children tend to be more controlling than parents of nonanxious children.

Behavioral Control

Parental control may take many forms. Behavioral control consists of behaviors parents use to manage, regulate, and supervise their children (Ballash et al., 2006). One study found that parents' behavioral involvement in their children's lives has led to children's perceived competence and understanding of control. Therefore, parental monitoring was associated with positive outcomes (Grolnick & Slowiaczek, 1994). A later study, however, found a more complicated link between parental monitoring and childhood anxiety; both extremely high and extremely low levels of parental involvement were associated with anxiety disorders in children (Colder, Lochman, & Wells, 2006).

Extreme parental involvement may become intrusive. Parental intrusiveness can manifest in three ways: providing unnecessary assistance to children, engaging in infantilizing behavior, and invading children's privacy. Wood (2006) found a correlation between high parent intrusiveness and high separation anxiety severity ratings. Parent intrusiveness was recorded based on the total number of seconds the parent engaged in intrusive or unnecessary physical assistance. Interestingly, this specific relationship between parent intrusiveness and separation anxiety did not extend to other types of anxiety disorders, such as generalized anxiety disorder or social phobia.

Wood's (2006) study demonstrated that intrusive parents who provide unnecessary assistance to their child, thereby restricting the child's autonomy, might actually promote anxiety in the child by limiting his or her mastery and sense of control. Because these children have fewer experiences with independent action and feelings of mastery, control, and self-efficacy, they will respond with anxiety when faced with novel tasks. As a way of avoiding anxiety, they tend to cling to their caregivers for assistance in novel situations and respond negatively to separation from caregivers.

Wood (2006) further discussed parents who engage in infantilizing behaviors, that is, parents who speak to their children using baby language and those who display excessive physical affection. Wood explained that this is intrusive because it forces children to function at an immature level. Similarly, parents who invade their children's privacy and cross boundaries place children in passive and immature roles, hindering their capacity for independent action.

Parental Anxiety

One study postulated that anxious parents experience anxiety as a result of observing their children struggle with new tasks (Capps, Sigman, Sena, Henker, & Whalen, 1996). In an effort to reduce their own anxiety, parents assume control over the task their child is performing. Muris and Merckelbach (1998) examined the relationship between parental control and anxiety symptoms in nonclinically anxious children. Children rated their parents in areas related to emotional warmth, rejection, control, and anxious rearing. A significant and positive relationship between anxious rearing and control was found, indicating that anxious parents are more likely to be controlling than nonanxious parents. Additionally, perceived parental control also predicted symptoms of SAD.

Parental Affection

Other forms of parental control may involve affectionate versus affectionless control. Two dimensions of parent behavior that contribute to the development of anxiety in children are warmth and control (Putnam, Sanson, & Rothbart, 2002). The combination of parental control and level of warmth appears to have a unique effect on anxiety. Affectionless control is characterized by high control coupled with minimal affection, whereas affectionate control involves high control coupled with affection. Mothers of anxious children exhibit significantly more control and less warmth than mothers of socially competent and aggressive children (Dumas, LaFreniere, & Serketich, 1995). Anxious mothers are significantly less warm and more controlling than nonanxious mothers (Whaley, Pinto, & Sigman, 1999). Furthermore, anxious mothers of anxious children are significantly more controlling than anxious mothers of nonanxious children. This suggests that behaviors exhibited by anxious mothers may be reciprocally influenced by their anxious children.

Parental control and low warmth appear to be a specific factor in parent-child interactions involving anxious children. Childhood anxiety is associated with parenting styles characterized by limited or inconsistent affection and extreme displays of control (Elizabeth et al., 2006). DiBartolo and Helt (2007) proposed that these specific parental characteristics instill feelings of helplessness in children, which may ultimately lead to symptoms of SAD. Although Dumas and colleagues (1995) found a significant correlation between affectionless control and anxious children, the research does not prove that parental affectionless control *causes* or *induces* anxiety in children. On the other hand, as suggested in Whaley and others (1999), there is a possibility that the child's personality and temperament elicit certain parenting styles.

Although parental displays of affection are determinants of the quality of later social and emotional adjustment in children, affectionate control, which involves displays of affection coupled with parental control, is also implicated in the pathogenesis of anxiety in children (DiBartolo & Helt, 2007). In a study examining social anxiety in nonclinical preschoolers, children were observed playing with same-age unfamiliar peers and completing a LEGO building task with their mothers. Parents of socially inhibited children were found to be highly controlling yet affectionate during the unstructured free play. On the other hand, these parents did not provide enough warmth or guidance during the structured LEGO task (Rubin, Cheah, & Fox, 2001). One hypothesis regarding affectionate control is that highly affectionate, overindulgent parents attempt to protect their child in response to their child's display of distress. This further suggests that parental control is elicited by anxious behaviors in children, and parents who respond with affectionate control maintain and reinforce anxiety in their children and perpetuate the cycle of unhealthy parent-child interactions.

Discipline

Other forms of parental control involve disciplinary measures. Power-assertive and punitive parents control their children's actions and discipline their children forcefully by yelling, hitting, and demanding obedience. A longitudinal study that followed a sample of 112 children from ages 2 to 4 years old concluded that overly involved protective and low warm-engaged (affectionless control) parenting predicted anxiety disorders in children. However, power-assertive punitive parenting did not predict anxiety in children (Bayer, Sanson, & Hemphill, 2006).

Psychological Control

Another form of control involves psychological attempts of parents to control their children's actions. One example of psychological control is a parent's use of guilt in an attempt to influence a child's behaviors. Although this tactic was found to be a mediating factor between family conflicts and adolescent anxiety, there has yet to be such a study on its effect on SAD in children (Ballash et al., 2006).

Cultural Differences

Cultural differences play a role in parental control and their effects on anxiety in children. Contrary to the research cited above that authoritarian parenting styles (high control and minimal affection) are associated with anxiety in children, authoritarian parenting styles were associated with better adjustment and academic performance for Asian Americans than were authoritative parenting styles (Steinberg, Lamborn, Dornbusch, & Darling, 1994). Authoritative parenting is characterized by warmth and acceptance in the context of clear rules and boundaries regarding acceptable behaviors (Ballash et al., 2006). On the other hand, authoritative styles were more beneficial for European-American achievement than first-generation Chinese Americans (Chao, 2001). Chao suggested that people from different cultures might respond differently to parental control due to their culture's perceptions of parental control. For example, Randolph (1995) pointed out that authoritarian parenting is associated with caring, love, and protection for African Americans and, therefore, is associated with assertiveness, independence, and competence among African-American children.

A recent study administered questionnaires to 2,893 Arab adolescents in eight Arab societies (Dwairy, Achoui, Abouserie, & Farah, 2006). These questionnaires measured mental health status, family connectedness, and parenting styles. Parenting styles were coded as authoritarian, authoritative, or permissive based on parental characteristics related to control, flexibility, and inconsistency, respectively. The study found that parental inconsistency was associated with the most negative effects: low family connectedness and lower mental health. Conversely, authoritative parenting was associated with higher family connectedness and better mental health. However, results showed that authoritarian parenting did not negatively affect mental health. Authoritarian parenting within an authoritarian culture may not have negative effects on the individual. The results suggest that parental inconsistency, as well as an overall inconsistency between parenting styles and the residing culture, may be harmful to the individual's mental health.

Paternal Factors

A major limitation of most studies regarding children with SAD is the use of only mother-child interactions. In fact, paternal psychopathology has also been shown to be a significant risk factor for the development of psychopathology in children (Whaley et al., 1999). Children characterized as having low tolerance for ambiguous situations were more likely to have fathers with authoritarian characteristics, as well as mothers who appeared overly protective and were reluctant to scold (Harrington, Block, & Block, 1978). Specifically, fathers were highly controlling, emotionally unsupportive, and impatient, while mothers were lacking in spontaneously expressed emotions and yet were not scolding. It is interesting to note that both parents demonstrated low expectations for their children. Additional research is needed to understand father-child interaction effects on children with SAD.

IMPLICATIONS FOR EDUCATORS

Prevention

Parent-child interactions, specifically those related to control, play a critical role in the development of SAD in children. Retrospective studies suggest that childhood SAD frequently precedes adult anxiety disorders, including panic disorders, agoraphobia, and major depressive disorder (Klein, 1995). Additionally, a 3.5-year follow-up study found that parents of children with SAD experienced a greater incidence of depression, obsessive-compulsive behavior, phobic anxiety, and general distress (Kearney, Sims, Pursell, & Tillotson, 2003). Therefore, treatment of SAD is necessary for the amelioration of child and family mental health and overall functioning.

It is important that adults work collaboratively and offer flexibility within their traditional roles. True collaboration requires adults to decrease their need for control and approach the team as equal partners. The family and others with whom the child comes in contact must actively participate along with school staff to create and implement an effective plan. Intervention plans must be developmentally appropriate and consider age, gender, experience, culture, ethnic background, and individual traits.

It is important to be aware of the early signs of extreme attachment, including excessive worry, nightmares, psychosomatic complaints, school reluctance or refusal, and fear of being alone. Leaving home or separating from loved ones can be a difficult transition, and the sheer magnitude of change can be overwhelming at any age. Building trust with new adults and in a new environment takes time, and adults need to demonstrate patience and the willingness to allow each child to set his or her own time frame for developing a trusting relationship.

Communication is essential in preventing separation anxiety. Parents are encouraged to talk to their child in a mature manner by describing the school environment, the expectations of the child, and the general schedule and avoid infantilizing talk. For example, the parent may say, "You're going to school! You'll be in your own classroom with chairs and toys and lots of other children. You will play, share, learn new things, have fun, and talk to your friends and teachers. You will also have lunch in school, and after snack time, I will come to pick you up to go home together." The timing of an explanation is important. For some children, explaining weeks in advance may create anxiety of anticipation, while other children may need the additional time to get accustomed to the idea. The tone of voice of the parent and the setting are to be considered. The child should be relaxed, and the parent should model excitement and pleasure. When children remain anxious, the teacher needs to give them time to discuss their emotions. Appropriate feeling words may need to be supplied to help validate the child's feelings. When children understand and identify their feelings, they become empowered to control their own actions.

The teacher may hold group or individual discussions with children experiencing anxiety due to separation. Writing letters, drawing pictures, or sending e-mails to parents will assist in encouraging children to express themselves. Children may feel connected to the parent by holding the letter or drawing, putting it in their bag, or mailing it. E-mail may allow the child to receive responses during the school day, which can reassure children that they are in contact with the parent. Reminders of home can sometimes be distracting or upsetting, so reading of e-mails must be scheduled appropriately.

Having a transitional object to foster a sense of security is common practice in preschool environments. Sometimes children have a favorite item that they may bring to school and are not required to share, such as a blanket, piece of blanket, or toy. Some parents will hand the child a personal item to indicate that they will return, such as a watch or set of keys. Teachers may post photographs of parents in the classroom or in small books, and children are permitted to seek comfort from the photos. Although many schools have a limited orientation time when parents are invited to stay in the classroom, some children may need extra time. In this case, a "mommy/daddy line" can be drawn on the floor with tape. It is an area where the parents may sit and observe or communicate with their child, but to avoid parent intrusiveness, no one is to cross the line. Children will begin to recognize that distance is acceptable.

The transfer of children's trust from a parent to a teacher is important. With young or anxious children, parents should be encouraged to spend time in the school interacting with the child and the teacher. Because anxious behaviors in parents may trigger anxiety in children, parents should model comfort in the environment. The amount of time that the parent stays may need to be decreased gradually. Parental warmth and affection is encouraged in a noncontrolling manner, and parents are advised to refrain from excessive affection. For children who are showing early signs of difficulty with parting, it may be possible to arrange for the child to leave the parent, instead of reverse. Perhaps another adult, such as a babysitter, neighbor, or relative, could take the child from home to school. If separation at home is not possible, then a parent area could be designated whereby separation and transition to school could be made easier.

Security is often based on a sense of control. Many early childhood programs have an orientation period when children arrive for shorter days before beginning full-time or a graduated lengthening of the school day. Also, when classes maintain consistent routines and schedules, children know what to expect, which increases their sense of mastery over their environment and reduces worry (Kim & Yeary, 2008). To increase self-efficacy, provide opportunities for children to experience success in the classroom. Future orientation occurs when the teacher announces in advance what activity comes next and what is expected. Clear and concise class rules that are stated in positive terms assist in children feeling safe and involved in the group. Children showing signs of distress may benefit from arriving early to become familiar with the classroom and materials before adjusting to the group. Other children may be less bewildered if they arrive with other children so they immediately feel part of the group. In these situations, the first activity of the day should be planned carefully. Some programs have a welcoming group activity, while others keep the early part of the day for free-choice activities that allow for staggered drop-off and gradual involvement in a group.

Children's comfort comes from a variety of developmentally appropriate practices. Being sensitive to the child's needs is paramount. The teacher can promote a worry-free classroom by being supportive of efforts, maintaining a calm reaction to unexpected events, modeling playfulness by being silly, encouraging children to join in at their own pace, and stressing the importance of each and every child. Some children may need proximity to the teacher to increase feelings of safety.

Interventions

Many children with SAD are treated successfully with cognitive-behavioral therapy (CBT). CBT is distinguished from behavioral therapy in that the latter technique focuses on the child's overt behaviors without considering the maladaptive thoughts that may be causing these behaviors, whereas CBT combines a behavioral approach with cognitive therapy and focuses on modifying maladaptive thoughts as a way of changing the child's behavior. CBT teaches children skills such as recognizing anxious feelings and physical reactions to anxiety and using coping strategies to increase self-efficacy. CBT approaches for treating children with SAD include exposure techniques, cognitive restructuring, relaxation training, social skills training, and operant conditioning.

Exposure is highly recommended for children exhibiting school reluctance, school refusal, and nonattendance (Lauchlan, 2003). Graduated exposure is a type of exposure in which the child is introduced to the school setting and separated from the caregiver gradually. Separation is increased gradually with the aim of desensitizing the child to the separation. When the time interval reaches the end of the school day, dismissal is a natural reward for attendance. The second type of exposure is flooding, where the child is forced to attend school without the parent, using escorts if necessary. The parents should not discuss their desire for the child to attend school but rather be firm yet considerate in their demand for attendance. Both of the exposure methods include supportive therapy to examine the child's fears and discuss coping strategies.

An important aspect of CBT occurs in the therapy environment, but it also can be incorporated in the school by teachers. Cognitive restructuring or self-statement training assists children in analyzing their reasons for anxiety by stating their negative expectations and pairing these statements with a positive perspective on the same experience. For example, a child may state, "The other children don't like me." The positive replacement statement can be, "I can make a friend." A plan may be devised for developing at least one friendship in the class and then extending this to include more friends.

Another form of CBT is relaxation training. Children learn to relax the body through breathing exercises and mental imagery. The relaxed state is paired with an anxiety-producing stimulus to retrain a child to eliminate physical distress while approaching separation. Social skills training gives children time to rehearse social situations and examine where they may have problems. It is important to include the family in treatment, as these methods can be practiced and reinforced at home, thus improving treatment efficacy and generalizability.

Operant conditioning can also be used by the school and family. Incentives for appropriate separation are provided and withheld for inappropriate behaviors. If a child is displaying reluctance to attend school, then the time spent at home during school hours should be as boring as possible, with schoollike activities provided. To extinguish SAD symptoms, the teacher should not attend to inappropriate behavior, while any behavior that exhibits adaptation to the school environment should be rewarded with praise and attention.

In addition, parent-child interaction therapy (PCIT), an empirically supported treatment for children with disorders and their families, incorporates the family throughout treatment (Brinkmeyer & Eyberg, 2003). The rationale behind PCIT is that improvements in parent-child interactions will help the child, as well as overall family functioning, improve. Standard PCIT treatment involves two phases: child-directed interaction (CDI) and parent-directed interaction (PDI). During CDI, parents are taught skills to increase warmth, responsiveness, attention, and praise when interacting with their children. The PDI phase is based on operant principles of behavior change, and parents are instructed to provide consistent positive and negative consequences based on their child's behaviors. PCIT treatment has demonstrated significant improvements in children's behaviors, parent stress level, and overall family functioning.

One study adapted PCIT for children with SAD by adding a new phase. The bravery-directed interaction (BDI) phase, designed to be implemented between the CDI and PDI phases, consists of several minisessions: the BDI Teach Session, the BDI Coach #1 Session, and the BDI Coach #2 Session (Pincus et al., 2005). During the BDI Teach Session, parents are educated about the nature and cause of anxiety, as well as factors that maintain anxiety in children. Specifically, parents are taught about ways that certain parenting behaviors or practices may reinforce separation anxiety. They are taught how to modify their own behaviors and the importance of exposing their child to separation experiences. During the BDI Coach #1 session, parents and children begin the process of exposure practice; the BDI Coach #2 session provides follow-up. Results included increased social reinforcement of brave behaviors, improved parent-child attachment, and decreased levels of parent anxiety.

Treating children with SAD requires that parents and school professionals work collaboratively throughout treatment. Teachers should work toward providing the child with a warm and comforting school environment by implementing consistent rules and structure within the classroom. Treatment should not just focus on the child in isolation but on overall family functioning as well. Treatments need to be modified depending on the child's age, intellectual level, culture, gender, experience, ethnic background, and individual traits. Educating parents about their role in the development of SAD and teaching positive parenting skills will help to prevent future occurrences of SAD.

EDUCATIONAL STRATEGIES

Prevention

- Encourage collaboration among all adults who work with the child.
- Be aware of early warning signs of excessive worry, reluctance, and psychosomatic complaints.
- Communicate maturely and openly with children about your expectations. Validate and accept their feelings without judgment.
- Maintain connections with the home without crossing boundaries. Example: Have children write letters to parents but not call them, since the latter demands an immediate response.
- Provide concrete cues for security without allowing intrusiveness. Examples: Children can bring a security object to school. Draw a "mommy/daddy line" that is not crossed.
- Prepare good-bye rituals that are sensitive, consistent, and brief.
- If problems persist, try to arrange that the child leaves the parent, instead of the parent leaving the child.
- Schedule orientation for the beginning of school. Allow some students to arrive early.
- Provide activities for success.
- Maintain consistent routines to increase children's sense of mastery over their environment. Transitions should be well planned, pleasant, and active and include future orientation and advance warnings.
- Create positive, meaningful class rules in a nonthreatening manner.
- Welcome all parents and children to a nurturing, warm educational setting.

Intervention

- *Cognitive behavioral therapy* focuses on modifying thoughts and behaviors by recognizing anxious feelings and using coping strategies. Techniques include exposure, flooding, cognitive restructuring, relaxation training, and operant conditioning.
- *Parent-child interaction therapy* incorporates the family throughout treatment. Parents are taught positive interaction skills and behavior management strategies. Parents of children with SAD are educated about the cause and nature of anxiety.

DISCUSSION QUESTIONS

1. What parent-child interactions may play a role in the development of SAD?

2. How can educators inform parents that their child displays problematic behaviors?

3. How can school professionals educate parents about parent-child interactions?

4. How can teachers create and maintain an effective relationship with parents, especially when the parent is contributing to the separation anxiety?

5. At what point is it necessary for teachers to intervene and develop an intervention plan for children exhibiting separation anxiety symptoms?

6. When might an intervention need to be modified for a particular child, and under what circumstances?

RESEARCH SUMMARY

The following parenting factors are related to separation anxiety disorder in children:

- *Behavioral control.* Parents who engage in behavioral control display excessive monitoring, assisting, intruding, infantilizing, and invading their child's privacy. These behaviors limit the child's independence and self-confidence.
- *Parental anxiety.* Anxious parents tend to be more controlling and less affectionate than nonanxious parents. Anxious children may elicit controlling behaviors in parents.
- *Parental affection.* Affectionless control and extreme affectionate control instill feelings of helplessness.
- *Discipline.* Power-assertive and punitive parenting has not been shown to be linked with SAD.
- *Psychological control.* Guilt as a manipulative parenting style is related to adolescent anxiety, but there is no study to date on its effect on younger children.
- *Cultural differences.* Families from different cultures respond differently to parenting styles depending on their culture's perceptions of parental control. Inconsistency between parenting styles and cultural expectations leads to conflict.
- *Paternal factors.* Most studies have examined mother/child interactions. When fathers have been studied, authoritarian characteristics lead to children having difficulty with ambiguous situations.

RESOURCES

Balaban, N. (2006). *Everyday goodbyes: Starting school and early care, a guide to the separation process.* New York: Teachers College Press.

Eisen, A. R., & Engler, L. B. (2006). *Helping your child overcome separation anxiety or school refusal: A step-by-step guide for parents.* Oakland, CA: New Harbinger.

Eisen, A. R., & Schaefer, C. E. (2005). *Separation anxiety in children and adolescents: An individualized approach to assessment and treatment.* New York: Guilford Press.

HANDOUT

SEPARATION ANXIETY DISORDER

Parents and educators can work together to prevent separation problems. Fear of leaving a parent is common among children through 6 years old. How can parents foster secure attachment and healthy separation?

- It is important to build trust with your young child by responding to his or her needs. When children cannot get what they want, parents should firmly and kindly explain why.

  Example: "I know you're thirsty, but soda is bad for your teeth at night. Drink water."

- Gradually introduce your child to doing things independently without your being completely involved in the activity.
- Avoid helping children with every task, especially when they are capable of doing it for themselves. Teaching children responsibility will boost their confidence.
- Encourage play opportunities where your child can practice getting along with children of the same age. Children need to learn to negotiate, compromise, and cope with failure.
- Communication with your child is vital. Include children in family discussions. Answer their questions. Ask them to explain things to you.

  Example: When your child calls you, respond, even if it is to say, "Please wait a minute." Be sure to get back to the child's request as soon as possible.

  Example: Ask your child what he or she likes about a particular TV show or toy or place.

- When your child is going to a new day care or school environment, familiarize yourself with the setting and teacher so you can describe it to your child in advance. Parents should model excitement and pleasure about the new adventure.

  Example: "Your new school has lots of toys, and you will make so many friends there."

- If parents are invited to stay for a while at the beginning of the school year, explain to the child that you will be staying and then leaving. Reassure your child that you will return later.
- Many schools have an orientation period of shortened days. Be sure to attend these sessions since they often include some time with the teacher in a small setting.
- Validate the child's feelings. Avoid telling children what to feel or not feel.

  Example: Say that you understand he or she feels fear or sadness, but it is okay.

- One way of avoiding an awkward entrance is to arrive early. This will give your child time to choose an area where they he or she feels comfortable and not to feel rushed.
- It is important that your child transfer trust from a parent to a teacher. Show support and respect for the teacher. Children will pick up on any discomfort that you feel, and they may translate that to fear.
- Many children need a concrete transitional object to carry with them in school.

  Example: Allow the child to choose a nonvaluable item from home to take to school. For instance, some teachers will encourage all children to bring in a photo of their families.

- Some teachers will conduct group or individual discussions about coming to school.
- Teachers may allow children to write letters or e-mails to their parents. If you receive a letter or e-mail, thank your child for his or her thoughtfulness.
- Encourage your child to follow the class rules and explain that the rules are to help and protect all of the children.
- Each parent and teacher can decide on an individual basis if it is better to leave unobtrusively or to have a good-bye ritual. Once you have left or said good-bye, you must stay out of the classroom. If necessary, stay nearby without intruding on the child's adjustment.

- If problems persist, you may have someone else take the child to school or take the child from you at the entrance to the school.
- If your child is demonstrating the following symptoms on a regular basis, speak to a professional: Excessive distress at separation, excessive worry that something terrible will happen, nightmares, complaints of aches and pains, fear of being alone, and reluctance or refusal to attend school are all signs of a more serious disorder such as separation anxiety disorder. These symptoms are especially concerning if your child is 6 years old or older.

5

Mood Disorders and Creativity

Sara Pollak-Kagan and Paul C. McCabe

Emily Dickinson is one of America's best-known poets, as well as the "quintessential example of the enigmatic artist with a tortured mind" (Ramey & Weisberg, 2004, p. 175). McDermott (2001) used her collection of letters as an autobiographical source to investigate the presence of a mental illness. He suggested that Dickinson had an affective disorder that could be divided into two separate 4-year blocks. During the first block (1858–1861), Dickinson had seasonal affective disorder (SAD). McDermott presented data showing that these years were characterized by increased output in the spring and summer and decreased output in fall and winter. During the second block (1862–1865), when Dickinson likely suffered from bipolar II disorder and hypomania, she seemed to produce a remarkably large quantity of writing.

McDermott further proposed that Dickinson's mood had several effects on her poetry. Panic attacks provided her with intense negative emotional experiences, which she used in her poetry. For example, her feelings of looming death brought on by the attacks might have been transmuted into the poems that focused on death. Likewise, during the winters of the SAD years, Dickinson's works were wrought with death themes. During the period of her reported hypomania, Dickinson's writing style underwent a change as noticed by scholars of her work. McDermott (2001), quoting the critical review of Miller, stated that her writing is seen as an almost constant stream of ideas, with a "sudden development of several simultaneously expanding metaphors, creating an experience that required a new kind of reading (21)" (p. 688).

INTRODUCTION

Relations between creativity and madness have been recorded since antiquity. Pre-Grecian mythology expressed a close relationship between the gods and madness. Aristotle thought that great artists, philosophers, writers, and politicians are susceptible to gloom. Until recently, modern concepts have emphasized the apparent similarity between the production of novel ideas and the unusual thought and behavior of persons with mental illness. This chapter will explore the assertion that children and adolescents with mood disorders may have increased creativity levels.

BACKGROUND

Link Between Bipolar Disorder and Creativity

Support for the idea of a connection between bipolar illness and creativity has been drawn from only a few empirical studies. Nancy Andreasen (1987) carried out psychiatric interviews with 30 writers-in-residence at the University of Iowa Program in Creative Writing and with 30 controls. An occurrence of bipolar illness was reported in 43% of the writer group and 10% in the controls. Moreover, Andreasen found that 80% of the writers had experienced an episode of either severe depression or manic depression. They also had experienced either a manic episode characterized by euphoria, increased energy, and poor judgment or milder "hypomania" at some time in their lives. The writers also reported significantly more first-degree relatives with creative achievements in a variety of fields, including literature, art, and music. Andreasen concluded that the breadth of creativity in these families suggests that a genetic link to creative success may be transmitted within families.

Kay Jamison (1989) studied a British sample of 47 prizewinning artists and writers, questioning them about their mood states and their treatment history. Jamison reported that 38% of the sample had sought treatment for mood disorders, a rate about 30 times that of the general population. Writers experienced the most problems with mood disorders, and of these, poets topped the list, with half of them reporting psychiatric intervention (i.e., medications and/or hospitalization) for depression and/or mania. Almost two thirds of the playwrights had been treated for mood disorders, mainly with psychotherapy. The rate for biographers was 20%, and for artists 13%. One third of the 47 reported that they experienced severe mood swings; the poets and novelists were particularly prone to mood swings. Jamison argued that the biographers, the least likely to be linked with "creative fire," reported no history of mood swings or elated states.

Shapiro and Weisberg (1991) set out to determine the association between creativity and bipolar disorders using a sample of accomplished creative individuals with cyclothymia (a mood disorder similar to but less severe than bipolar disorder) and in relatives of persons with bipolar disorder. It was hypothesized that individuals with cyclothymia or demonstrating a tendency toward bipolar disorder would have higher creativity scores. Seventy-two undergraduate students at Temple University volunteered to participate. The results showed no difference in creativity scores between the participants meeting the criteria for cyclothymia and those who scored normally. A multiple regression analysis was performed on the data, and creativity scores of individuals meeting the criteria for hyperthymic pattern (that is, characterized by subsyndromal-elevated mood with few or no symptoms of depression) were significantly higher than those of the cyclothymic, dysthymic, or euthymic pattern groups. However, it is unclear whether this group represents people with a tendency toward bipolar disorder or just energetic people. Hyperthymia is not considered a disorder by the *DSM-IV-TR*, but an ostensibly unipolar hypomania is considered a risk factor for bipolarity. Clearly, a much larger sample of individuals meeting the criteria for a hyperthymic pattern is required to determine if subtle differences exist between elevated mood in typical individuals and those with a family history of bipolar disorder.

Interestingly, it was the combination of the two dimensions, hypomania alternating with depression, that accounted for the greatest proportion of the variance in creativity scores, suggesting that a depressive state has a suppressive effect on creativity. This is consistent with the work of Schuldberg (1990), who found that hypomanic personality traits and impulsivity in university students were positively correlated with creativity.

Other studies addressing the role of emotion on creativity have found that positive affect, not depression, is connected with the creative process. In an investigation of the emotions that occur during creative writing, Brand (1989) found that writers did not report great mood swings or feelings of distress, depression, or rage while writing. Similarly, in a pilot program with a small sample of graduate creative writing students, Shapiro and Weisberg (1991) found a noteworthy positive correlation between positive affect and creative ideation but no connection between negative affective states and any part of the creative writing process. With regard to poets, research suggests that although they share unusual experiences similar to those of individuals diagnosed with schizophrenia, they are less likely to manifest anhedonia (i.e., lack of pleasure-seeking activity) and social withdrawal reported in patients with schizophrenia (Nettle, 2006b; Rawlings & Locarnini, 2008).

Similar evidence was reported in a study of clinically identified individuals with bipolar disorder or unipolar major depressive disorder, who were matched with creative discipline controls (artists and writers with no psychiatric diagnosis) and healthy controls. Subjects were administered a number of creativity measures. Results indicated that individuals with bipolar disorder and healthy creative controls scored higher than healthy controls on a measure of artistic appreciation that reflects greater creativity. In addition, creative controls scored significantly higher than individuals with unipolar major depressive disorder on a figural test of divergent thinking, a presumed cognitive contributor to creativity. The results suggest that individuals with bipolar disorder exhibit a more diverse appreciation of art, while those with unipolar depression exhibit a more restricted ability to engage in creative problem solving (Santosa et al., 2007).

The relationship between temperament and creativity with individuals with bipolar was also investigated (Strong et al., 2007). Factor analysis was used to consolidate the subscales of several personality and temperament measures, and the resultant factors were used to measure creativity parameters in a sample of individuals with bipolar disorder, individuals with unipolar major depressive disorder, creative discipline controls, and healthy controls. The results indicated that the personality factors neuroticism/ cyclothymia/dysthymia and openness were differentially related to creativity.

Neuroticism provides access to negative affect and may facilitate openness to creative or divergent ideas, while cyclothymia facilitates variability of affect. Openness reflects a temperament-personality feature that facilitates cognitive flexibility and thus encourages creative thinking. Other studies have supported the finding that hypomanic personality features are more prevalent among highly creative artists and musicians as compared to other specialized professions, such as scientists (Rawlings & Locarnini, 2008).

Neurobiological and Genetic Model

Studies examining the neurobiological mechanism underlying creativity suggest a dominant role of three brain structures: the frontal lobe, the temporal lobes, and the mesolimbic system. The neurotransmission system primarily implicated with elevated mood and psychotic thinking is the dopaminergic system, especially the mesolimbic and cortical pathways. Both neurobiological and pharmacological evidence has supported an association of these pathways with motivational, emotional, and cognitive processes and, indirectly, with the processes of creativity (Rybakowski, Klonowska, Patrza, & Jaracz, 2006).

Individuals with bipolar mood disorders tend to be more emotionally reactive, which may also present as greater emotional sensitivity. This, together with a lack of inhibition due to compromised frontal lobe processes, may allow for unrestrained and unusual forms of expression with fewer inhibitory processes that respond to accepted norms and customs. Such individuals are more open to experimentation and risk-taking behavior, which may lead to creative forms of expression. The waxing and waning between manic and depressive states has been hypothesized as facilitative of freer expression of ideas and an unusual "kaleidoscopic" perspective of the world (Jamison, 1993).

Molecular-genetic studies investigating genetic determinants of creativity processes in association with psychiatric conditions have identified a heritable spectrum with widespread prevalence across cultures. Some researchers have proposed that creativity, and the cognitive, emotional, and psychological states that appear to encourage creativity, can be considered an evolutionary and genetic advantage to the species (Andreasen, 1987; Richards, 1997). In citing twin concordance, adoption, and family risk studies, Wilson (1992) noted that the strong genetic component in bipolar illness may "prevail at five hundred times the adjusted mutation equilibrium rate" (p. 88). A high prevalence beyond the expected mutation rates supports the hypothesis of genetic continuity, such that certain characteristics with adaptive benefits will propagate in the species through the process of natural selection.

Wilson (1992) suggested that a flourishing of artistic modes in Western cultures is not idiosyncratic but rather a result of genetic determination, as creative individuals reproduce and endow their offspring with creative personalities as well as underlying psychological processes. Evidence for this includes studies on courtship models, in which creativity in artistic domains serves to attract mates (Nettle, 2006a). Women are likely to rate creativity as attractive during the most fertile phase of the menstrual cycle (Haselton & Miller, 2006), and poets and visual artists have significantly more sexual partners than controls (Nettle & Clegg, 2006). As genetic features of creativity and openness are passed to offspring, so also is the propensity for psychological processes that may include extreme manifestations of mood, thought, and personality. Additional research is needed exploring the genetic origins of creativity, its link to mood disorders such as bipolar disorder, and the potential adaptive benefit to the species.

IMPLICATIONS FOR EDUCATORS

Educators are encouraged to develop a curriculum with ample opportunities for creative behaviors. They can create assignments that call for original work, independent learning, self-initiated projects, and experimentation. To provide opportunities for creative learning, educators can use curriculum materials that provide progressive warm-up experiences, develop procedures that lead to divergent cognitive processes, and employ activities that make creative thinking both legitimate and rewarding.

The following are recommendations for educators and parents to foster and nurture creativity in children:

- Children can be taught to appreciate and be pleased with their own creative efforts.
- Educators can be respectful and even encouraging of the unusual questions children ask.
- Educators can be respectful of children's unusual ideas and solutions, for children will see many relationships and resolutions that their parents and teachers miss.
- Educators can show children that their ideas have value by listening to their ideas and considering them. Children are encouraged to test their ideas by sharing them with others. They should be given credit for their ideas.
- Teachers can provide chances for children to learn, think, and discover without worry of immediate evaluation. Constant evaluation, especially during practice and initial learning, makes children afraid to use creative ways to learn. Educators should accept their honest errors as part of the creative process.
- Educators can establish creative relationships with children, that is, encouraging creativity in the classroom while providing adequate guidance and structure.
- Creativity in childhood is analogous to play; it is necessary to develop children's minds and allows them to organize and embellish their sense of the world.

Conversely, adults "kill" creativity in the following ways:

- Insisting that children do things the "right way." Teaching a child to think that there is just one right way to do things decreases innovation. Although many educational goals require the mastery of a specific skill or behavior, there are often many ways to learn and master the skill.
- Pressuring children always to be realistic or, worse, to stop imagining altogether. When educators or parents label a child's flights of fantasy as "silly" or a "waste of time," they often stifle creativity and hurt the child's feelings.

- Making comparisons with other children. This is a subtle pressure on a child to conform, yet the essence of creativity is freedom to conform or not to conform.

EDUCATIONAL STRATEGIES

- Educators are encouraged to develop a curriculum with ample opportunities for creative behaviors. They can create assignments that call for original work, independent learning, self-initiated projects, and experimentation. Educators can use curriculum materials that provide progressive warm-up experiences, develop procedures that lead to divergent cognitive processes, and employ activities that make creative thinking both legitimate and rewarding.
- Educators should be respectful of the unusual questions children ask and the unusual ideas and solutions that they generate.
- Educators can provide chances for children to learn, think, and discover without worry of immediate evaluation. Educators should accept honest errors as part of the creative process.
- Creativity in childhood is analogous to play; it is necessary to develop children's minds and allows them to organize and embellish their sense of the world.
- Educators should avoid teaching a child to think that there is just one right way to do things. Although many educational goals require the mastery of a specific skill or behavior, there are often many ways to learn and master the skill. Innovation comes from learning new ways to solve problems.
- Educators should also avoid being too grounded in pragmatism or, worse, to labeling a child's flights of fantasy as "silly" or a "waste of time." Doing so stifles creativity and hurts the child's feelings.

DISCUSSION QUESTIONS

1. How can creativity be elicited and fostered in all children, regardless of the presence of mental illness?

2. How can creative activities help children to express their emotions?

3. Might there be an evolutionary and adaptive benefit for humans to have intense mood changes? How might creativity be important for success of the species?

4. What are some of the challenges of fostering creativity in individuals who are suffering intense mood disorders? What precautions might be necessary?

5. Can you imagine a situation where treatment of an individual with a mood disorder might be delayed to prolong a period of creativity to encourage the production of an important artistic work? If so, what tension might exist between ethical concerns versus contribution to society?

RESEARCH SUMMARY

- The notion that mood disorders increase or enhance creativity is still hypothetical, as no studies have identified a causal connection and studies showing correlational evidence are equivocal.
- The biological mechanisms underlying such a relationship remain tentative, and researchers have not yet identified a neural pathway or shared biochemical process that explains why creativity and mood disorder might coexist.
- One refutation of the hypothesis is that many people with mood disorders are not more creative or artistic, and many artists and creative individuals are not affected by mood disorders. Therefore, the relationship, if one exists, is complex and influenced by a number of as yet unidentified factors.
- There is a concern that romanticizing such a serious medical condition is dangerous, placing a burden on sufferers to be creative or even to refuse treatment. Thus, although society may benefit from the creative works of its so-called mad geniuses, this benefit must be balanced against the cost to the individual—which is extraordinarily high when considering that at least one in five sufferers of bipolar disorder attempt suicide.
- Mood disorders are a treatable condition, and most patients report that their quality of life improves dramatically after starting psychotherapy and medication.

RESOURCES

Music and art therapy improves the quality of life for children and adults with disabilities or illnesses. Music and art therapy interventions can be designed to manage stress, alleviate pain, express feelings, and improve overall psychological functioning. Many of these activities and recommendations can be adapted for use at home.

American Art Therapy Association: www.arttherapy.org

American Music Therapy Association: www.musictherapy.org/faqs.html

The National Institute of Mental Health (NIMH) Web site offers up-to-date information about bipolar disorder:

www.nimh.nih.gov/health/publications/bipolar-disorder/complete-publication.shtml

The following books focus on understanding bipolar disorder in children and adolescents:

Anglada, T., & Hakala, S. M. (2008). *The childhood bipolar disorder answer book: Practical answers to the top 300 questions parents ask.* Naperville, IL: Sourcebooks.

Lombardo, G. T. (2008). *Understanding the mind of your bipolar child: The complete guide to the development, treatment, and parenting of children with bipolar disorder.* New York: St. Martin's Griffin.

HANDOUT

USE OF CREATIVE MEDIUMS WITH CHILDREN AND ADOLESCENTS WITH MOOD DISORDERS

Parents and educators can use art and music to help children express feelings and emotions. Art can be used to help children communicate specific concerns. Sometimes this approach may be met with denial and resistance. Yet often the artwork that is created is quite revealing. It can be used to allow children to express themselves through their choice of media. It is often best to allow children to choose spontaneously the topic/subject of the artwork. From a child's choice of subject, process and media, and ability to solve problems as they occur, the parent or educator can learn a lot about the cognitive and psychological processes of the child. The parent or educator can then use that information to help the child discuss how to solve problems, generate solutions, and cope with others.

Both music and art can be used to channel children's energy. Educators and parents often struggle to find the balance between knowing when to encourage and when to set limits or add structure to the process.

A child who is depressed may be encumbered in melancholy or irritable feelings, or the child may be withdrawn and resistive, requiring significant time to trust and express himself or herself. Art and music therapy helps children pull themselves from the withdrawn state and assists in gaining trust. Often, what cannot be expressed by children can be rendered into an artistic medium, and an astute parent or educator can use this rendering as a porthole into a child's inner world.

Furthermore, a child with the diagnosis of depression or bipolar disorder may be lacking in self-confidence. A parent or teacher can build on children's talents in art or music to help boost their confidence in themselves. Children should be encouraged to draw, sculpt, sing, or play an instrument if this is how they seem to shine. Children with bipolar disorder may be partial to creative mediums and activities during the hypomanic phase and should be encouraged to use art or music as a healthy form of expression and outlet for their energy.

SECTION II

Psychopharmacology

6

Atypical Antipsychotic Use in Children and Adolescents With Autism Spectrum Disorders*

A Review for Educators

Steven R. Shaw and Tamara Dawkins

Franco is a 9-year-old who has a long-standing diagnosis of Sotos syndrome with many behavioral features similar to autism. Sotos is a genetic disorder marked by large stature, intellectual disabilities, speech and language disorders, and weak muscle tone. A recent psychological evaluation showed that his current intellectual functioning is consistent with severe to profound intellectual disabilities. In addition, Franco has significantly delayed speech and language. He currently uses 16 understandable spoken words. His receptive vocabulary appears to be more advanced than his expressive vocabulary.

*Adapted from Dawkins, T., & Shaw, S. R. (2006). Atypical antipsychotic use in children and adolescents with autism spectrum disorders: A review for school psychologists. *Communiqué, 35*(1), 21–24. Copyright by the National Association of School Psychologists, Bethesda, MD. Use is by permission of the publisher. www.nasponline.org

> Like many persons with Sotos syndrome, Franco is much taller than any other student in his classroom. Over the last 6 months, Franco has become increasingly irritable, oppositional, and physically aggressive to adults and peers. Several efforts were made to conduct a functional behavioral analysis and behavior improvement plan, but Franco was resistant to interventions. The severity of the aggressive behaviors appeared to become worse at school, but Franco's parents even reported that they feared for the safety of Franco's younger sister due to the increased severity of the aggression at home. As a result of this increased aggression and resistance to classroom interventions, Franco was taken to a developmental pediatrician for medical intervention.
>
> Franco was given a trial of stimulant medications (Adderall and then Concerta) without noticeable effects on behavior. Due to his severe and frightening behaviors, the physician prescribed a low dose of Risperdal. Franco tolerated the medication well, showing few side effects. In addition, there appeared to be a reduction in aggressive and oppositional behaviors.
>
> Consider the following: Given the apparent effectiveness of the Risperdal trial, should efforts to find an effective behavior intervention plan be changed? What information could educators provide to parents and physicians that would be helpful in monitoring the outcomes of this medication trial? What are the potential long- and short-term positive effects of this medication for Franco?

INTRODUCTION

Atypical antipsychotic medications are a complex new approach to medical treatment of behavior problems in children with autism spectrum disorders. Educators can benefit from understanding the commonly used medications from this class of drugs, how these medications work, their potential positive outcomes, and related behavioral and educational side effects. Atypical antipsychotics can have both positive and negative effects on student performance. The response to these medications varies dramatically from student to student. As such, it is incumbent on educators to know what to look for and to monitor the effects of these medications.

BACKGROUND

Intensive early behavioral interventions are the treatment of choice for children with autism and many other developmental disabilities, as these children can demonstrate symptoms such as aggression, hyperactivity/impulsivity, self-injurious behaviors, and irritability. Providing effective treatments as early as possible is a primary goal of educators working with children with autism spectrum disorders (ASD). Consistent with this goal, physicians are increasingly prescribing atypical antipsychotic medications to children with ASD and many other developmental disabilities. Intensive early intervention may also include medications to assist in managing problem behaviors.

The early prescription of psychotropic medications is controversial (Correll, 2008). This is especially so in the case of powerful medications, such as atypical antipsychotic medications, which have significant and fairly common short-term side effects and unknown long-term effects. Atypical antipsychotic medications are approved for use in older children and adolescents with bipolar disorder and early onset psychotic symptoms. One atypical antipsychotic (i.e., Risperidol) is also approved to treat irritability, aggression, and self-injurious behaviors in children aged 5 to 18 years who have been diagnosed with ASD (Chavez, Chavez-Brown, & Rey, 2006). Atypical antipsychotic medications are frequently prescribed off-label (i.e., in a manner not approved by the U.S. Food and Drug Administration) for preschool-aged children diagnosed with autism, bipolar disorder, attention deficit/hyperactivity disorder, early-onset schizophrenia, psychotic disorders, intellectual disabilities, and other developmental disabilities.

Antipsychotic medications have long been used in the treatment of severe adult psychopathologies, such as schizophrenia. The first generation of antipsychotics includes such medications as Mellaril (thioridazine), Thorazine (chlorpromazine), and Haldol (haloperidol). The latest generation of antipsychotic medication is fast becoming the choice of physicians in the treatment of problem behaviors across various clinical groups of children and adolescents (Patel et al., 2005). One in five visits to a pediatric psychiatrist results in a prescription for an atypical antipsychotic medication (Carey, 2006; Curtis et al., 2005). Atypical antipsychotics are favored over their predecessors because they produce fewer neurological side effects, such as tardive dyskinesia and extra pyramidal symptoms (EPS). Atypical antipsychotics include medications such as Zyprexa (olanzapine), Resperdal (respiridone), Clozaril (clozapine), Seroquel (quetiapine), and Geodon (ziprasidone).

The Effects of Atypical Antipsychotics on Symptoms of ASD

The effectiveness of atypical antipsychotics in improving the core features of ASD, such as social interaction and communication and the reduction of repetitive behaviors, has not been proved consistently (Toren, Ratner, Laor, & Weitzman, 2004). According to some reports, the use of risperidone may reduce stereotypic behaviors (Matson & Dempsey, 2008). However, in one reported case, stereotypic behaviors increased for a child prescribed risperidone (Perry, Pataki, Munoz-Silva, Armenteros, & Silva, 1997). Improvements in communication and social relatedness are also reported in children diagnosed with autism and administered risperidone or olanzapine (Potenza, Holmes, Kanes, & McDougle, 1999). Researchers often fail to find improvements in language ability in persons with ASD who are prescribed atypical antipsychotics. However, in two studies, researchers did find a reduction in verbal perseveration and stereotypic use of language (Zuddas, Ledda, Fratta, Muglia, & Cianchetti, 1996). Thus, although language ability many not improve with the use of atypical antipsychotics, reductions in stereotyped use of speech and decreases in verbal perseveration may lead indirectly to improvements in communication for persons with ASD.

Children with ASD display numerous maladaptive behaviors that are similar in presentation to those in adults with psychotic features (Selengut

Brooke, Wiersgalla, & Salzman, 2005). Therefore, physicians have prescribed atypical antipsychotics to children and adolescents with ASD. Though the use of these medical interventions in ASD has been carried out ahead of research reports on the effectiveness of these medications, there is now evidence that the use of atypical antipsychotics may be an effective pharmacological treatment option for children and adolescents to improve a number of symptoms associated with ASD (Hellings et al., 2005).

Aggression. Atypical antipsychotic medication use in children and adolescents is often productive in the treatment of aggressive behaviors. Because aggression is among the many behaviors associated with ASD, atypical antipsychotics are prescribed for children and adolescents with ASD. There are reports that some children diagnosed with ASD display less physical aggression toward people and property when prescribed risperidone, olanzapine, or clozapine. Although atypical antipsychotics are useful for the treatment of aggressive behaviors in persons with ASD, the long-term utility of these medications may be limited. For example, the effects of clozapine on aggression diminished after 5 months of use in one child with ASD despite increases in dosage, suggesting that these medications may lose their potency in some patients over time (Zuddas et al., 1996). In addition to reports of efficacy in treating aggressive behaviors, atypical antipsychotics have also been associated with a reduction in self-injurious behaviors in children and adolescents with ASD. Thus, atypical antipsychotics are likely a reasonable short-term treatment for both aggressive and self-injurious behaviors. Atypical antipsychotics may promote and sustain behaviors that are more appropriate over a longer period when used in combination with behavioral therapies.

Hyperactivity. Some children with ASD display hyperactive behavior. Researchers report positive outcomes for the treatment of hyperactivity in persons with autism through the administration of atypical antipsychotics (Aman & Langworthy, 2000). Risperidone is associated with decreased overreactive and explosive behaviors in children with ASD. Clozapine improves both hyperactivity and fidgetiness, whereas olanzapine is associated with decreased sensory-motor hyperactivity. These results are promising. However, the effects of atypical antipsychotics on hyperactivity may not be apparent for some time. In one study, olanzapine was linked with decreases in hyperactivity after 8 weeks of use but not after 4 weeks of treatment (Potenza et al., 1999). Therefore, families and health care professionals need to be patient once the atypical antipsychotic is first administered.

Mood. Individuals with ASD often display abnormal mood and affect. A number of studies show that atypical antipsychotics stabilize affect. Researchers report improvements in blunted affect with the use of clozapine (Zuddas et al., 1996). Improvements in anxiousness and nervousness, depression, irritability, and fearfulness have been found with the use of risperidone and olanzapine. In addition, olanzapine has been shown to be of additional benefit in the improvement of restlessness and increasing calmness (Potenza et al., 1999).

Cognition. There are few studies on the effects of atypical antipsychotic medication use and cognitive functioning in persons with autism. Purdon, Jones, and Labelle (1994) investigated the cognitive ability of two children diagnosed with ASD prior to and during treatment with risperidone. The researchers found that one child demonstrated improvements in general intellectual ability, memory, executive functioning, and verbal ability with the use of risperidone. The effects of the medication on cognition were less evident for the other child in the same study, though this participant showed slight improvements as well. Although few studies have been conducted in this area, reports suggest some improvement in cognition with no decline in cognitive ability occurs with atypical antipsychotic use in children with behavior disorders and low IQ (Aman, Buitelaar, De Smedt, Wapenaar, & Binder, 2005; Snyder et al., 2002).

Side Effects

Although the use of atypical antipsychotic medication in children and adolescents with ASD seems to hold promise, the potential for side effects presents challenges. There is a risk of developing tardive dyskinesia (involuntary, repetitive movements) while taking atypical antipsychotic medication, though this risk is less than what is found with the use of typical antipsychotic medication. In addition, neuroleptic malignant syndrome, a rare but life-threatening reaction to antipsychotic medication, has been reported (Isbister, Balit, & Kilham, 2005). The syndrome is characterized by fever, muscular rigidity, altered mental status, and autonomic dysfunction. Another common side effect of atypical antipsychotics is the risk of increased blood sugar levels, which may lead to problems such as diabetes. Many of the side effects associated with atypical antipsychotics are common to all medications of this group, though some side effects are more common to one medication than to another. Although studies of the side effects associated with atypical antipsychotic medication use in children and adolescents with autism is conducted via case studies and small samples, these studies have found side effects in persons with ASD that are similar to those in persons with schizophrenia (Fedorowicz & Fombonne, 2005).

Clozapine. The Food and Drug Administration (FDA) does not approve clozapine for use in children, yet it is prescribed and studied in children and adolescents with autism. Side effects associated with clozapine (also known as Clozaril) use in children and adolescents with ASD include sedation, transient enuresis (involuntary urination), seizures, agranulocytosis (dangerous reduction in white blood cells), constipation, and hypersalivation (Zuddas et al., 1996). In addition to these side effects, the FDA acknowledges reports of headache, lightheadedness, dizziness, fever, blood clots in the lung, liver disease, and rapid heart rate.

Olanzapine. Olanzapine is marketed under the name Zyprexa. The most commonly reported side effects of olanzapine use in children with autism are sedation and weight gain (Potenza et al., 1999). Constipation, dizziness, upset stomach, increased appetite, restlessness, and dry mouth have been reported in other clinical populations.

Risperidone. Since its introduction in 1996, risperidone (marketed under the name of Risperdal) has been the most studied of the atypical antipsychotics. A number of side effects associated with the use of risperidone in children and adolescents diagnosed with autism have been uncovered. The most commonly known side effects are somnolence, excessive appetite, nausea and vomiting, excessive saliva, dizziness or loss of balance, and weight gain (Matson & Dempsey, 2008). Increased prolactin levels (a hormone associated with lactation) in female and male users is also a common side effect of risperidone (Hellings et al., 2005). However, this side effect is reversible, as prolactin levels return to normal once the medication is discontinued. Initial insomnia and anxiety are common problems among children with autism that may be exacerbated by the use of risperidone. Other associated side effects include nausea, upset stomach, rash, runny nose, changes in vision, agranulocytosis (dangerously low white blood cell count), and hepatotoxicity (liver damage).

Quetiapine. Quetiapine is marketed under the name Seroquel. Side effects associated with quetiapine use in children and adolescents with autism include weight gain, sedation, and possibly seizures (Martin, Koenig, Scahil, & Bregman, 1999). Additional side effects include headache, agitation, dry mouth, constipation, pain, vomiting, upset stomach, low blood pressure and dizziness, increased heart rate, fainting, cataracts, low thyroid level, elevated cholesterol and/or triglycerides, increase or decrease in body temperature, and difficulty swallowing.

Ziprasidone. Ziprasidone is marketed under the name Geodon. Little research has been carried out on the efficacy and side effects of ziprasidone use in children and adolescents with ASD. Ziprasidone is associated with sedation, weight gain, and in some cases weight loss (McDougle, Kem, & Posey, 2002). Other side effects associated with ziprasidone include low blood pressure and dizziness, increased heart rate, fainting, seizures, increase or decrease in body temperature, difficulty swallowing, nausea or upset stomach, rash, diarrhea, increased cough and runny nose, and restlessness.

Conclusion

Atypical antipsychotics represent significant improvements over the first generation of antipsychotics. Nonetheless, they are not without risks. Although off-label prescription practices are common for psychopharmaceutical use with children, atypical antipsychotics may have severe short-term unintended effects and the long-term effects are unknown. The cognitive and behavioral side effects of atypical antipsychotics have not been studied in sufficient detail. Given that one of five visits to a pediatric psychiatrist results in the prescription of an atypical antipsychotic, the number of children who may experience side effects is potentially quite high (Curtis et al., 2005).

Yet for many children with ASD, atypical antipsychotics bring about considerable improvement of many of their symptoms. This class of medications has the potential to dramatically improve the quality of life for children with ASD and their families.

IMPLICATIONS FOR EDUCATORS

Children treated with atypical antipsychotic medications experience improved behavioral symptoms, such as decreases in aggression, hyperactivity/impulsivity, and self-injurious behaviors (Cheng-Shannon, McGough, Pataki, & McCracken, 2004). Consequently, these medications are useful in the treatment of behaviors associated with ASD in children, adolescents, and adults (Dinca, Paul, & Spencer, 2005). Yet atypical antipsychotics are prescribed off-label for young people diagnosed with bipolar disorder, psychotic disorders, and developmental disabilities. Researchers have begun to study this class of drugs in children as young as preschool age (Aman & Madrid, 1999). Research on atypical antipsychotic use in children and adolescents with ASD is conducted mainly through case studies. The inconsistent use of behavioral measures across studies makes generalization of findings difficult. Despite these concerns, atypical antipsychotic medications continue to be prescribed to children and adolescents with ASD in increasing numbers (Curtis et al., 2005). Given the limitations of the research concerning both long- and short-term safety and side effects, educators, school nurses, and school psychologists are on the front line when it comes to monitoring the effectiveness and side effects of atypical antipsychotics in children with ASD (DuBois, 2005). Monitoring language and cognitive changes, as well as being aware of the possible side effects, is a critical role for educators of children prescribed atypical antipsychotics.

EDUCATIONAL STRATEGIES

Keep careful notes and observations of children's behavior. Report changes to parents immediately.

- Motor skills, such as walking speed, quality of gait, fine motor coordination, apparent joint stiffness, and running skills, may change.
- Increases in appetite frequently occur and need to be monitored, as weight gain is common.
- Changes in speech, aggression, mood, activity level, and responsiveness to directions might occur.

The child's response to classroom interventions may change as well.

- Behavioral interventions that may not have been effective in the past may be more effective after medications.
- Speech and language therapies may be more effective after medications due to improvements in language or improvements in the ability to follow directions.
- Changes in overactivity and on-task behaviors often lead to improved classroom behaviors.

DISCUSSION QUESTIONS

1. Is the risk of atypical antipsychotics worth the positive benefits in most cases? What factors might assist in making the decision to medicate a particular child?

2. What do educators need to look for in terms of side effects of atypical antipsychotics?

3. How might antipsychotic interventions interact with behavioral and classroom interventions? In a positive manner? In a negative manner?

4. To what degree can antipsychotics improve school-based performance?

5. How can educators create an effective relationship among parents and medical professionals?

RESEARCH SUMMARY

- Atypical antipsychotic medications are widely administered to children with ASD, bipolar disorder, and ADHD. Yet the only FDA-approved use for children is risperidone for children 5 to 17 years old with ASD.

- The common and severe side effects of first-generation antipsychotic medications are reduced with atypical antipsychotics, but side effects sometimes still occur.

- The research on atypical antipsychotic medication and children shows mixed results. There is substantial evidence that aggression, overactivity, and mood improve. Language and cognition do not seem to improve significantly.

- The long-term side effects of atypical antipsychotics for children are not known.

- Weight gain and impaired motor skills are among the common short-term side effects.

- Although atypical antipsychotic medications are commonly administered to children, there is insufficient research to address their overall safety and effectiveness in this population. As such, parents and educational professionals must be especially vigilant in observing positive and negative changes in behavior.

RESOURCES

The U.S. Food and Drug Administration has fact sheets on a variety of antipsychotic medications:

www.fda.gov/Drugs/DrugSafety/PostmarketDrugSafetyInformation forPatientsandProviders/ucm111085.htm

The U.K. Medicines and Health Care products Regulatory Agency, the British version of the FDA, has a slightly different view of antipsychotic medications:

http://www.mhra.gov.uk/Safetyinformation/Generalsafetyinformation andadvice/Product-specificinformationandadvice/Antipsychoticdrugs/ index.htm

This medical book describes the use and problems in the use of antipsychotics for several populations, including children with developmental disabilities:

Ellenbroek, B. A., & Cools, A. R. (Eds.). (2000). *Atypical antipsychotics.* Boston: Birkhäuser Verlag.

HANDOUT

USE OF ATYPICAL ANTIPSYCHOTIC MEDICATION WITH CHILDREN AND ADOLESCENTS

As with all medications, it is important to follow the instructions of the physician and all written instructions that come with medications. Do not forget to give/take medication as directed. Atypical antipsychotics can be extremely effective in controlling a variety of behaviors. There is evidence of positive effects on aggression, mood, hyperactivity, and cognition when administered to children with autism and other developmental disabilities. Much of the research is preliminary, however; the scope of positive effects of all antipsychotic medications is not yet known. Also, there are important side effects that need to be monitored.

- The Food and Drug Administration (FDA) does not approve ***clozapine*** for use in children, yet it is prescribed and studied in children and adolescents with autism. Side effects associated with clozapine (also known as Clozaril) use in children and adolescents with autism include sedation, transient enuresis (involuntary urination), seizures, agranulocytosis (dangerously low white blood cell count), constipation, and hypersalivation.
- ***Olanzepine*** is marketed under the brand name Zyprexa. The most common reported side effects of olanzepine use in children with autism are sedation and weight gain.
- ***Risperidone***, marketed under the brand name Risperdal, has been the most studied of the atypical antipsychotics. The most common known side effects are somnolence, excessive appetite, nausea and vomiting, excessive saliva, dizziness or loss of balance, and weight gain. Initial insomnia and anxiety are common problems among children with autism that may be exacerbated by the use of risperidone. Other associated side effects include nausea, upset stomach, rash, runny nose, changes in vision, agranulocytosis, and hepatotoxicity (liver damage).
- ***Quetiapine*** is marketed under the brand name Seroquel. Side effects associated with quetiapine use in children and adolescents with autism include weight gain, sedation, and possibly seizures.
- ***Ziprasidone*** is marketed under the brand name Geodon. Side effects associated with ziprasidone include low blood pressure and dizziness, increased heart rate, fainting, seizures, increase or decrease in body temperature, difficulty swallowing, nausea or upset stomach, rash, diarrhea, increased cough and runny nose, and restlessness.

Atypical antipsychotics often play an important role in improving the behavior of children with developmental disabilities. Medications can make schooling more effective and dramatically improve home life. Yet side effects can be severe if medications are not administered exactly as recommended. Many parents may change dosage, forget to give medications one day then give double the next, or stop giving medication altogether. These are never good ideas for any medication, and with antipsychotics, the side effects can be serious.

Both parents and educators can help to monitor dosage, administration adherence, and behavior to generate detailed reports for the prescribing physician or psychiatrist. This information can be helpful in adjusting dosage or medication to maximize symptom reduction while minimizing side effects. Discuss any concerns that you might have with your physician.

7

Tardive Dyskinesia With Typical and Atypical Antipsychotic Medications in Children and Adolescents*

Daniel Farrell, Janine Fischer, and Paul C. McCabe

A 14-year-old boy with autism, Jeremiah, was brought to a pervasive developmental disorders clinic because of increasingly aggressive and disruptive behavior. His aggression had started earlier in childhood but had become progressively more dangerous with age. Previous medications used to manage his aggression included psychostimulants, selective serotonin reuptake inhibitors, tricyclic antidepressants, buspirone, and secretin. Jeremiah had never received any antipsychotic medications. To treat his aggression, the antipsychotic medication risperidone was started at 0.5 mg/day and was increased gradually to a dose of 3 mg/day

---

after 16 months. Shortly after achieving this dose, Jeremiah's behavior improved dramatically—he demonstrated decreased aggression and less hyperactivity, improved language functioning, and increased sociability.

By the 23rd month of treatment, symptoms of tardive dyskinesia began to appear. Jeremiah developed a jerking of his trunk and abdomen, and he was reported to be moving his shoulders and trunk in a writhing motion throughout the day. Examination revealed Jeremiah had periodic choreic movements of his shoulder and trunk; no oral, lingual, or buccal (cheek) movements were observed, and no other neurological abnormalities were found. The use of anticholinergic agents and vitamin E did not improve his dyskinesia, and a reduction of risperidone to 2 mg/day resulted in the re-emergence of aggressive behavior. Discussions with Jeremiah and his family about the risks and benefits of continuing risperidone therapy led to a decision to continue risperidone at 3mg/day with the addition of benztropine 2 mg twice daily and a vitamin E supplement. Jeremiah's behavior appeared to benefit from this drug regimen.

INTRODUCTION

Prescriptions of antipsychotic medications for children have increased dramatically, rising almost fivefold from 8.6 out of 1,000 children in 1995–96 to 39.4 out of 1,000 children in 2001–02 (Cooper et al., 2006). Antipsychotic medications are used to treat a variety of childhood problems, yet relatively few studies demonstrate conclusive evidence of these medications' efficacy and whether their effects are worthwhile, given the potentially serious side effects they may cause (Rani, Murray, Byrne, & Wong, 2008). One such side effect, tardive dyskinesia, is of particular concern.

BACKGROUND

Symptoms and Diagnosis

Tardive dyskinesia (TD) is a part of a larger group of symptoms known as extrapyramidal symptoms (EPS). Besides TD, EPS include Parkinsonian tremors, rigidity, akathisia, and dystonia. TD is one of the most common side effects of medications used to treat a variety of psychiatric and developmental conditions. Despite many similar symptoms, TD must be differentiated from other neurological disorders, including Tourette syndrome, chronic motor tic disorder, Huntington's chorea, Wilson's disease, and Meige's syndrome (Margolese, Chouinard, Kolivakis, Beuclair, & Miller, 2007).

According to the *Diagnostic and Statistical Manual of Mental Disorders* (4th ed., text revision, American Psychiatric Association [APA], 2000), the diagnosis of neuroleptic-induced tardive dyskinesia involves choreiform (rapid, jerky, nonrepetitive), athetoid (slow, sinuous, continual), or rhythmic (stereotyped) movements of the tongue, jaw, or extremities developed in association with the use of neuroleptic (antipsychotic) medication for at least a few months. *Tardive* indicates a delayed and chronic reaction; this separates TD from spontaneous dyskinesia, a movement disorder not related to antipsychotic medications (Shirzadi & Ghaemi, 2006). *Neuroleptic medication* refers to antipsychotic medications with dopamine antagonist properties. There are two different types of TD: treatment-emergent TD and withdrawal-emergent TD (Rodnitzky, 2003). In most cases, withdrawal-emergent TD will disappear on its own as the neuroleptic medication is discontinued.

TD involves various involuntary movements, usually in the face, lips, tongue, and jaw. An early sign and common feature of TD is fine, wormlike gesticulating of the tongue while it sits at rest in the mouth. As the condition worsens, the tongue may come in and out of the mouth at irregular intervals, and the individual may repeatedly lick or smack the lips and press the tongue against the cheek to form a bulge. Involuntary movements can also be seen in the extremities and the trunk, but these are less common. The individual's fingers may display stereotypic movements, which are more noticeable when the fingers are held in extension. The individual's fingers may look as though they are playing a piano, and toes and feet may display irregular movements as well. Movements in the trunk can consist of shoulder shrugging, twisting, or extension of the trunk and pelvic thrusting or rotating. Involuntary movements of the face and mouth occur in about 75% of individuals who are affected by TD, while extremity involvement occurs in about 50% and trunk involvement in about 25% of cases. All three areas are affected in about 10% of cases. In mild cases, the person may not even be aware of the movements (Sachdev, 2000). However, TD is often quite noticeable to both the individual and observers. It can make the person's speech unintelligible, increase the likelihood of falling, and lead to respiratory distress if it affects diaphragm muscles. For these and other reasons, it often leads to shame, guilt, anger, and depression (Margolese, Chouinard, Kolivakis, Beuclair, & Miller, 2007).

TD first became of interest in the 1970s and 1980s, when it was identified as a common and often debilitating side effect of antipsychotic medications. Renewed interest in TD came about with the introduction of new "atypical" antipsychotics in the 1990s. Atypical antipsychotic medications revolutionized the treatment of psychiatric conditions such as schizophrenia, mental retardation, autism, and bipolar disorders, as they tended to produce significantly fewer serious side effects, including TD (Lalonde, 2003). The most common and significant side effects with atypical antipsychotic medications include sedation and weight gain (Silva, Matzner, Diaz, Singh, & Dummit, 1999). Although the risk of TD is reduced with atypical antipsychotics, TD remains a potential side effect when high dosages are prescribed.

TD has been broadly investigated in adults, but very few studies have examined the condition in children despite the increased use of antipsychotics with this population (Conner, Fletcher, & Wood, 2001). Response to medications in children may be different than in adults due to developmental factors that can modify the way in which the drug is metabolized. Neurotransmitter systems undergo change with age. For example, the ratio between the different types of dopamine receptors increases. The varying effect of medications due to these developmental changes in dopamine receptor ratios is largely unknown. In addition, animal models suggest that psychotropic medications can result in permanent biochemical and physical receptor changes in the developing brain. Is it not clear if this holds true for humans as well (Vitiello & Jenson, 1995).

The difference between traditional and atypical antipsychotics is their affinity and binding properties with respect to the dopamine receptor.

Atypical antipsychotics bind more loosely to dopamine receptors than dopamine itself and release rapidly from these receptors. Traditional antipsychotics, on the other hand, bind more tightly to the receptors than dopamine. Atypical antipsychotics, therefore, bind to the receptor and then dissociate quickly to allow for more normal dopamine neurotransmission. Thus, traditional antipsychotics remain attached to the receptor longer, accumulate in the brain tissue, and are more likely eventually to lead to TD. Atypical antipsychotics are less fat soluble, are released rapidly from the receptors and brain tissue, and appear less likely to cause TD (Seeman, 2002).

Shirzadi and Ghaemi (2006) proposed a way to classify atypical antipsychotics based on their dopamine receptor binding affinity. Within the atypical antipsychotic group, different medications have different binding affinities, and these seem to be related to the potential EPS side effects. Clozapine and quetiapine are low-affinity atypical antipsychotic medications. The low-affinity medications are less potent and bring about fewer EPS symptoms, but they are more likely to cause weight gain. Olanzapine is a middle-affinity atypical antipsychotic. High-affinity atypical antipsychotics would include risperidone, ziprasidone, and aripiprazole. The high-affinity medications have more EPS potential but tend to bring about less weight gain.

Specific populations are more prone to developing TD. Rates are higher for children with autism and mental retardation (Conner et al., 2001) and for individuals with child-onset schizophrenia (Kumra et al., 1998). In addition, lower IQ, higher baseline Abnormal Involuntary Movement Scale scores (AIMS; Guy, 1976), and female gender may increase the risk of TD (Conner et al.).

Prevalence of TD

There is evidence that TD is significantly more prevalent with the use of traditional antipsychotic medications than atypical antipsychotics, but few studies directly compared these medications (Conner et al., 2001). Estimates of TD in adults using antipsychotics range from 3% to 70%, with a median prevalence of about 24% in individuals treated with traditional antipsychotics (Sachdev, 2000). Although atypical antipsychotics may be less prone to instigating TD, they are not risk-free. A study of 95 children in a residential treatment facility aged 7 to 21 compared the prevalence of TD in persons treated with traditional and atypical antipsychotic medications. Prevalence in the group treated with traditional antipsychotics was approximately 14% and in the group treated with atypical antipsychotics, approximately 4%. This is consistent with other studies investigating atypical antipsychotic medications (Conner et al.).

In a study examining the efficacy of risperidone prescribed to children with autism and its potential to bring about TD, approximately 15% of the patients developed withdrawal emergent dyskinesia, but there was no incidence of TD (Malone, Maislin, Choudhury, Gifford, & Delaney, 2002). The study's short duration, including a follow-up at 6 months, limits the implications of the results. In fact, most studies with children have been of a relatively short duration, limiting the availability of evidence of TD impact with long-term antipsychotic medication use.

Another concern with studies reporting the incidence of TD may be the criteria researchers use to diagnose TD; some researchers may be reporting subthreshold criteria. Gebhardt et al. (2006) studied 93 adolescents with schizophrenia or schizoaffective disorder primarily treated with atypical antipsychotics. The researchers found that mild symptoms of movement disorders were relatively high, at 39.8%. They also found a prevalence rate of 5.4% for individuals fulfilling the criteria for TD. These results are consistent with other studies investigating atypical antipsychotic medications. However, if subthreshold criteria were included for this study, TD symptoms appeared in 11.8% of patients. Thus, even though atypical antipsychotic medications have a lower incidence rate of TD that fully meets the diagnostic criteria, they may still be producing subthreshold symptoms at near the rate of traditional antipsychotics.

Although few antipsychotic medications have been tested in double-blind, placebo-controlled studies in pediatric populations, they are increasingly being prescribed to children under the age of 18. One data review indicated that from 1995 to 2002, antipsychotic medications were prescribed in over 5.5 million outpatient visits to medical professionals by children 2 to 18 years old, reflecting a fivefold increase in the number of antipsychotic prescriptions to children. Of those children, the mean age was approximately 12 years (Cooper et al., 2006). Similar findings by Doey, Handelman, Seabrook, and Steele (2007) noted that up to 12% of antipsychotic prescriptions written by surveyed Canadian doctors were for children under the age of 18. Antipsychotic medications are often prescribed to treat disorders for which they have not been indicated, such as behavioral and affective disorders. In addition, there are virtually no data on safety regarding drug-to-drug interactions when children are prescribed more than one psychotropic medication, yet such treatment frequently occurs (Jenson, Bhatara, & Vitiello, 1999).

Treatment of TD

There is no effective treatment of TD. The best way to bring about remission is to discontinue the medication causing the condition. If the medication cannot be stopped, then it is advised to prescribe the smallest dose that will still produce a beneficial effect. Atypical antipsychotics are presently the drugs of choice to treat many disorders due to reduced risk of TD. However, antioxidants have also been used for both prevention and treatment of TD. One such antioxidant is vitamin E, and 9 of 11 studies demonstrated a beneficial effect to using vitamin E, although the studies were of short duration. Nevertheless, vitamin E carries virtually no risk and may be worth taking as a supplemental treatment when a patient is prescribed an antipsychotic medication (Sachdev, 2000).

For managing TD caused by a traditional antipsychotic, Margolese, Chouinard, Kolivakis, Beauclair, Miller, and Annable (2007) suggested gradually switching the patient to an atypical antipsychotic. They also suggested suppression therapy with a traditional antipsychotic, which consists of reducing the level but increasing the number of daily doses to keep the level of medication consistent. However, suppression therapy is recommended only for short-term use, especially when the patient is switching to an atypical antipsychotic. Margolese and colleagues strongly warned against stopping all medications, because psychotic symptoms typically re-emerge and are often worse than before the patient started taking medication.

IMPLICATIONS FOR EDUCATORS

With the increase of medications being prescribed to pediatric populations, school staff are in an optimal position to monitor medication efficacy and adverse side effects. The school can play an important role in helping children and adolescents monitor their medical treatment, particularly given past evidence indicating that physicians may not inform their patients properly about potential side effects. In a survey of clinicians in England, 48% of respondents informed less than half of their patients about the risk of tardive dyskinesia (Chaplin & Potter, 1996). When asked why, most responded that they feared noncompliance with the medications. Recent studies in Canada have found better informed-consent and monitoring practices. One study by Schachter and Kleinman (2004) found that 78% of respondents routinely disclosed information about TD. Another recent study of Canadian physicians indicated that almost 44% use a scale such as the Abnormal Involuntary Movement Scale (AIMS) to monitor TD symptoms (Doey et al., 2007). Despite the trend of increasing disclosure of adverse effects and monitoring of TD when using antipsychotic medications, a significant percentage of patients are still not being offered informed consent and monitoring for TD.

TD can influence school performance. Because of the tongue and mouth involvement, it can lead to speech abnormalities (Sachdev, 2000). Social interactions may also be affected, especially in childhood and adolescence when peer relations play an important role. Given the unusual nature of the symptoms, there is significant potential for teasing. Educators should be aware of these potential consequences and intervene early if TD behaviors manifest.

TD movements can fluctuate over time. For instance, they may increase with heightened emotional or stressful states and decrease with relaxation. They can fluctuate from day to day or hour to hour. Distracting tasks, such as finger tapping or mental arithmetic, can bring out movements that otherwise may not be noticeable (Sachdev, 2000). Because symptoms of TD can fluctuate based on circumstances and over time, the physician may not get an accurate picture of TD in the child during an office visit. The school team, including the psychologist and child's teacher, can monitor behaviors over time and in varying circumstances when movements may be most noticeable.

TD is most commonly measured by AIMS, which is presented in Table 7.1. This scale contains 12 items and uses a standardized rating procedure, on a 5-point scale, to evaluate TD in the face, extremities, and trunk (Malone et al., 2002). It is recommended that formal AIMS assessment of TD be conducted every 3 months with a patient taking antipsychotic medications (Silva et al., 1999). School psychologists and school nurses would be well suited to use this tool, even if on a more informal basis. Working with families and physicians, the school is in a position to maximize safety and efficacy while minimizing negative side effects for children taking psychotropic medications.

Table 7.1   Abnormal Involuntary Movement Scale (AIMS)

Patient Name:		Date of Visit:			
MOVEMENT RATINGS: Rate highest severity observed. Rate movements that occur upon activation one less than those observed spontaneously. Circle movement as well as code number that applies.		**RATER**	**RATER**	**RATER**	**RATER**
		Date	**Date**	**Date**	**Date**
Facial and Oral Movements	**1. Muscles of Facial Expression** (e.g., movements of forehead, eyebrows, periorbital area, and cheeks, including frowning, blinking, smiling, grimacing)	0 1 2 3 4	0 1 2 3 4	0 1 2 3 4	0 1 2 3 4
	2. Lips and Perioral Area (e.g., puckering, pouting, smacking)	0 1 2 3 4	0 1 2 3 4	0 1 2 3 4	0 1 2 3 4
	3. Jaw (e.g., biting, clenching, chewing, mouth opening, lateral movement)	0 1 2 3 4	0 1 2 3 4	0 1 2 3 4	0 1 2 3 4
	4. Tongue Rate only increases in movement both in and out of mouth, *not* inability to sustain movement. Darting in and out of mouth.	0 1 2 3 4	0 1 2 3 4	0 1 2 3 4	0 1 2 3 4
Extremity Movements	**5. Upper (arms, wrists, hands, fingers)** Include choreic movements (i.e., rapid, objectively purposeless, irregular, spontaneous) and athetoid movements (i.e., slow, irregular, complex, serpentine). Do *not* include tremor (i.e., repetitive, regular, rhythmic).	0 1 2 3 4	0 1 2 3 4	0 1 2 3 4	0 1 2 3 4
	6. Lower (legs, knees, ankles, toes) (e.g., lateral knee movement, foot tapping, heel dropping, foot squirming, inversion and eversion of foot)	0 1 2 3 4	0 1 2 3 4	0 1 2 3 4	0 1 2 3 4
Trunk Movements	**7. Neck, shoulders, hips** (e.g., rocking, twisting, squirming, pelvic gyrations)	0 1 2 3 4	0 1 2 3 4	0 1 2 3 4	0 1 2 3 4
Global Judgments	**8. Severity of abnormal movements overall**	0 1 2 3 4	0 1 2 3 4	0 1 2 3 4	0 1 2 3 4
	9. Incapacitation due to abnormal movements	0 1 2 3 4	0 1 2 3 4	0 1 2 3 4	0 1 2 3 4
	10. Patient's awareness of abnormal movements. Rate only patient's report.				
	No awareness	0	0	0	0
	Aware, no distress	1	1	1	1
	Aware, mild distress	2	2	2	2
	Aware, moderate distress	3	3	3	3
	Aware, severe distress	4	4	4	4

MOVEMENT RATINGS: Rate highest severity observed. Rate movements that occur upon activation one less than those observed spontaneously. Circle movement as well as code number that applies.		RATER	RATER	RATER	RATER
		Date	**Date**	**Date**	**Date**
Dental Status	**11. Current problems with teeth and/or dentures?**	No Yes	No Yes	No Yes	No Yes
	12. Are dentures usually worn?	No Yes	No Yes	No Yes	No Yes
	13. Edentia?	No Yes	No Yes	No Yes	No Yes
	14. Do movements disappear in sleep?	No Yes	No Yes	No Yes	No Yes

Source: Department of Health and Human Services; Public Health Service; Alcohol, Drug Abuse, and Mental Health Administration; NIMH Treatment Strategies in Schizophrenia Study, ADM-117, Revised November 1985.

CODE: 0 = None 1 = Minimal, may be extreme normal 2 = Mild 3 = Moderate 4 = Severe

EDUCATIONAL STRATEGIES

- Appropriate school personnel should be aware of all medications the student may be taking and their potential side effects. This can be accomplished by asking specific questions upon enrollment and on information update forms and by creating a safe, judgment-free environment for parents to disclose information.
- Make sure the school has appropriate resources to understand the student's diagnosis and potential side effects of medications. Resources can include the *DSM-IV-TR*, the *Physician's Desk Reference*, the *Pill Book*, and related texts.
- Educate teachers and other school personnel about the side effects of all medications the student is taking. This can be done by the child's teacher, school psychologist, nurse, or other individual who is familiar with medications' potential side effects.
- If a student is taking antipsychotic medications, the school psychologist or nurse should take periodic observations. Using a standard protocol, such as the Abnormal Involuntary Movement Scale (AIMS), is recommended.
- With family consent, actively reach out to the student's doctors to share observations, behavioral data, and concerns. Educators should work with the child, parents, doctors, and therapists to develop a treatment plan with strategies for the home, community, and educational settings.
- When students who are taking medications develop school problems, the school team should rule out side effects of the medication. For example, if a student develops articulation errors or begins to have difficulty forming letters, or is manifesting unusual motor behaviors, side effects of the medication should be considered before beginning speech or occupational therapies.

DISCUSSION QUESTIONS

1. What implications might tardive dyskinesia have for a student in school? What information do teachers need to have about a child's potential or present side effects?

2. What coping mechanisms might you teach to a student with tardive dyskinesia? What types of classroom accommodations might be needed in an IEP or Section 504 plan to help the student access the appropriate curriculum?

3. What responsibility do school psychologists and educators have to warn parents of the side effects of both traditional and atypical antipsychotics? Is doing so overstepping the bounds of the educational field to trespass in the medical field, or is it providing a service that doctors may have overlooked?

4. Many children with psychiatric disorders have been diagnosed with multiple disorders and are on a veritable cocktail of medications. If a student at your school was diagnosed with bipolar disorder, began taking a traditional antipsychotic (such as Haldol), and is now being diagnosed with Tourette syndrome, what, if anything, should you say to the parents? What might be the academic ramifications for a child with multiple diagnoses and medications?

RESEARCH SUMMARY

*   Tardive dyskinesia (TD) is a part of a larger group of symptoms known as extrapyramidal symptoms (EPS). TD is one of the most common side effects of antipsychotic medications.

*   The diagnosis of neuroleptic-induced tardive dyskinesia involves choreiform (rapid, jerky, nonrepetitive), athetoid (slow, sinuous, continual), or rhythmic (stereotyped) movements of the tongue, jaw, or extremities developed in association with the use of antipsychotic medication for at least a few months.

*   Prescriptions of antipsychotic medications for children have increased fivefold, rising from 8.6 out of 1,000 children in 1995 to 39.4 out of 1,000 children in 2002.

*   Antipsychotic medications are used to treat a variety of childhood problems, yet there are relatively few studies demonstrating conclusive evidence of these medications' efficacy, their potential for serious side effects, the impact of drug-to-drug interactions, and the long-term implications of prolonged medication use in children.

*   In a review of research, the median prevalence of TD in patients using traditional antipsychotics was 24%. Atypical antipsychotics have been found to cause TD in approximately 4% of cases.

*   There is some evidence that milder symptoms of TD, which do not rise to the full diagnostic criteria of TD, are more prevalent than noted with atypical antipsychotics.

- Doctors may not be fully informing all patients and parents/guardians about the potentially serious side effects of antipsychotics, perhaps because they fear patients may choose not to take such medications. Also, many clinicians are not using a standard protocol to monitor movement-related side effects.

RESOURCES

Parker, J. N., & Parker, P. M (Eds.). (2002). *The official patient's sourcebook on tardive dyskinesia: A revised and updated directory for the Internet age; A reference manual for self-directed patient research.* San Diego, CA: Icon Health.

This Web site may be a helpful resource to families who are dealing with movement disorders, including tardive dyskinesia:

Worldwide Education and Awareness for Movement Disorders (WE MOVE): www.wemove.org

HANDOUT

TARDIVE DYSKINESIA

Antipsychotic medications are being used to treat several disorders in children today, including psychosis, Tourette syndrome, bipolar disorder, autism, and more. Antipsychotic, or neuroleptic, medications can be broken down into two categories: traditional (or typical) and atypical. One of the potential side effects of these medications is tardive dyskinesia.

Tardive dyskinesia (TD) is a movement disorder that is characterized by repetitive, meaningless, and involuntary movements of the limbs; fingers; toes; or oral muscles, including the lips and tongue. TD can be difficult to diagnose. This is partially due to its having similar symptoms as other neurological disorders, including Tourette syndrome, chronic motor tic disorder, Huntington's chorea, Wilson's disease, and Meige's syndrome. TD's symptoms can also range from very mild to debilitating. In milder cases or in the early stages, it may go undiagnosed, even by trained professionals.

- TD often starts with a fine, wormlike twitching of the tongue and may progress to involuntary licking or smacking of the lips, irregular protruding of the tongue, or pressing the tongue against the cheek to create a bulge.
- In other extremities, fingers may look as though they are playing a piano, toes or feet may display irregular movements, shoulders may display shrugging motions, the trunk may twist, and the pelvic area may thrust or rotate.
- Because TD can affect a person's speech, may make the person fall, or otherwise cause the person to be negatively noticed by peers, it can lead to shame, guilt, anger, and even depression.

TD is most often seen in patients who take traditional antipsychotics, a group of neuroleptic medications first developed in the 1950s. They were found to reduce psychotic symptoms but had significant side effects, including TD. Traditional antipsychotics include chloropromzine (Thorazine), haloperidol (Haldol), and thioridazine (Mellaril). In the 1980s, atypical antipsychotics were developed. Atypical antipsychotics often minimize the extrapyramidal symptom side effects, though they may have other side effects, such as drowsiness and weight gain. Atypical antipsychotics include aripiprazol (Abilify), clozapine (Clozaril), olanzapine (Zyprexa), perphenazine (Trilafon), risperidone (Risperdal), ziprasidone (Geodon), quetiapine (Seroquel), and paliperidone (Invega).

There is no agreed-upon or consistent way to alleviate TD, though it is most often associated with long-term or high doses of neuroleptic medications. Individuals with TD may switch to an atypical antipsychotic, take a physician-supervised drug holiday, or add a supplement such as vitamin B6 or E to the routine. Atypical antipsychotics are not without risk of causing TD, but evidence suggests the risk is less. Making any changes to prescribed medications should be done only under the supervision of the prescribing doctor.

Physicians should warn individuals and parents of all side effects and use standardized protocols, such as the Abnormal Involuntary Movement Scale (AIMS), to follow potential side effects. It is also important for parents to know that many neuroleptic medications are being prescribed to children despite a lack of research into their long-term effects. They are also being prescribed for disorders that they have not been scientifically proven to manage. There is ample anecdotal evidence that neuroleptic medications may help these disorders, but additional empirical research is needed to support it. Parents, the medical community, and educators should work closely together and maintain clear lines of communication when treating children with neuroleptic medications to share information about treatment and observed side effects.

8

Recent Advances in the Medical Management of Children With Attention Deficit/ Hyperactivity Disorder

John S. Carlson, Angela Maupin, and Tara Brinkman

Jasmine is a 7-year-old girl in the first grade who was first diagnosed with ADHD in kindergarten. Conjoint behavioral consultation was undertaken in an attempt to improve on-task behavior during group time, transitions from one activity to another, and self-control. Although data collection across baseline and treatment

(Continued)

(Continued)

conditions demonstrated some improvement, Jasmine's behavior continued to create management issues for her teacher, barriers to her learning, and problematic social interactions with her peers. Her mother also reported that Jasmine's inattention, hyperactivity, and impulsivity were problematic at home, including during the morning routine, at the dinner table, and when she played with her siblings and neighbors. She also reported that Jasmine had become more oppositional and noncompliant with parental requests.

After learning about the continued challenges at school, her mother decided that she would like to consult with Jasmine's pediatrician about a possible medication trial. A copy of the conjoint behavioral consultation report was provided to the doctor. The physician confirmed a diagnosis of ADHD and prescribed a 6-week trial of Concerta. After 2 days of treatment, her teacher reported many changes in Jasmine's impulsive behavior, as she demonstrated greater self-control and focus, especially during group times in the classroom. After 1 week of treatment, Jasmine's mother reported to her teachers that Jasmine's behavior at home was dramatically improved and that the family could finally eat dinner together without Jasmine getting up from her chair repeatedly. In addition, she indicated that Jasmine was responding much more appropriately when compliance with requests was needed (e.g., putting her clothes in the laundry room).

INTRODUCTION

The evidence base for the medication management of core symptoms (e.g., inattention, hyperactivity, impulsivity) of attention deficit/hyperactivity disorder (ADHD), a neurodevelopmental disorder of childhood, has clearly been demonstrated within the literature. Dosage titration and close monitoring of medication effects is necessary to ensure an individual's optimal response and to improve functioning at school. The majority of prescribed medications for ADHD fall within the class of medications called central nervous system stimulants or psychostimulants (e.g., methylphenidate [MPH], dextroamphetamine, or mixed amphetamine salts). Stimulant treatment for ADHD symptoms has been researched since the early 1930s. Considerable changes with respect to formulation and intended duration have recently occurred. This includes the use of long-acting medicines, typically in extended release forms (e.g., Concerta, Adderall XR, Metadate CD, Focalin), and the emergence of a skin-patch delivery system (i.e., Daytrana). Other advances in the medication treatment of ADHD include (a) an increased focus on non-stimulant-based medicines (e.g., selective norepinephrine reuptake inhibitors) such as atomoxetine (Strattera), (b) the use of ADHD medications to improve functioning in preschool and adult populations, (c) comparative and combined treatment studies on pharmacological and psychosocial approaches to ADHD, (d) the use of ADHD drugs in combination with other medicines to address coexisting disorders, and (e) the use of novel medication treatments for ADHD symptoms (e.g., Clonidine, extended-release guanfacine, modafinil, metamantine).

BACKGROUND

Psychostimulants

Over 200 controlled trials of psychostimulants within school-aged populations have consistently demonstrated a 60% to 80% response rate on multiple cognitive and behavioral measures. Changes in core symptoms (i.e., inattention, hyperactivity, impulsivity) have been reported in as many as 80% to 90% of those treated within a closely monitored treatment approach. Less research has been conducted with preschool populations, yet similar efficacy data (i.e., 65% to 75% response rate) is reported within at least nine controlled trials in preschoolers.

A prominent effect that stimulant treatment has on children with ADHD is an increase in dopamine levels within the brain (Kollins & March, 2007). The neurobiological substrate believed to cause ADHD appears to be appropriately targeted by psychostimulants, and in turn the core features of the disorder are improved. Stimulant drugs have also been shown to be effective for peripheral features of ADHD, such as academic problems, aggression, and social skill deficits (Biederman & Spencer, 2008). Long-term effects on core and peripheral features of ADHD have not been reported reliably, and the consensus is that these medicines have only short-term effects on the core symptoms.

Stimulant drug treatment with intensive monitoring at school and home for the purpose of appropriate dosage titration is more effective in improving core symptoms of ADHD than behavioral approaches, cognitive-behavioral therapy, parent training, educational interventions, or medication practices typically implemented by community-based physicians (Biederman & Spencer, 2008). Combined treatment approaches involving medication, parent training, and classroom management appear to be most efficacious for children experiencing comorbid conditions (e.g., coexisting symptoms of anxiety, depression, oppositional behavior, difficulty in parent-child interaction; Rappley, 2005). Moreover, combining behavior therapy with medication seems to offer a greater likelihood of improved functioning and be accepted better by parents and may allow for a decrease in dosage of stimulant drugs (APA, 2007).

Short-term side effects of stimulant drugs are mild and most commonly involve loss of appetite, sleep disturbance, and weight loss (Lerner & Wigal, 2008). Other side effects may include irritability, stomachache, headache, exacerbation of psychosis and tics, and mild increase in blood pressure and heart rate. Contraindications, or reasons to consider alternative treatments, might include growth or weight concerns, mild anxiety, tension, agitation, glaucoma, use of monoamine oxidase inhibitors (a type of antidepressant), seizures, and tics. Long-term treatment studies also indicate continuation of adverse effects across time that appear to be mild and of little health concern, most often including decreased appetite, mild/transient growth suppression, and clinically insignificant increases in blood pressure and heart rate.

Stimulant medications have long been recognized as effective treatments for youth diagnosed with ADHD. However, alternatives to stimulant treatment are needed for some children. For example, adverse events such as growth suppression, insomnia, irritability, mood changes, tics, and poor appetite are cited as reasons for MPH discontinuation. Because stimulants are considered a controlled substance with abuse potential and, thus, have strict prescription guidelines, some are hesitant to turn to this form of treatment, especially those who may have a family history of substance abuse. Furthermore, the Food and Drug Administration (FDA) has recently told companies who produce stimulants to add warnings regarding the possibility of cardiovascular effects and the potential emergence of psychiatric problems. Thus, substantial motivation to examine alternative pharmacological treatments exists. One of these medicines, atomoxetine (Strattera), has been recently approved by the FDA for treatment of ADHD in children and adults.

Atomoxetine

Atomoxetine is a selective norepinephrine reuptake inhibitor. Unlike the stimulant medicines, it does not require the prescription practices associated with a controlled substance (e.g., extensive documentation, frequent doctor's visits). Support for the safety and efficacy of atomoxetine in the treatment of children and adolescents diagnosed with ADHD is limited when compared to that for the stimulants. Less than a dozen randomly controlled treatment studies in childhood populations (ages 6 to 18) have been reported within the literature, eight of which were reviewed by Barton (2005). Unlike the MPH literature, limited information exists regarding the developmental differences in treatment response to atomoxetine across populations. One meta-analytic study, however, reported atomoxetine to be equally effective and tolerated in children when compared to adolescents (Wilens, Kratochvil, Newcorn, & Gao, 2006). Rappley's (2005) recent review of atomoxetine studies indicated that over 1,000 children and adults have been treated to date and that approximately 60% of those treated demonstrate meaningful changes. No long-term effects of atomoxetine have been reported, yet there is no reason to believe that this medicine will differ from stimulants in demonstrating a lack of sustained outcomes.

Atomoxetine's primary mechanism of action is on norepinephrine and dopamine levels within the prefrontal cortex of the brain. This is a significant benefit over MPH, as it is believed to reduce abuse potential (Barton, 2005). Treatment with atomoxetine typically results in symptom reduction within 1 week, yet full effects do not occur until after 4 weeks. This contrasts with the psychostimulants, which typically demonstrate effects on classroom behavior shortly after ingestion (e.g., 30 minutes). Once-daily administration of atomoxetine in the morning results in symptom improvement well through the evening into the next morning. Initial atomoxetine doses should not be rapidly increased to prevent side effects such as sedation and lethargy; it is important for classroom teachers to be aware of these side effects (Wilens, 2008).

Across multiple studies, the most commonly observed adverse effects are nausea, vomiting, fatigue, decreased appetite, and mood swings. Consistent with the psychostimulants, the most significant side effect concerns for children taking atomoxetine are weight loss and possible slowing of growth (Rappley, 2005). Atomoxetine can also increase heart rate and blood pressure and may result in the development of tics. The potential for side effects in those taking atomoxetine necessitates close monitoring at school and home. The costs and benefits of this treatment must be considered, especially in light of recent FDA "black-box" warnings regarding the possibility of atomoxetine causing liver damage or an increase in suicidal ideation.

Novel and Alternative Medicines

Parents sometimes try nonprescriptive approaches prior to turning to psychoactive medications, such as methylphenidate or atomoxetine, to treat their children's inattentive, hyperactive, and impulsive behavior. It is important for school personnel to be informed of the use of such treatments. Many of these alternative treatments have been investigated, but none has demonstrated efficacy. Examples of these ineffective treatments include caffeine (Carlson, Kruer, Ogg, Mathiason, & Magen, 2007) and St. John's wort (Weber et al., 2008).

A number of novel medications have also been investigated in the treatment of ADHD. Modafinil, a drug used to treat narcolepsy, has demonstrated some improvement in ADHD symptoms in children and adolescents (Amiri et al., 2008). Guanfacine (Intuniv), an antihypertensive (blood pressure) drug, has been shown to have significant benefits for children diagnosed with ADHD (Biederman et al., 2008) and is currently being considered for FDA approval. Clonidine, another of the antihypertensive drugs, has been used in combination with MPH to counteract the side effect of sleep disturbance with some effectiveness (Palumbo et al., 2008). Many antidepressants have been investigated in the treatment of ADHD, albeit with limited effectiveness. One of these, reboxetine (Edronax), has recently been found to improve ADHD symptoms (Tehrani-Doost, Moallemi, & Shahrivar, 2008). Finally, a drug used to treat Alzheimer's disease called memantine was recently reported as demonstrating promise in the treatment of ADHD (Findling et al., 2007).

New formulations of existing psychostimulants continue to come on the market as existing ADHD treatments continue to be refined. Lisdexamfetamine (Vyvanse), an extended-release version of dextroamphetamine, was recently FDA approved for ADHD treatment. Dexmethylphenidate extended-release capsule (Focalin) has also been found to be effective in reducing ADHD symptoms and improving academic performance within a limited number of studies to date (e.g., Silva et al., 2008). In addition to new formulations of existing medicines, new psychostimulant drug delivery systems have emerged. Daytrana, a transdermal patch of MPH for children, has significantly improved ADHD symptoms (Findling et al., 2008) and provides an alternative for those who are unable to benefit from daily medicines.

Although limited research support exists for medicines other than stimulants and atomoxetine, parents, school personnel, and medical professionals need to attend to these advances for three important reasons. First, physicians will often prescribe medications off-label, and practice has been known to lag behind research within the field of child psychiatry. Clinicians and teachers working with children should not be surprised when they hear of the use of these novel medicines. Second, the use of new medications or alternatives to psychostimulants and atomoxetine indicate that not all children respond to the medicines traditionally prescribed for ADHD. Third, children's response to medication is important to measure across multiple settings, and the efficacy of a medication for a particular child needs close scrutiny via valid and reliable measures (Madaan et al., 2008). In sum, the use of novel medications and formulations further illustrates that medications being used today to treat ADHD might be far different from those in the near and distant future.

Conclusion

Recent advances in the medical management of ADHD provide a glimpse into the future. Changes in delivery systems of the drugs that have been found to be effective will continue. Medications that improve ADHD symptoms but do not have abuse potential, do not require stringent prescription oversight, and have fewer side effects on appetite and sleep will continue to be developed. (See Table 8.1 for a list of FDA-approved medications.) According to the latest evidence base, psychostimulants demonstrate the approach with the best cost-benefit ratio for treating ADHD in children and adolescents.

Table 8.1   FDA-Approved Medications for ADHD

Trade Name	Generic Name	Class of Medication	Approved Age	Year Approved
Adderall	Amphetamine	Stimulants	3 and older	1996
Adderall XR	Amphetamine (extended release)	Stimulants	6 and older	2001
Concerta	Methylphenidate (long acting)	Stimulants	6 and older	2000
Daytrana	Methylphenidate (transdermal patch)	Stimulants	6 and older	2006
Dexedrine	Dextroamphetamine	Stimulants	3 and older	1976
Dexedrine Spansule	Dextroamphetamine (long acting)	Stimulants	3 and older	2002
DextroStat	Dextroamphetamine	Stimulants	3 and older	2001
Focalin	Dexmethylphenidate	Stimulants	6 and older	2001
Focalin XR	Dexmethylphenidate (extended release)	Stimulants	6 and older	2005
Intuniv ER	Guanfacine (extended release)	Antihypertensive	6 and older	Pending
Metadate CD	Methylphenidate (continuous delivery)	Stimulants	6 and older	2001
Metadate ER	Methylphenidate (extended release)	Stimulants	6 and older	1999

Trade Name	Generic Name	Class of Medication	Approved Age	Year Approved
Methylin	Methylphenidate	Stimulants	6 and older	2002
Methylin ER	Methylphenidate (extended release)	Stimulants	6 and older	2000
Ritalin	Methylphenidate	Stimulants	6 and older	1955
Ritalin LA	Methylphenidate (long acting)	Stimulants	6 and older	2002
Ritalin SR	Methylphenidate (sustained release)	Stimulants	6 and older	2001
Strattera	Atomoxetine	SNRI	6 and older	2002
Vyvanse	Lisdexamfetamine	Stimulants	6 and older	2007

SNRI = Selective norepinephrine reuptake inhibitor.

IMPLICATIONS FOR EDUCATORS

Psychotropic medications are often prescribed to school-aged populations due to dysfunction within the school setting. School personnel are the eyes and ears of understanding how ADHD symptoms impact a child's school functioning. Psychopharmacological interventions for ADHD can have profound effects on classroom behavior. Both desired effect and side effect data are essential to monitor within the school setting, given the amount of time children spend in this context. The role of schools is also essential prior to medication initiation, as a failure to respond to school-based psychosocial interventions should be documented and families can share those data with their physicians. Establishing clear target behaviors for medication treatment can help guide school personnel's observations and reports to help facilitate parents' and physicians' decisions to maintain, modify, or discontinue medication treatment. Performance at school can be assessed by classroom teachers, teacher aides, or school psychologists. Homework completion, time on-task, and daily behavior reports document specific outcomes, which can be examined to see if changes in core features of ADHD (inattention, hyperactivity, impulsivity) are improved enough to reduce dysfunction in academic performance.

Knowledge about the types of medications used to treat ADHD and other childhood mental health disorders is essential for school personnel, given the significant increase in the use of these treatments in school-aged populations. Understanding how medicines work, their targeted symptoms, their positive and negative effects, and the timing of effects are important for those within a treated child's environment. In addition, awareness of the rapidly changing world of pediatric psychopharmacology is essential, because the medications used to treat ADHD today are not likely to be the same medications used decades from now.

EDUCATIONAL STRATEGIES

- Educate parents, teachers, and other school personnel about the most common types of medications used to treat ADHD, their intended effects, and their side effects.
- Implement classroom-based interventions with integrity and collect progress-monitoring data on reducing inattention, hyperactivity, and impulsivity so that "failure to respond" to psychosocial treatments has been established prior to a family's consultation with a physician.
- Work collaboratively with families and their physicians to provide important behavioral records and observations from the school setting pertaining to both intended and side effects of medication treatment.
- Homework completion, time on-task, and daily behavior reports document specific outcomes, which can be examined to see if changes in core features of ADHD (inattention, hyperactivity, impulsivity) have improved.

DISCUSSION QUESTIONS

1. Is the risk of medication treatments for ADHD worth the positive results in most cases? Why?

2. What are the important target behaviors to monitor at school and home when a child is prescribed a stimulant-based medication for treatment of ADHD?

3. What side effects of medications for ADHD do educators need to look for?

4. How might stimulant-based treatments for ADHD differ from non-stimulant-based treatments for ADHD?

5. To what degree can medications for ADHD improve school-based performance? What additional skills or behaviors might need to be taught alongside medication treatment?

6. How can educators create an effective relationship among parents and medical professionals to ensure adequate medication monitoring when treating ADHD?

RESEARCH SUMMARY

- Psychotropic medications, specifically psychostimulant medications, are very effective in the short-term treatment of ADHD, especially when combined with psychosocial treatments.
- Psychostimulants demonstrate the best cost-benefit ratio in treating ADHD in children and adolescents, according to the latest evidence base.
- Intensive monitoring of medication treatment outcomes across multiple settings can lead to improved dosage titration practices and, ultimately, greater efficacy of medication treatments.

- School personnel can play a vital role in helping provide school-based functioning data to parents and physicians to help them in their decision to initiate, maintain, alter, or discontinue medication treatment.
- Evidence is emerging for the effectiveness of a number of alternatives to psychostimulants (e.g., atomoxetine), and new medicines that address current weaknesses of existing treatments are on the horizon for addressing ADHD symptoms.

RESOURCES

The Food and Drug Administration (FDA) provides a series of psychotropic medication fact sheets, including fact sheets on all drugs approved for treating ADHD:

www.fda.gov/Drugs/DrugSafety/PostmarketDrugSafetyInformation forPatientsandProviders/ucm111085.htm

The National Institute of Mental Health (NIMH) has published a detailed booklet that describes ADHD symptoms, causes, and treatments and provides information about getting help and coping with ADHD:

www.nimh.nih.gov/health/publications/attention-deficit-hyperactivity-disorder/index.shtml

An ADHD advocacy group called Children and Adults with Attention Deficit/Hyperactivity Disorder has a helpful Web site that discusses multiple treatment approaches:

www.chadd.org

HANDOUT

RECENT ADVANCES IN THE MEDICAL MANAGEMENT OF ADHD

A diagnosis of ADHD, a neurodevelopmental disorder, requires a thorough assessment of a child's behavior across multiple contexts. Teachers and school personnel are essential to provide information at both the diagnostic and treatment-monitoring stages. A comprehensive developmental history is important to establish the pervasive and chronic nature of symptoms associated with ADHD. Alternative explanations (such as learning problems, sleep problems, stress, anxiety, depression, substance abuse) should be ruled out prior to a diagnosis; doing so requires close collaboration among home, school, and community settings. Prior to initiating medication treatment, parents are strongly advised to consult with school personnel to develop a behavior intervention plan, which should include teacher and parent input and involvement. If this behavioral approach to treating inattention, hyperactivity, and impulsivity is ineffective, then parents are encouraged to meet with their family physician regarding medication treatment to be initiated in combination with continued behavior plans at home and school.

A number of medications have clearly demonstrated efficacy in the short-term treatment of ADHD. The majority of these medicines are from a class of medications called psychostimulants, but increased attention has been given to nonstimulant medicines in recent years. Side effects associated with these medicines are typically minimal in comparison to the significant improvements seen at school and home. However, all medications currently used to treat ADHD have some serious, though rare, side effects associated with them. Parents and teachers should be aware of medication side effects via consultation with a child's physician. Upon beginning medication treatment, parents should do the following:

- Work closely with your physician to determine the most appropriate medication treatment, including the type of medication to be used (stimulant versus nonstimulant), the characteristics of that medicine (long acting versus short acting), and the goals or behaviors to be targeted for treatment (inattention, hyperactivity, impulsivity, work completion).
- Give medication as directed by the treating physician.
- Treatment adherence issues should be conveyed to school personnel so they can provide observational and narrative data about the treatment's impact on classroom behavior.
- Monitor a child's response to medication across multiple contexts by involving key school personnel.

Performance at school can be assessed by the classroom teacher, a teacher aide, or school psychologists. Homework completion, time on-task, and daily behavior reports are specific outcomes that can be examined to see if changes in core features of ADHD (inattention, hyperactivity, impulsivity) are improved enough to reduce dysfunction in academic performance. Monitoring for adverse effects is also essential: Loss of appetite, sleep disturbance, irritability, and mood changes should be closely watched for within the home and school settings.

9

Polypharmacy Prescription Practices in School–Aged Populations

Challenges and Considerations

John S. Carlson

Charlie is a 9-year-old boy in the third grade who was first diagnosed with ADHD in kindergarten. Charlie's classroom performance has decreased significantly in the past 3 months following a change in stimulant dose resulting from his visit with a new physician. Charlie's deviant and acting-out behavior at school has worsened, and he demonstrates greater difficulty with self-regulation. From communications with his mother, his teacher has concluded that changes are pervasive across settings; the recent behavioral decline is affecting both his classroom behavior and functioning at home.

Data collection efforts were undertaken at both home and school to examine closely the current nature of Charlie's challenges and possible functions for these behavioral problems. As communication with Charlie's mother continued, it was determined that Charlie has been staying up late into the night playing video games. Two weeks of targeting a number of ecological changes, including

(Continued)

(Continued)

removing the gaming system from his room, failed to improve Charlie's sleep patterns substantially, however, as he continued to stay up late into the night. It is determined that Charlie may be experiencing insomnia resulting from the change in stimulant dosage, and a lower dose is prescribed.

Unfortunately, Charlie's hyperactive, impulsive, and inattentive behaviors became even more problematic. His physician decided to return his dose to the previous level and to prescribe clonidine to help him go to sleep at night. After 2 weeks of a combined treatment approach, Charlie's sleep has improved dramatically and his self-regulation skills are once again evidenced within the classroom setting. Home and school functioning has returned to levels seen prior to the change in stimulant dose 3 months ago.

INTRODUCTION

Physicians commonly employ two or more psychotropic medications (termed *polypharmacy*, *copharmacy*, *combined pharmacotherapy*, or *concomitant medication treatment*) to treat one or more mental health conditions in children (Zonfrillo, Penn, & Leonard, 2005). This practice has been found to be especially prevalent within vulnerable populations, such as children receiving psychotropic medication who are also being served within the foster care system (Breland-Noble et al., 2004). Polypharmacy prevalence rates within that subgroup of children have been reported to be as high as 72.5% (e.g., Zito, Safer, Sai, et al., 2008). Such practices raise a number of ethical concerns. The knowledge base for many pediatric psychopharmacological treatments when used alone is limited, and even less support exists regarding the efficacy of psychotropic medications used concurrently (Safer, Zito, & dosReis, 2003).

The use of combined medications highlights the urgent need for future investigations of both intended and side effects associated with these prescription practices. The potential for adverse events via drug-drug interactions and the distinct way that young children metabolize medications makes the issue of polypharmacy important for school-based personnel due to legal and safety reasons. We must first "do no harm" as we work to create "good" within the lives of those who are unresponsive to psychosocial treatments or educational interventions that have been carried out carefully and with clearly established integrity.

When families choose to use medication treatment approaches for their children, school psychologists and educators are in a position to collaborate with physicians to understand how psychotropic medication treatments, single or multiple, may be negatively or positively influencing a child's functioning at school, at home, and/or in the community. The psychopharmacological agents commonly employed within school-aged populations clearly target classroom behaviors, social interactions, and readiness to benefit from instruction. Gathering data about changes in these behaviors is essential to the risk-benefit analysis required to determine if a polypharmacy approach is necessary.

BACKGROUND

Overview and Definitions

Polypharmacy refers to the use of more than one medication by an individual. It is a widespread practice within behavioral health care. Improving the social, occupational, academic, and family functioning of children is often the impetus for a physician's consideration of the risks and rewards associated with combining medications. A technical report from experts in the field (National Association of State Mental Health Program Directors, 2001) specifies the rationale for physicians' use of more than one medication as the need to do the following:

- Address a complex array of symptoms
- Treat multiple illnesses concurrently
- Speed up the therapeutic benefits of a drug
- Normalize functioning
- Augment the impact of a preceding drug
- Control or prevent conditions that often have specific phase lengths or reoccur, such as mania or depression
- Prevent or treat the side effects that arise from monotherapy
- Target the lack of previous treatment effectiveness

Five categories cover the broad array of different situations and circumstances that surround this type of prescription practice. These include same-class polypharmacy, multiclass polypharmacy, adjunctive polypharmacy, and augmentation. *Total pharmacy* is the fifth term used to describe polypharmacy and refers to the total number of pharmacological agents a person is currently taking. It differs substantially from the other four categories, as it takes into consideration the ingestion of both prescription and nonprescription medications, such as over-the-counter medicines (e.g., cold medicines) and illicit substances (e.g., marijuana).

Risks Associated With Polypharmacy

There are a number of inherent risks when children take multiple medications, including the increased likelihood of side effects or adverse events. In addition, a more challenging set of circumstances arises when using more than one medicine, and issues related to a link between treatment complexity and compliance may arise. One significant challenge when adding medication to an existing medication is the lack of clarity that may emerge regarding whether each medication is having its intended effects. This has clear implications for the need for close monitoring. Using more than one medication to treat a condition may also directly result in the need to use yet another medicine, as there appears to be a compounding effect from polypharmacy approaches.

Expenses associated with more than one prescription are also an important consideration, as the cost of treatment may affect one's ability to use or access the treatments prescribed. Such costs must also be considered from a larger systems perspective, as two or more prescriptions may create a burden on health insurance plans and, ultimately, affect future generations via increased health care costs.

Safety and efficacy issues arise within combined medication treatments due to a bias toward not publishing results of studies that demonstrate negative results. In addition, it is challenging to decipher the changes attributed to one medication when two are used within empirical studies, and there is an overextension of data from adult populations to implications for treatment within childhood populations (Safer et al., 2003). In sum, the limited evidence base in place to support polypharmacy in children must be weighed with the unknown long-term treatment effects that multiple medications may have on a young child's developing brain.

Assumptions Associated With Polypharmacy

Parents who choose a psychopharmacological treatment approach often feel that they have no other choice, given the level of dysfunction caused by their child's symptoms or the family's available resources and supports. The assumption when the family's physician prescribes two or more medications is that the parents' feelings of helplessness and hopelessness have persisted as a result of a lack of improvement seen within a monotherapy approach. School personnel also need to consider the decision-making process demonstrated by the prescribing physician. School psychologists and educators can help verify diagnostic assessments, differential diagnosis, and the presence of existing data that clearly show a lack of response to prior treatments. In addition, a "rational copharmacy in psychiatry" is important to consider as progress-monitoring strategies are developed within the school setting to communicate treatment response back to the family and their treating physician (Preskorn & Lacey, 2007, p. 100). The criteria supporting the selection of a polypharmacy approach include the following:

- Knowledge that a combined medication approach will positively affect the disorder or symptoms
- Evidence that a combined approach is more effective, including being more cost-effective, than a monotherapy approach to treatment
- Certainty that a combined approach will not have significantly greater safety or tolerability risks than monotherapy
- Knowledge that the drugs will not interact negatively within the child's body
- Confidence that the drugs will interact in a way that augments a response
- Evidence that the drugs are believed to have only one mechanism of action
- Knowledge that drugs do not have broad-acting, the same, or opposite mechanisms of action within child and adolescent populations
- Evidence that a drug's effects on the body have been investigated in children and that the drug has a simple metabolism, an intermediate half-life, and linear pharmacokinetics

Some have argued that that use of the term *"rational" polypharmacy* is extremely premature within childhood populations, given the considerable lack of evidence in support of a combined treatment approach

(Safer et al., 2003). Additional data are needed to support polypharmacy practices in children.

Medication Use in School-Aged Populations

Significant mental health challenges affect one in every five children, and the prevention and intervention of psychiatric disorders has been identified as a national priority (U.S. Department of Health and Human Services, 1999). Consistent with this movement, psychotropic medication prescriptions within school-aged populations have increased dramatically during the recent decade within both outpatient and inpatient service delivery systems (Najjar et al., 2004). Population prevalence rates of psychotropic medications have been found to be consistently higher in the United States (6.7%) when compared to other countries (e.g., Germany, 2.0%), leading many to believe that policy and government regulation largely account for these differences (e.g., Zito, Safer, de Jong-van den Berg, et al., 2008).

Medication Use Within Vulnerable Populations

Without psychotropic medication treatments, many with psychiatric conditions would go untreated or be undertreated, resulting in significant impairment and limited opportunities for typical development. The majority (71%) of children ages 3 to 12 years with severe mental illness (i.e., psychiatrically hospitalized children in the United States) have a prescription history involving at least one psychotropic medication (Zakriski, Wheeler, Burda, & Shields, 2005). Those within long-term residential treatment care between the ages of 5 and 19 have rates closer to 90% (Connor, Ozbayrak, Kusiak, Caponi, & Melloni, 1997). In those ages 9 and younger, almost half treated within a psychiatric inpatient unit have a history of medication treatment (Lekhwani, Nair, Nikhinson, & Ambrosini, 2004). This is despite the fact that these young children are at significantly greater risk for adverse drug responses and that few medications other than psychostimulants are approved for use within this age group. The use of psychotropic medication treatments by families and care providers is remarkable when considering the limited evidence base available for the majority of psychotropic treatments used in children.

Prevalence of Polypharmacy in Childhood Populations

An increase in the frequency of using multiple medications (e.g., 4.7% in 1987 to 13.6% in 1993) to treat one or more childhood mental health conditions has been reported (Martin, Van Hoof, Stubbe, Sherwin, & Scahill, 2003; Olfson, Marcus, Weissman, & Jensen, 2002). Within specific medication classes, such as treatments for ADHD, rates have increased as much as fivefold (from 5% to 25%) within a 5-year time frame (Bhatara, Feil, Hoagwood, Vitiello, & Zima, 2002). Recent polypharmacy prevalence rates are estimated to be nearly 33% for children on psychotropic medication as observed within large samples of Medicaid and state insurance plans (e.g., dosReis et al., 2005). At this rate, nearly half of those on psychotropic medication may be expected to be prescribed combined medication treatments within the next 5 years.

Cultural Considerations and Polypharmacy

The increase in combined medication treatment rates is not confined to physicians practicing in the United States; the use of multiple medications to treat children's mental health challenges has been reported across the world. For example, data from a child and adolescent outpatient clinic population in Turkey indicate that more than 25% were prescribed medication and, of those, 10% were prescribed two or more medications (Aras, Varol Tas, & Unlu, 2007). Most common were prescriptions for both a selective serotonin reuptake inhibitor (SSRI; e.g., fluoxetine) and a benzodiazepine, which is a member of the anxiolytic (antianxiety) class (e.g., alprazolam). Data from India indicate that 39% of children seen within a child and adolescent psychiatry clinic were prescribed a psychotropic medication (Russell, George, & Mammen, 2006). Of the treated children, 52% were receiving more than one medication. Data from those seen within an inpatient psychiatric setting in Finland indicated that 43% were prescribed medication, with 36% of those treated with a combined pharmacotherapy approach (Sourander, 2004). The most common combined approach involved an antipsychotic with an SSRI (31%). In addition, the use of two antipsychotics to treat one psychiatric disorder was quite common (23%).

Interventions

Combined Medication Approaches. Medication treatments in combination have been used to treat the majority of childhood disorders, including disruptive behavior disorders, mood disorders, anxiety disorders, psychotic disorders, and pervasive developmental disorders (Zamvil & Cannon, 2002). Stimulants plus mood stabilizers have been used to treat bipolar disorder. Stimulants plus SSRIs have been used to treat unipolar depression. Stimulants with anxiolytics (anti-anxiety medications) or SSRIs have been used to treat anxiety disorders. In addition, aggression has been targeted with combined stimulant/antipsychotic approaches. In children treated for ADHD, it is common to prescribe a stimulant during the day and clonidine (i.e., an alpha agonist) at night to help with stimulant-induced sleep problems. The rationale for these combined treatment practices within childhood populations is typically summarized as the need to (a) address issues of comorbidity or co-occurring symptoms, (b) reduce symptoms that are harmful to the patient or others, (c) combat emergent side effects that develop from the primary medication treatment, and (d) normalize the target behaviors and symptoms so that development may proceed in a more age-appropriate manner. Leaders within the field of child psychiatry (as reviewed by Safer et al., 2003) have noted that the following situations would be justifiable for using more than one psychotropic medication:

- Use of antidepressant plus a stimulant for comorbid ADHD and depression
- Use of clonidine to treat stimulant induced insomnia
- Use of ADHD medication and a mood stabilizer in comorbid ADHD and bipolar disorder

- Use of two or more medications to treat ADHD and Tourette syndrome or obsessive-compulsive disorder (OCD)
- Use of two or more medications to treat major depression with psychotic features
- Use of two or more medications to treat comorbid anxiety disorders and major depression
- Use of another medication when there is a first-line treatment for the condition (e.g., ADHD)
- Antidepressants with lithium for bipolar disorder
- Lithium augmentation for untreatable depression
- Lithium and antipsychotics for acute psychoses
- Lithium and anticonvulsants for untreatable mania
- Sustained-release methylphenidate with short-acting methylphenidate to increase impact at drug onset
- Methylphenidate and a late afternoon neuroleptic for severely hyperactive children
- Addition of another medication for those who show partial response to methylphenidate and have a disruptive behavior disorder
- Augmentation with anxiolytic or antipsychotic to SSRIs for those with treatment-resistant OCD
- Use of additional medication in combination with SSRI for those with treatment-resistant depression

It is important to note that these clinical recommendations have no empirical support to justify their use and further research is necessary for these polypharmacy practices to be continued.

Monitoring Combined-Medication Treatments. Given the limited evidence for use of multiple medications within school-aged populations, it is essential that school psychologists, educators, and other school personnel have a clear understanding of both the treatment approach being attempted and its rationale. Researching answers to the following questions is essential prior to developing progress-monitoring strategies within the school, home, or community setting (Pruitt & Kiser, 2004):

- What empirical evidence exists for the indication/symptoms being treated?
- What safety or tolerability concerns exist for the prescribed medication(s)?
- What treatment compliance issues are important to consider?
- How will the treatment progress be monitored, according to the family and the family's physician?
- How are risks and benefits going to be analyzed, shared, and discussed across settings?

With these responses in mind, school psychologists and educators can apply medication evaluation approaches found within the literature (e.g., Carlson, 2008) to a polypharmacy approach. It is essential that data collection begin prior the onset of medication treatment or any medication augmentation. This will allow for the collection of baseline data to which future data can be compared for progress-monitoring purposes.

IMPLICATIONS FOR EDUCATORS

Psychotropic medications are often prescribed to school-aged populations due to dysfunction within the school setting. School psychologists and other school personnel can play a key role in monitoring the effects of medication(s) so that physicians and families have the data necessary to make decisions about medication treatment initiation, modification, and/or discontinuation. The more educators are aware of the frequency of polypharmacy in school-aged populations, the types of medicines prescribed concurrently, the rationale behind such practices, and the potentially deleterious effects that may arise within the school setting, the better they will be able to communicate with families and physicians regarding classroom-based observations of targeted symptoms and emergent side effects. Educators' skills and training in consultation, collaboration, and working as a team are essential to efficient and effective home–school communication. Given the importance of balancing the costs and benefits of using multiple psychotropic medications in children, educators remain in a key position to develop ecological and behavioral interventions that work so that children's functioning at school is not targeted with medication treatments. Demonstration and documentation of a failure to respond to these psychosocial interventions at school is an important role for educators to play in the treatment of children with mental health challenges.

EDUCATIONAL STRATEGIES

- Educate parents, teachers, and other school personnel about the most common types of medications used to treat mental health problems in children.
- Implement classroom-based interventions with integrity and collect progress-monitoring data so that it is clear that the child demonstrates a "failure to respond" to psychosocial treatments prior to initiation of a mono- or combined-medication therapy approach.
- Work collaboratively with families and their physicians to provide important behavioral records, data, and observations from the school setting pertaining to both intended and side effects of medication treatments.
- Discuss any concerns about a child's responsiveness to medications immediately with the child's parents, school nurse, school psychologist, and physician. Some medication side effects are serious and should be reported immediately.

DISCUSSION QUESTIONS

1. Why do physicians decide to use more than one psychotropic medication to treat children, despite a lack of evidence for such a practice?

2. What are the risks of using more than one psychotropic medication to treat children's mental health challenges? Are these worth the potential advantages of changing target symptoms? Why?

3. What are the important target behaviors to monitor when a child is prescribed two or more medications?

4. What side effects do educators need to look for in children treated with polypharmacy approaches?

5. How might using clonidine concurrently with a psychostimulant for ADHD have different effects than using just a psychostimulant?

6. To what degree can medications used in combination improve school-based performance? How might they be detrimental to school-based performance?

7. How can educators create an effective relationship among parents and medical professionals to ensure adequate medication monitoring when multiple medications are prescribed to a student?

RESEARCH SUMMARY

- Many children across the world are treated with more than one medication in an effort to improve a child's mental health functioning across home, school, and community settings. Such practices also appear to be on the rise. As stated succinctly by the American Academy of Child and Adolescent Psychiatry (2001):

  > Little data exist to support advantageous efficacy for drug combinations, used primarily to treat co-morbid conditions. The current clinical "state-of-the-art" supports judicious use of combined medications, keeping such use to clearly justifiable circumstances. Medication management requires the informed consent of the parents or legal guardians and must address benefits vs. risks, side effects and the potential for drug interactions.

- The majority (71%) of children ages 3 to 12 years with severe mental illness (i.e., psychiatrically hospitalized children in the United States) have a prescription history involving at least one psychotropic medication. Those within long-term residential treatment care between the ages of 5 and 19 have rates closer to 90%.

- Examples of polypharmacy practice include the following:
  - The use of stimulants plus mood stabilizers to treat bipolar disorder
  - Stimulants plus SSRIs used to treat unipolar depression
  - Stimulants with anxiolytics or SSRIs used to treat anxiety disorders
  - Stimulants with antipsychotics to treat aggression
  - Prescribing a stimulant during the day for ADHD and clonidine (i.e., an alpha agonist) at night to help with stimulant-induced sleep problems

- The increase in combined medication treatments is not unique to the United States. Data from studies of clinic populations in Turkey, India, and Finland find two or more medications used to treat 12.5%, 20.2%, and 15.4% of children and adolescents, respectively. Most common were prescriptions for both a selective serotonin reuptake inhibitor and a benzodiazepine, an antipsychotic with an SSRI, and the use of two antipsychotics to treat one psychiatric disorder.

RESOURCES

The Food and Drug Administration (FDA) provides a series of psychotropic medication fact sheets, including on all those drugs approved for treating common psychiatric disorders in childhood:

www.fda.gov/Drugs/DrugSafety/PostmarketDrugSafetyInformation
forPatientsandProviders/ucm111085.htm

The National Institute of Mental Health (NIMH) has put together a detailed booklet that describes ADHD symptoms, causes, and treatments and provides information about getting help and coping with this condition. ADHD treatments are commonly combined with other medications in pediatric populations.

www.nimh.nih.gov/health/publications/adhd/summary.shtml

HANDOUT

POLYPHARMACY PRESCRIPTION PRACTICES IN SCHOOL-AGED POPULATIONS

Any childhood psychiatric diagnosis requires a thorough assessment of the child's behavior across multiple contexts. A comprehensive developmental history is essential to understanding the pervasive and chronic nature of the symptoms impacting the child's functioning. Classroom observations and an interview with the child may also be helpful to clarify the diagnosis and to identify target behaviors for treatment.

All psychiatric conditions in children should be initially addressed via psychosocial or behavioral approaches. After failing to demonstrate change with treatments that have been carried out with integrity and as intended, then alternative treatment approaches might be considered. Further data collection is necessary for progress monitoring and to examine changes that may occur when medication is used in combination with other treatments, especially when used with other medication approaches. Few situations warrant the use of multiple medications to treat a mental health condition. Work closely with the child's physician to justify the rationale for a combined medication treatment approach and clearly define the behaviors that should be targeted for progress monitoring within the school setting. Ask the physician questions and insist on getting answers to the following questions and be sure to share these with school personnel:

- What empirical evidence exists for the indication/symptoms being treated?
- What safety or tolerability concerns exist for the prescribed medication(s)?
- What treatment compliance issues are important to consider?
- How will or should the treatment progress be monitored?
- How are risks and benefits going to be analyzed, shared, and discussed across settings?

Working with the school psychologist and the child's teacher to monitor the child's response to a combined medication treatment approach across multiple contexts is important given the lack of evidence for this prescription practice. The classroom teacher can assess and report performance within the classroom. Homework completion, time on-task, social relations, and daily behavior reports may be specific outcomes that should be examined to see if changes occur in the core symptoms targeted for treatment. Identifying and monitoring potential adverse effects is also essential.

10

Educational Implications of Commonly Used Pediatric Medications

Larry M. Bolen and Michael B. Brown

School psychologist Tamika Peters was asked to consult about a second-grade teacher about Kyla, a student with a history of learning and attention problems. Kyla has struggled to acquire basic academic and social skills in the classroom. She was diagnosed with asthma last year and has been on several medications the last few months in an effort to control her asthma. Kyla often wheezes and has difficulty breathing both in the classroom and during physical exertion. Kyla was most recently prescribed a beta-2 agonist drug that often causes nervousness and restlessness.

To gather information on the possible effects of medication, the school psychologist had both Kyla's teacher and parents complete the Medication Side Effects Screening Form (see Figure 10.1). Based on the information collected, Kyla's parents were advised to talk further with their pediatrician about the potential medication side effects. Given Kyla's challenges in school and the possible influence of medications on her school performance, her pediatrician has chosen to continue medication for 2 more weeks. Another Medication Side Effects Screening Form will be completed, and if the side effects do not fade away, then a new medication with a different side effects profile will be prescribed.

Figure 10.1 Medication Side Effects Screening Form: Kyla

MEDICATION SIDE EFFECTS SCREENING FORM

Name: ___Kyla O.___   DOB: ___23 Nov 2002___   Age: ___7___

Health Status:

Does the child have any symptoms of the following acute or chronic illnesses?

Cough _____ Cold _____ Headache _____ Stomachache _____ Earache _____

Asthma ___X___ Other respiratory problem _____ Fever _____ Other _____

List any prescription or over-the-counter medications the student is taking.

terbutaline sulfate (Bricanyl Turbuhaler)

Possible Medication Side Effects (check all that apply):

_____	Dizziness	_____	Reduced psychomotor speed
_____	Fatigue/lack of energy	__X__	Anxiety
_____	Nausea	_____	Aggressive behavior
_____	Sleep disturbance	_____	Depression
__X__	Tremors	__X__	Hyperactivity
__X__	Difficulty with concentration	__X__	Irritability
_____	Drowsiness/decreased alertness	_____	Moody
__X__	Inattention	_____	Oppositional behavior
_____	Memory impairment	_____	Other (specify)

Medication Side Effects Ratings:

Specify the side effects from the list above that cause the most difficulty.
  Overactivity, difficulty concentrating, nervousness

Specify student-reported side effects from the list above.
  Kyla told the teacher that she just cannot sit still any more. Her feet shake with extra energy throughout the day. These are all new behaviors for Kyla. Although Kyla has had difficulty in school prior to the new medication, her current behaviors make it difficult for Kyla to keep pace. She is falling further behind her classmates.

Actions and Interventions:

Recommended actions/interventions based on potential medication side effects.

_____ Postponement of formal psychoeducational assessment

__X__ Recommendation for accommodation to 504 Team or IEP Team

_____ Classroom interventions to assist teacher in working around side effects

__X__ Consultation, education, or further information gathering with parent

__X__ Consultation with health care provider about current medication and/or alternative medical interventions

_____ Behavioral interventions to reduce need for medication (e.g., relaxation training)

_____ Other intervention (specify):

INTRODUCTION

All medications have the potential for side effects—effects that occur beyond or in addition to the desired therapeutic effect of the drug. The medications frequently used for common childhood illnesses are no exception. Although these medications are regularly used, their short- and long-term impact on school performance may not be fully appreciated by students, parents, health care providers, or educators. For example, medications might affect learning and memory, interrupt the child's attention span and concentration, or cause loss of stamina and drowsiness during class. Educators benefit from understanding the effects on school performance of frequently prescribed and over-the-counter medications for a variety of common physical disorders affecting children and adolescents.

BACKGROUND

Children experience a variety of routine illnesses during the school years, and 31% of school-age children have chronic health-related problems ranging from mild to severe. Up to one third of these students have medical consequences significant enough to interfere with school performance (Newacheck & Halfon, 1998). Respiratory illnesses, recurrent ear infections, and asthma are the most frequently occurring chronic health conditions affecting children (Charles, Pan, & Britt, 2004). Asthma accounts for the most number of days absent from school for students in the United States (Thompson & Gustafson, 1996).

Medication is frequently used to treat these common illnesses of childhood and adolescence. Some of the commonly used medications are prescribed by a health care provider, and parents may also rely on the use of over-the-counter medication. More than 95 million packages of over-the-counter (OTC) medication for cough and colds are purchased yearly (Consumer Healthcare Products Association, 2007). OTC medications are used to treat a variety of other symptoms, including fever, headache, stomachache, allergies, and insomnia.

Of children experiencing a chronic illness, 45% fall seriously behind in their schoolwork, which often contributes to negative feeling toward school (Theis, 1999). Of students at the high school level identified as Other Health Impaired, 35% receive failing grades. School performance is affected by absences due to the illness or the physical side effects of treatment (i.e., nausea, stomachaches), and the students fall behind in their work (Geist, Grdisa, & Otley, 2003; Shiu, 2001). Although there is a paucity of empirical studies examining the effects of the commonly used medications on school learning, it is likely that the medications used to treat these common illnesses have an effect on students' ability to do well in school.

Medication Issues

Few studies in the literature document the impact of the effects of these commonly used medications on children's school performance, and many of these studies were done some years ago (Eiland, Jenkins, & Durham, 2007). Each of the commonly used medications has side effects that have the potential to disrupt school performance. Several nonspecific side effects are common across many categories of drugs, while certain important issues are specific to treatments for specific disorders.

Nonspecific Medication Side Effects. Drug side effects can occur in the physiological, cognitive, or behavioral domains. Examples of nonspecific side effects include the following:

- Dizziness
- Fatigue/lack of energy
- Nausea
- Sleep disturbance
- Difficulty with concentration/inattention
- Drowsiness/decreased alertness
- Inattention
- Memory impairment
- Tremors or reduced psychomotor speed
- Anxiety/depression
- Aggressive or oppositional behavior
- Hyperactivity
- Irritability/mood instability

Nonspecific side effects can have a significant effect on school performance either singularly or in combination with one another. For example, antihistamines may cause hyperactivity, drowsiness, or difficulty with attention that could affect the child's ability to work effectively in class. Nonspecific side effects may be a target of either accommodation or intervention, as appropriate.

Issues Specific to Medications for Treatment of Asthma. Asthma is acute respiratory distress caused by inflammation and swelling of the airway lining that results in obstruction or narrowing of the airway. Asthma is the most common chronic illness among children younger than 18 years in the United States (Drotar, 2006). Asthma can have a number of adverse effects on school achievement. One survey of teachers of children with asthma found that over half of these students were moderately underachieving and 15% demonstrated serious learning deficits. Problems in mathematics (23.7%), language (18.6%), spelling (18.6%), reading (23.7%), and handwriting (25.4%) were most commonly identified (Naude & Pretorius, 2003).

A number of medications are used to treat asthma. Asthma medications are commonly grouped into quick-relief (rescue) drugs, such as fluticasone (Flovent) and budesonide (Pulmicort), and long-term (controller) medications, such as albuterol (Ventolin, Proventil; Martin, Scahill, Charney, & Leckman, 2003). Medication side effects may cause symptoms such as the following:

- Tremors affecting fine motor control
- Aggressive or oppositional behavior

- Memory impairment
- Mood instability
- Anxiety, worry
- Nausea
- Inattentiveness
- Hyperactivity or agitation

Children with chronic asthma may be passive and easily fatigued in the classroom, resulting in poor attending skills, which are often mistaken as symptoms of attention disorders (Celano & Geller, 1993). Long-term treatment with any of the corticosteroid medications may result in a variety of side effects that can affect school achievement (Naude & Pretorius, 2003). Children with chronic moderate to severe asthma may therefore be at considerable risk for school difficulties.

Issues Specific to Medications for Pain, Headaches, and Fever. Headaches are a frequent complaint of children in both primary and secondary schools. Analgesic drugs are used to reduce pain, and antipyretic drugs are prescribed to reduce fever; drugs that are effective in treating pain are typically also effective in reducing fever. Aspirin, acetaminophen (Tylenol), naproxen sodium (Aleve), and ibuprofen (Motrin) are among the most commonly prescribed analgesic/antipyretic medications. These drugs can be found in single-ingredient preparations as well as combined with other medications in multisymptom allergy, cough, cold, and flu remedies. Children who are prescribed analgesics are generally not at great risk for deleterious side effects that affect school performance. Normal dosage of aspirin and related drugs may, however, cause nausea, vomiting, diarrhea, or gastrointestinal bleeding in some children (Amann & Peskar, 2002).

Some children may be prescribed anticonvulsant medication for the treatment of migraine. Gabapentin (neurontin), topiramate (Topamax), levetiracetam (Keppra), and zonisamide (Zonegran) are the four anticonvulsant medications most commonly used for migraine headache. Anticonvulsants are associated with a number of potential side effects, such as hyperactivity, fatigue, irritability, cognitive processing difficulty, and emotional lability. These side effects are usually reversible by either discontinuation or dose reduction (Eiland, 2007). Likewise, behavioral and cognitive effects generally diminish when dosage is discontinued following short-term therapy. Residual effects may continue under long-term treatment with a concomitant negative effect on academic achievement (Loring & Meador, 2004).

Antipyretics and analgesics account for a large number of overdoses; the American Association of Poison Control Centers reported that of all overdoses of OTC products, 66% involved acetaminophen, 19% involved ibuprofen, and 15% involved aspirin. Toxic symptoms from aspirin-related medications can include tiredness, rapid breathing, seizures, vomiting, bleeding, and coma (Amann & Peskar, 2002). Educators and mental health professionals should be aware of this potential when working with students who have the potential for accidental or purposive overdose.

Issues Specific to Medications for Cough and Colds. Cough and cold medications frequently contain a combination of drugs that aim to treat a variety of symptoms of the cold and flu. The combination of drugs might include a decongestant, cough suppressant, antihistamine, expectorant, and/or an analgesic/antipyretic. The physiological effects of common cold and cough medicines can disrupt children's school performance. For example, cough and cold medication may exacerbate sedative effects, affecting alertness, concentration, and psychomotor speed (Connor & Meltzer, 2006; Martin et al., 2003; Woo, 2008). Commonly experienced side effects that may affect school performance include the following:

- Slowing of psychomotor speed
- Increased heart rate and dysrhythmia
- Sedation and dizziness
- Headaches
- Dry mouth
- Decreased alertness, drowsiness, and sedation
- Nausea and gastrointestinal upset
- Fatigue
- Irritability
- Depression

OTC cough and cold medicines that contain decongestants may have serious health consequences for children with hypertension, congenital heart disease, or diabetes. Topical decongestants (sprays and drops) produce vasoconstriction and shrinkage of the nasal tissues yet typically result in little systemic absorption when used as directed (Woo, 2008). Despite the relative safety of dextromethorphan, a common ingredient in OTC medicines, there have been cases of its "recreational" use, as well as death by overdose. Although generally nonaddictive, dextromethorphan use can result in a substance-dependence syndrome, and parents and educators should be aware of its abuse potential (Murray & Brewerton, 1993). Serious adverse physical effects rarely occur following overdose of diphenhydramine (e.g., Benadryl), chlorpheniramine (e.g., Chlor-Trimeton), and brompheniramine (e.g., Dimetapp Allergy; Eick, Blumer, & Reed, 2001).

IMPLICATIONS FOR EDUCATORS

Understanding the use and effects of frequently used medications is important for school psychologists, counselors, and educators. School personnel can utilize a variety of direct and indirect strategies to assist students who may have school-related symptoms as a result of medication use.

Assessment

Obtaining a developmental history, including a medical history, is typically a part of formal evaluations for special services, but may also be useful when conducting informal assessments that lead to direct interventions. It is important to ask about OTC medications and common childhood illnesses as a potential factor in poor school performance. The Medication Side Effect Form (see Figure 10.2 on page 102) provides a convenient method for gathering information about common childhood illnesses, medications, and potential medication side effects. Collecting this information is important to understanding the factors that may be affecting students' behavior or school performance.

Once potential medication side effects are identified, it may be beneficial to assess specific behaviors or attributes that medication may be affecting. For example, school psychologists can utilize standardized instruments and rating scales, along with more informal data collection methods (e.g., interview or direct behavior observation), to develop an understanding of students' situations. Monitoring protocols can be designed to address the needs of individual students and provide an excellent review of a variety of measures and procedures that can be used to assess the effects of medications across important domains (DuPaul, Coniglio, & Nebrig, 2004).

Intervention

No interventions are specific to potential side effects of frequently prescribed medications. Some medication side effects will require accommodations that "work around" the symptom. For example, interventions for temporary side effects will likely include tolerating the side effects for the short period of treatment or, if necessary, scheduling important tasks around the period of treatment (e.g., postpone formal psychoeducational assessment or other high-stakes testing). School personnel should also collaborate with other health care providers in the school (e.g., the school nurse or the school-based health center staff) when issues of medication side effects arise.

School personnel will find that the interventions that they typically use for analogous symptoms caused by other factors will be useful for dealing with medication side effects. Many pediatric psychology interventions are based on sound theory and practice, although very few studies are aimed at empirically validating the efficacy of interventions (Spirito & Kazak, 2006). Many useful intervention strategies for health-related problems in the school setting can be used for medication side effects as well (Drotar, 2006; Kratochwill, Cowell, Feeney, & Sannetti, 2004).

Advocacy and Education

Although school personnel should not give medical advice, they nonetheless should be aware of issues surrounding the use and effects of frequently used pediatric medications. School psychologists, counselors, nurses, and social workers working with children who are using these medications can inform teachers and parents about their potential side effects. Teachers may also benefit from assistance in developing a method to monitor the effects and side effects of medication (DuPaul et al., 2004). Parents should be encouraged to discuss the possible effects of medication on school performance with their child's health care provider.

School psychologists and school nurses should consider providing informal and formal training programs for school staff on these issues. Education and school-based health care professionals often require continuing professional development programs and training, and medication and medication side effects is a potentially valuable topic for a training program. Arranging for collaborative training with fellow school-based health providers is also a great way to build collaboration and to get others in the schools thinking more about the impact of health issues on school achievement (Brown, 2008). The *PDR Concise Drug Guide for Pediatrics* (2008) and *Medications for School-Age Children: Effects on Learning and Behavior* (Brown & Sawyer, 1998) are additional resources that will provide useful background information in this area.

Conclusion

Medication is regularly used to treat the common illnesses of childhood and adolescence. Although many medications are commonly used, their short- and long-term impact on school performance may not be fully appreciated by students, parents, health care providers, or educators. Understanding the uses and effects of frequently used medications is important for contemporary role of school personnel. Educators are capable of assisting students, parents, and colleagues in understanding this important area of children's health and serve students whose school learning may be affected by medication side effects.

EDUCATIONAL STRATEGIES

- Collaborate with other health care providers (e.g., the school nurse or the school-based health center staff) when issues of medication side effects arise.
- Use established intervention procedures to develop individual accommodations via the 504 Team or IEP Team to assist teachers.
- Develop classroom interventions to assist teachers in working around students' side effects. Interventions typically used for analogous symptoms caused by other factors are often useful for dealing with medication side effects as well.
- Interventions for short-term side effects include tolerating them for the short period of treatment or scheduling important tasks around the period of treatment (e.g., postpone formal psychoeducational assessment or high-stakes assessment).
- Apply behavioral interventions (e.g., relaxation training) to reduce the need for medication or to improve subjective reactions to symptoms.
- Provide ongoing consultation with parents and contact with the child's health care providers to obtain additional information and/or discuss alternative medical interventions.

DISCUSSION QUESTIONS

1. Advertisements for medications must list all side effects, even the most uncommon. How might this affect parents' perception of the frequency and severity of side effects?

2. Serious side effects are relatively uncommon yet are the focus of many Web sites, books, and investigative television reports. Are the

popular media reports improving the awareness and understanding of medication side effects or contributing to excessive and unwarranted fear in parents?

3. How can we help teachers and other educators understand educational side effects of medications?

4. Few studies have been conducted of interventions specifically for side effects of commonly used pediatric medications. What are some possible reasons for this?

5. Are children good reporters of side effects? How might their reports be influenced by lack of knowledge, bias, or other confounding factors?

RESEARCH SUMMARY

- Of school-age children, 31% have chronic health-related problems.
- Respiratory illnesses, recurrent ear infections, and asthma are the most frequently occurring chronic health conditions affecting children.
- School performance is affected by both the side effects of the medication and absences due to the illness.
- Asthma accounts for the most number of days absent from school for students in the United States.
- Children with chronic moderate to severe asthma are at considerable risk for school difficulties; they can have poor attending skills, which are often mistaken as symptoms of attention disorders.
- Cough and cold medications have sedative effects affecting alertness, concentration, and psychomotor speed.
- Children prescribed anticonvulsant medication for migraine are at risk for cognitive impairment and learning difficulties.

RESOURCES

The National Institutes of Health (NIH) and U.S. National Library of Medicine publish the MedlinePlus Web site:

"Over-the-Counter Medicines": www.nlm.nih.gov/medlineplus/overthecountermedicines.html

www.otcsafety.org

The "leading makers of OTC medicines" have formed the CHPA Educational Foundation to "help families safely and effectively use OTC medicines":

www.otcsafety.org

In addition, the FDA publishes information about drug availability and safety at its Web site:

www.fda.gov/Drugs/DrugSafety/default.htm

HANDOUT

A GUIDE TO MEDICATION SIDE EFFECTS

All medications have the potential for side effects—effects that occur beyond or in addition to the desired effect of the drug. Although most children experience few or moderate side effects, parents should be alert for these symptoms. Most medication side effects are temporary and go away once the medication is discontinued or switched to a different medicine.

Common Side Effects

_____ Dizziness

_____ Fatigue/lack of energy

_____ Nausea

_____ Sleep disturbance

_____ Tremors

_____ Difficulty with concentration

_____ Drowsiness/decreased alertness

_____ Inattention

_____ Memory impairment

_____ Reduced psychomotor speed

_____ Anxiety

_____ Aggressive behavior

_____ Depression

_____ Hyperactivity

_____ Irritability

_____ Moody

_____ Oppositional behavior

Tips for Parents

- Your physician and pharmacist are the best sources of information about medication.
- Ask your physician and pharmacist about common side effects of medications your child is prescribed so that you know what you might expect.
- All prescribed medication has a package insert that contains a complete list of side effects under a section called "Adverse Reactions."
- Inform your medical professional about all other medications your child is taking, including over-the-counter medications, herbal remedies, and vitamins.
- Keep a detailed record of when your child starts, stops, or changes dosages.
- Report any new or unexplained symptoms to your physician.
- Alert your child's teachers when your child is taking or changing medication.

Figure 10.2   Medication Side Effects Screening Form

MEDICATION SIDE EFFECTS SCREENING FORM

Name: _____ DOB: _____ Age: _____

Health Status:

Does the child have any symptoms of the following acute or chronic illnesses?

Cough _____ Cold _____ Headache _____ Stomachache _____ Earache _____

Asthma _____ Other respiratory problem _____ Fever _____ Other _____

List any prescription or over-the-counter medications the student is taking.

Possible Medication Side Effects (check all that apply):

_____ Dizziness	_____ Reduced psychomotor speed
_____ Fatigue/lack of energy	_____ Anxiety
_____ Nausea	_____ Aggressive behavior
_____ Sleep disturbance	_____ Depression
_____ Tremors	_____ Hyperactivity
_____ Difficulty with concentration	_____ Irritability
_____ Drowsiness/decreased alertness	_____ Moody
_____ Inattention	_____ Oppositional behavior
_____ Memory impairment	_____ Other (specify)

Medication Side Effects Ratings:

Specify the side effects from the list above that cause the most difficulty.

Specify student-reported side effects from the list above.

Actions and Interventions:

Actions/interventions that may be warranted based on potential medication side effects.

_____ Postponement of formal psychoeducational assessment

_____ Recommendation for accommodation to 504 Team or IEP Team

_____ Classroom interventions to assist teacher in working around side effects

_____ Consultation, education, or further information gathering with parent

_____ Consultation with health care provider for additional information and/or alternative medical interventions

_____ Behavioral interventions to reduce need for medication (e.g., relaxation training)

_____ Other intervention (specify):

Dietary Control and Supplement Use

11

Dietary Modification in the Treatment of Autism Spectrum Disorders*

Caryn R. DePinna and Paul C. McCabe

Andre is a 3-year-old boy diagnosed with autism. He is nonverbal, displays impaired social relatedness and stereotypical movements (flapping and rocking), and has difficulty adjusting when presented with a change in his routine. Andre's mother, Mrs. Smith, has sought out early intervention services since his diagnosis and is now starting to look into alternative interventions to supplement her son's treatment.

While researching interventions for autism on the Internet, Mrs. Smith discovered information about dietary modification, specifically a diet that eliminates gluten (wheat) and casein (dairy). The Internet sources and parent advocacy groups report that this diet can help to reduce a child's atypical behaviors associated with autism. Mrs. Smith becomes very excited after finding this information and goes to Andre's pediatrician for more information. The pediatrician explains how dietary modification is implemented and the theory behind it. He also explains that the research available on this intervention is still in the beginning stages and is inconclusive. In

*Adapted from DePinna, C., & McCabe, P. C. (2008). Food allergies and autism: The gluten-free/casein-free hypothesis. *Communiqué, 36*(5), 10–11. Copyright by the National Association of School Psychologists, Bethesda, MD. Use is by permission of the publisher. www.nasponline.org

addition, the pediatrician provides Mrs. Smith with a list of resources to get more information and a list of foods that are gluten- and casein-free. He encourages Andre's parents to do more research and make an informed decision about whether or not to implement dietary modification with their son.

Parents may be faced with this same decision, as many parent advocacy groups support dietary modification. Also, it can be an appealing intervention because it gives parents a sense of control over their child's treatment. Parents must decide what is best for their child and family, while taking into consideration all the information available on dietary modification.

INTRODUCTION

Dietary modification in the treatment of autism spectrum disorders (ASD) is an alternative intervention that has recently received increased attention from the media and parent advocacy groups. Dietary modification, or more specifically the gluten-free/casein-free (GFCF) diet, eliminates all wheat and dairy products from the child's diet. This intervention is based on the hypothesis that eliminating gluten and casein from the diet will reduce the behavioral symptoms associated with autism. Researchers theorize that children with autism have abnormal digestive systems and are not able to metabolize foods containing gluten (wheat) and casein (dairy). Researchers hypothesize that when gluten and casein are not metabolized or completely broken down during the digestive process, this leads to a measurable effect on the child's behavior. Some researchers believe that eliminating foods with gluten and casein from the diet of children with ASD will decrease problem behaviors. Currently, research on this intervention is inconclusive and lacks empirically valid findings.

BACKGROUND

Researchers have investigated the effects of dietary modification since the 1920s. The GFCF diet hypothesis originated from research indicating that children on the autism spectrum have an abnormal digestive system (Cade et al., 1999; Reichelt, Saelid, Lindback, & Boler, 1986). This research is based on the opioid-excess hypothesis, in which it is argued that foods with gluten (wheat) and casein (dairy) are not metabolized or broken down completely in some individuals. Evidence supporting this finding in individuals with ASD is based on the increased levels of peptides present in their urine (Shattock & Whiteley, 2002). When gluten and casein are not completely broken down during the digestive process, peptides, which are short chains of amino acids, remain in the digestive tract and are absorbed into the bloodstream. These peptides are hypothesized to become biologically active and be treated as neuropeptides by the brain. As neuropeptides, they stimulate an opiate-like effect and potentially cause and/or contribute to behaviors associated with ASD (Shattock & Whiteley; Wakefield et al., 2002). Some researchers believe that eliminating gluten and casein from the diet of children with ASD will decrease problem behaviors by preventing and/or reducing the entrance of the opiate peptides into their bloodstreams (Sun & Cade, 1999; Sun, Cade, Fregly, & Privette, 1999).

The GFCF Diet

Several studies have investigated the effects of GFCF diet on the behavior of children with ASD. Survey research has reported positive results from gluten- and casein-free dietary interventions (Klaveness & Bigam, 2002; Rimland, 2000; Shattock, 1995). In addition, a number of case studies have reported findings that gluten- and casein-elimination diets have reduced the symptoms associated with ASD (e.g., Cade et al., 1999; Knivsberg, Reichelt, Nodland, & Hoien, 1995; Knivsberg, Wiig, Lind, Nodland, & Reichelt, 1990; Reichelt, Ekrem, & Scott, 1990; Whiteley, Rodgers, Savery, & Shattock, 1999). However, methodological weaknesses in the studies limit the generalizability and robustness of the findings (DePinna & McCabe, 2008).

For instance, Knivsberg and colleagues (1990) evaluated the effectiveness of the GFCF diet on 15 children with autism. After 1 year on the diet, the children were observed to have a decrease in autistic behaviors and normalized urinary peptide levels. However, serious limitations of the study were no control group and a relatively small sample size, thus limiting generalizability. In addition, the participants received two types of diets, depending on their age of onset of autism. It is unknown if the variation in diet had any effect on the urinary peptide behaviors and/or autistic behaviors.

Whiteley and colleagues (1999) conducted a study aimed at investigating the short-term effects of a gluten-free diet on children with ASD. Twenty-two children diagnosed with ASD and other communication disorders (including Asperger syndrome, autism, semantic pragmatic disorder, and dyspraxia) made up the treatment group. Six children diagnosed with autism made up a control group and were not involved in any dietary intervention. In addition, 5 children diagnosed with autism were studied separately as a challenge group who had gluten reintroduced into their diets after previously following a gluten-free diet for 6 months. The treatment group followed the diet for 5 months. Pre- and postdiet data were collected, including parent and teacher interviews, observations, psychometric assessments, and urinary profiling. After 5 months, the children on the gluten-free diet showed an improvement in their behavior. However, there was no significant decrease in urinary peptides levels when compared to the control group or to the group that reintroduced gluten into their diets. Thus, dietary intervention may not change the peptide levels in the body.

Knivsberg, Reichelt, Hoien, and Nodland (2002) conducted a controlled study that evaluated the effects of a GFCF diet on autism. The participants in this study were 20 children diagnosed with ASD who also had urinary peptide abnormalities (10 were randomly placed in the control group and 10 in the experimental group). After 1 year on the diet, the experimental group showed a reduction in autistic behavior, an improvement in their socialization, and increased nonverbal cognitive abilities compared to controls. This study suggests that dietary intervention may help treat the symptoms of autism spectrum disorders.

A study conducted by Elder and colleagues (2006) investigated the effects of a GFCF diet on urinary peptide levels and the severity of autistic symptoms. It also evaluated the role of parent behavior in influencing the therapeutic and placebo effects of the diet. After 12 weeks, there were no significant differences in autistic symptoms or urinary peptides between the experimental and control groups. In addition, there were no significant differences in observed parent behaviors between the experimental and control group, as measured by in-home observations that recorded the way parents interacted with their children and how they reacted to their child's behavior. The findings indicated that parents consistently acted the same way toward their children, regardless of research group membership.

In studies that use parent behavioral ratings to assess behavior, parental behavioral influence is frequently an experimental confound. This occurs when parents rate their child's behavior based on their belief that the intervention is successful. Although there was no significant difference in parent behavior between groups, several parents reported that they observed improvements in their child in areas including language, hyperactivity, and frequency of tantrums, despite the lack of confirmatory data to support these claims. Interestingly, more than half of the parents decided to keep their children on the GFCF diet after the conclusion of the study, despite the lack of data supporting the diet. This suggests that parents believe that the diet may have a positive effect despite contradictory evidence. Parental opinion regarding intervention efficacy can be extremely influential when the data collection relies heavily on parent behavior ratings (Elder et al., 2006).

Seung, Rogalski, Shankar, and Elder (2007) retrospectively examined the data collected by Elder and others (2006) and specifically focused on analyzing the verbal communication of children with autism. Of the 15 children who participated in the study by Elder et al., results from 13 children were analyzed in this study. The study employed double-blind crossover methodology. The participants were randomly assigned to one of two groups, one that followed the GFCF diet for 6 weeks and then a regular diet for 6 weeks and another that followed a regular diet for the first 6 weeks and then the GFCF diet for 6 weeks. The children were provided with premade meals throughout the study, and both parents and researchers were blind to which diet the children were following. Results of this investigation showed that there were no significant improvements in the children's verbal communication after the gluten-free casein-free diet. It is imperative that studies are rigorously designed with the necessary blinded controls to yield results that are replicable and empirically valid (McCabe & DePinna, 2008).

Research Limitations

The body of research examining the effects of GFCF diets on the behaviors associated with ASD is still in its infancy and is based largely on survey and case study research. The use of these research methods rather than double-blind, experimentally controlled studies contributes to methodological and validity limitations. Additionally, these studies do not take into account the effects of other treatments that the child may be receiving while participating in the study or survey (e.g., applied behavior analysis, speech therapy, vitamin therapy, occupational therapy, intensive special education, etc.). It is also important to consider the variation in symptom constellation and severity that is characteristic of autism spectrum disorders. Furthermore, the current body of research does not report insight into how dietary intervention affects varying degrees of behavior or how children on contrasting ends of the autism spectrum differentially respond to the diet. Many of these limitations have led researchers to investigate further the effects of a GFCF diet on ASD employing more scientifically rigorous research designs.

Some of the questions left unanswered by the extant literature require further investigation before the GFCF hypothesis can be supported as an efficacious treatment. For instance, do all children on the autism spectrum display urinary peptide abnormalities? Past research has indicated that many children on the spectrum have been found to have this digestive abnormality; however, it is unknown whether it is a diagnostic symptom of ASD or a correlate. Another unanswered question concerns whether severity of behaviors is a factor in the effectiveness of dietary interventions. More specifically, can a GFCF diet be more effective if the symptoms are less severe? It is possible that children on different ends of the spectrum are differentially responsive to the diet. Another issue that requires further examination is the contamination of results caused by other interventions. Many past studies included children who were participating in targeted educational and behavioral programs for children with ASD. Some studies did not indicate and control for the other types of treatment the participants were receiving. Without knowledge of these interventions and the ability to control or match for them, it is impossible to conclude that symptom improvements were due to GFCF dietary intervention rather than other intervention strategies. Future research needs to explore how dietary interventions compare with other empirically supported interventions for autism spectrum disorders, as well as their efficacy when used in combination.

Conclusion

The research available on dietary intervention and amelioration of autism symptoms is inconclusive. In addition to the gluten- and casein-free diet, other dietary interventions that have been investigated include the additive-free diet, the sugar elimination diet, fatty acid supplementation, the allergen-free diet, and megavitamin therapy. There is currently no recommended dietary intervention for the treatment of autism due to the equivocal research results. The American Academy of Pediatrics (Gidding et al., 2006) recommends that parents help their children follow general dietary recommendations, including a diet rich in fruits and vegetables, whole grains, low-fat and nonfat dairy products, beans, and fish and lean meat.

IMPLICATIONS FOR EDUCATORS

With 1 in 150 children being diagnosed with an autism spectrum disorder, it is important that educators stay up-to-date on the research and potential interventions for ASD. It is very likely that educators will come into contact with a child following the GFCF diet, given the media attention and the rise in the number of children diagnosed with autism spectrum disorders. Educators can better support the child if they understand the rationale for diet and how to assess the child's behavior before and after this intervention. It is also important for educators to be informed about this research because parents often rely on their child's school as a resource. Educators can provide information to parents and refer them to the appropriate professionals.

If the GFCF diet is implemented as a formal academic intervention, then it will need to be documented on the Individualized Education Plan (IEP), along with any other interventions that the child is receiving. Parents are usually responsible for providing the child's diet, including lunch and snacks, but educators will need to monitor whatever food products are available in the classroom and lunchroom. Educators will also need to discourage children from sharing foods, especially among older children who often like to "swap" their food. In addition, many classroom materials may contain wheat products and will need to be replaced with wheat-free alternatives. This includes Play-Doh, paints, markers, glue, paste, tape, stickers, and stamps. All service providers in the school (e.g., speech therapist, occupational therapist) will need to follow these dietary procedures. If the child's teacher or therapists anticipate a project or assignment that will involve gluten-based materials (e.g., making a pasta necklace), they need to give parents sufficient advanced notice so they can send in gluten-free substitutes. Educators, therapists, and parents should stay in close communication and work together to discuss the best interventions for the child, as well as devise strategies to document progress from those interventions.

EDUCATIONAL STRATEGIES

- Provide an appropriate educational environment that meets the needs of the child.
- Provide parents with resources and research pertaining to autism spectrum disorders and empirically valid interventions.
- Stay abreast on research and new findings related to ASD and the GFCF diet.
- Support families whether or not they choose to use dietary modification with their child.
- Ensure that children on elimination diets are not excluded from classroom activities that involve food by keeping extra gluten- and casein-free foods available.
- Make sure parents have ample time to supply the classroom and their child with GFCF snacks and classroom materials (glue, markers, molding dough, etc.).
- Encourage parents to consult with their pediatrician before starting a dietary intervention with their child.

DISCUSSION QUESTIONS

1. Much of the research on dietary modification and autism is inconclusive. Why is it important for educators to be critical of research findings and methodology that is used in research design? How can educators communicate problematic research design effectively to parents?

2. Children with dietary modifications can easily become isolated during lunchtime or during classroom activities that involve food. These times are often opportunities for children to interact socially with their peers. How can teachers aid students so they are not left out or isolated during these activities?

3. What are some reasons why dietary modification and other alternative treatments for autism spectrum disorders receive a lot of attention from the media and parent advocacy groups despite insufficient research support?

4. If a parent decides to put a child on a GFCF diet, what are the possible pros and cons of following this diet?

RESEARCH SUMMARY

- One out of every 150 children is diagnosed with an autism spectrum disorder each year.
- The gluten-free/casein-free (GFCF) diet eliminates all wheat and dairy products from the child's diet.
- Researchers theorize that children with autism have abnormal digestive systems and are not able to metabolize foods with gluten (wheat) and casein (dairy products) and that eliminating gluten and casein from the diet will reduce the behavioral symptoms associated with autism.
- This hypothesis is based on increased levels of peptides present in the urine of individuals with ASD. When gluten and casein are not completely broken down during the digestive process, peptides, which are short chains of amino acids, remain in the digestive tract and are absorbed into the bloodstream. These peptides are hypothesized to become biologically active and be treated as neuropeptides.
- As neuropeptides, they stimulate an opiate-like effect on the brain and are hypothesized to cause and/or contribute to behaviors associated with ASD.
- The body of research examining the effects of GFCF diets on the behaviors associated with ASD is still in its infancy, is based largely on survey and case study research, and is inconclusive. Additional research is needed using more rigorous methodologies that control for rating biases and alternative treatments that the children are receiving.

RESOURCES

Autism Network for Dietary Intervention (ANDI): www.autismndi .com. This organization's Web site offers many resources for parents about implementing a gluten-free casein-free diet.

The Centers for Disease Control and Prevention (CDC): www.cdc .gov/ncbddd/autism/index.htm. The CDC provides information to parents about autism spectrum disorders and links to related resources.

Autism Speaks: www.autismspeaks.org. This advocacy group provides support to parents and conducts research about autism.

The GFCF Diet Support Group: http://gfcfdiet.com/NewpageDirectory6 .htm. This gluten-free casein-free diet Web site has a directory of gluten- and casein-free foods and brand-name products.

The following is a comprehensive handbook for parents and professionals that provides information about diagnosis, assessment, and treatment of and intervention for autism spectrum disorders:

Volkmar, F. R., Paul, R., Klin, A., & Cohen, D. J. (Eds.). (2005). *Handbook of autism and pervasive developmental disorders* (3rd ed.; Vols. 1–2). Hoboken, NJ: John Wiley and Sons.

HANDOUT

DIETARY MODIFICATION: THE GLUTEN-FREE CASEIN-FREE DIET

- This diet eliminates all wheat (gluten) and dairy products (casein) from the child's diet.
- It is based on a hypothesis that removing gluten and casein proteins from the child's diet will reduce the behavioral symptoms associated with certain disorders, especially autism.
- Research on the effectiveness of dietary modification is still in the beginning stages. Several case studies and parental surveys have found that a gluten- and casein-free diet can be effective in reducing the behaviors associated with autism. These studies have many limitations, and the findings cannot be generalized due to the methodological problems.
- Further empirically valid research is needed to determine if dietary modification has a reliable effect on a child's behavior.

Other things to consider:

- Always consult with your child's pediatrician before implementing any type of dietary intervention.
- It is also a good idea to speak with a nutritionist to ensure that your child is getting a balanced diet that provides the necessary nutrition.
- When implementing dietary modification, speak with your child's teacher. Send in food to keep in the classroom for birthday parties and class celebrations so your child can participate.
- Keep in mind that many classroom materials contain wheat products; these include Play-Doh, glue, paste, markers, stickers, tape, and so on. Parents who place their child on a gluten-free casein-free diet are responsible for providing substitute materials for their child to use in the classroom. It is important to have frequent communication with the teacher to prepare for upcoming activities and obtain the necessary materials.
- If needed, provide your child's teacher with information about the gluten-free casein-free diet so he or she is informed and can explain it to the other children in the class.

12

The Prevention of and Interventions for Eating Disorders*

Catherine Cook-Cottone

Megan is 15 years old and in the 10th grade. Megan has been struggling with an eating disorder for some time. She is returning to school this fall after inpatient treatment over the summer. Her teachers describe her as an ideal student. She always wears a smile, is a high achiever, dresses impeccably, and is caring and sensitive of the needs of others. She comes from an achievement-oriented family committed to education and sports. Megan is the older of two children. Her younger brother was born with cerebral palsy and is considered a high-need child both medically and emotionally. In addition, Megan's mother struggled with her weight when she was younger and complained often and intensely for the year after delivery of each child about her weight. She is always on a diet.

Megan's early development was somewhat unremarkable in regard to medical concerns. She suffered the occasional cold. Developmental milestones were accomplished as expected; some even described her as precocious. She was frequently described as a passionate little girl; as her mother stated, "When she feels things, she feels them very deeply." Interestingly, at school, her behavior has been ideal, marked with emotional control and compliance. Megan received straight As and perfect attendance awards from kindergarten through Grade 5 (10 years old).

(Continued)

*Adapted from Cook-Cottone, C., & Scime, M. (2006). The prevention and treatment of eating disorders: An overview for school psychologists. *Communiqué, 34*(5), 38–40. Copyright by the National Association of School Psychologists, Bethesda, MD. Use is by permission of the publisher. www.nasponline.org

(Continued)

Notably, she is known to work slowly and methodically. When pressed to do academic work quickly, Megan often becomes stressed and makes more errors. Megan is also a good soccer player. She was selected for the travel team every year (up until the year she got sick). Megan's two favorite things about soccer were winning and running. Her coaches were driven and could be critical.

Megan's best friend, Molly, was of a very slight stature and did not enter puberty for several years after Megan. At a December sleepover in their eighth-grade year at Molly's house, the two young girls had a long conversation about their bodies with Molly's older sister. Megan was now 5'3" and 145 pounds. Molly's sister let them look through her magazines, photo albums, and yearbooks. Molly's sister told Megan that if she wanted to really look good, she would need to lose a few pounds. She gave Megan a self-help diet book that she said had worked for her. The book recommended a 1,200-calorie-a-day diet emphasizing protein and fiber intake. Megan was thrilled and started her diet that night.

Within a month, Megan had dropped 15 pounds. On a 5'2" frame, this was quite noticeable. She now weighed 130 pounds. Megan liked the feeling of being thinner and was getting lots of compliments. Her soccer coach commented that the weight loss would help her performance and encouraged her in her efforts. Her coach was also impressed by Megan's recent increase in commitment to soccer and the mileage she was putting in for her training. Megan was running five miles a day during the week (on top of soccer practice) and seven to nine miles on the weekends. Megan liked the feeling of being in control. In 2 more months, she dropped another 10 pounds (now 120 pounds). She was getting compliments from everyone: coaches, teachers, friends, and boys.

The weight loss continued. By March, she was at 105 pounds. In early March, Megan was out with her mother shopping for vacation swim suits. When her mother saw her in her suit, she was shocked at Megan's weight loss and told her she looked too thin. By June, Megan was down to 90 pounds, and she clearly did not look okay. Teachers in her eighth-grade team referred her to the student study team. The school psychologist called home to voice the concerns of Megan's teachers and peers. He encouraged Megan's parents to take her to a physician. Her mother finally took her to a pediatrician, who recommended an eating disorder specialist. The family told the school nothing.

Despite treatment, Megan continued to drop weight. The medical doctor had encouraged the parents to pursue outpatient counseling with someone who worked with eating disorders, as well as a nutritionist, and they complied. By the summer of ninth grade, Megan was too thin to play soccer, and her doctor prohibited all exercise until she gained weight. She weighed 78 pounds. She was enrolled at the treatment center to stabilize her weight.

After 12 weeks as an inpatient, Megan put on 12 pounds and was released. She was placed on a strict meal plan, and her parents monitored her meals. Megan has been starting to grow weary of her restricted life and is beginning to talk in therapy. She is beginning to eat more on her own and acknowledges that when eating, she feels better emotionally and physically. She is getting ready to go back to school and resume her life activities.

INTRODUCTION

Eating disorders and eating-disordered behavior are among the top psychological and health concerns for children and adolescents. Often thought to be culturally driven, eating-disordered behavior is characterized by an intense preoccupation with body size and shape, pathological fear of gaining weight, compulsive pursuit of thinness, and severe disturbance in eating behavior (*Diagnostic and Statistical Manual of Mental Disorders*, 4th ed., text revision, American Psychiatric Association [APA], 2000). Behavioral symptoms include self-starvation, food restriction, purging of food, and/or a cyclic binging and purging of food. These symptoms evolve over time from a set of behaviors designed to control body shape and size into clinical disorder affecting all aspects of a child's or adolescent's life (Cook-Cottone & Phelps, 2006). Symptoms affect psychological and social development, school performance, and physiological health (Hoek & van Hoeken, 2003). Despite over 25 years of research, these disorders are still difficult to prevent and treat.

BACKGROUND

The *DSM-IV-TR* currently lists both anorexia nervosa and bulimia nervosa as the major diagnostic areas of eating disorder (ED). Notably, it also lists "eating disorders not otherwise specified" to include disorders of eating that do not meet the criteria for any specific ED. Further, binge-eating disorder is included among the criteria sets and axes provided for further study in the *DSM-IV-TR*. This proposed disorder is associated with recurrent episodes of binge eating, subjective and behavioral indicators of impaired control and associated distress, and the absence of purging or compensatory behaviors. Eating disorders are known to present along with depressive disorders, obsessive-compulsive disorder, personality disorder, anxiety disorders, and/or substance abuse (*DSM-IV-TR*).

Mental health practitioners and researchers are looking to the educational system for help in improving the effectiveness of prevention and intervention initiatives. Federal wellness mandates have also recognized schools as playing a substantial role in the promotion and maintenance of the health of children. Key practices include timely and efficient risk identification, implementation of effective prevention programs, and support of out-of-school treatment efforts (Cook-Cottone & Phelps, 2006).

Body dissatisfaction and dieting, the two strongest predictors of eating-disordered behaviors, have become nearly normative (e.g., Cook-Cottone & Phelps, 2006). The prevalence rate for anorexia nervosa (AN) is 0.3% for young women and approximately 0.03% for males. The prevalence rate for bulimia nervosa (BN) is estimated at 1% in young women and 0.1% in young men (Hoek & van Hoeken, 2003). From 1953 to 1999, the mortality rate for those diagnosed with AN averaged around 5% (Steinhausen, 2002). In a study of the survivors of AN, less than 50% recovered, 30% improved but were not considered recovered, and 20% remained chronically ill (Steinhausen). Outcomes have been relatively promising for those diagnosed with BN, with evidence of up to 75% of those diagnosed not meeting criteria at 5 years (Ben-Tovim, 2003). However, recent innovations in prevention intervention are promising. School-based prevention and treatment-support efforts have produced positive results (e.g., Cook-Cottone, Kane, Scime, & Beck, 2004).

Etiology Research Brief

Though etiology is not well understood, researchers are working toward an integrated, comprehensive model that accounts for the variables associated with eating disorders (Myers, Wonderlich, Norton, & Crosby, 2004). Researchers have found the persistence of symptoms, despite prevention and treatment, distinctively challenging. Notably, ED symptoms are manifest with frequent relapse, are associated with psychiatric comorbidity, and often result in significant medical complications (Herzog & Eddy, 2007).

Neurological Findings. More recent evidence implicates neurological features in etiology (Cook-Cottone, 2009). Specific findings have indicated both statelike and traitlike characteristics associated with the risk and development of EDs (Duchesne et al., 2004). That is, some evidence points to predisorder neurological tendencies that may place children and adolescents at risk. Neurological issues also arise once the individual is symptomatic. Researchers are working to disentangle these findings. Tchanturia, Campbell, Morris, and Treasure (2005) reported that there have been comparatively fewer neuropsychological studies of eating disorders than of any of the other major psychiatric disorders.

Dysfunctional inputs to key neural control networks may emanate from the cortex and hippocampus (Pearson, Goldklang, & Striegel-Moore, 2002). To date, associated neurological features of BN include impulsivity and attention deficits (e.g., Tchanturia et al., 2005). Individuals who struggle with BN often manifest symptoms associated with a particular set of disorders and behavioral syndromes (Steiger & Bruce, 2007). According to Steiger and Bruce, these include panic disorder, dramatic-erratic personality disorders, alcohol and substance abuse and dependence, novelty seeking, impulsivity, and affect instability.

Other Contributing Factors. Other risk factors related to onset include many well-researched areas in the biological, psychological, social, and cultural realms. At the individual level, these factors include self-regulation, dieting and set-point-related physiological disruptions, pubertal onset, and the disordered development of self-concept (Jacobi, Paul, deZwaan, Nutzinger, & Dahme, 2004). Gender is also a strong risk factor because only a small proportion of clinical cases are male. However, both genders show increases in incidence in specific weight-sensitive athletic or social contexts (e.g., boxing, dancing, gymnastics; Patel, Greydanus, Pratt, & Phillips, 2003). At the interpersonal level, eating disorders are associated with a variety of familial factors, such as low levels of parental attunement, low communication, and physical and sexual abuse (Wonderlich et al., 2000). In some cases, specific family characteristics may protect against eating-disordered behavior and encourage the development of emotional regulation and problem solving (Wisniewski & Kelly, 2003).

Media influence is considered an important factor. In a now-famous study, Becker, Burwell, Gilman, Herzog, and Hamburg (2002) measured the eating-disordered behavior of two cohorts of Fijian adolescents: one cohort had been exposed to television for only a few weeks, while the other cohort had been exposed for 3 years. Of those who had been exposed for 3 years, 11% reported engaging in self-induced vomiting, 74% reported feeling fat, 69% stated they had dieted to lose weight, and 29% were assessed to be at risk for clinical-level eating disorder. This is in contrast to the group only recently exposed who reported no eating-disordered behavior and general satisfaction with their bodies.

Prevention and Intervention Support

School personnel, coaches, dance instructors, and family members can play a key role in facilitating ecological continuity of care for children and adolescents with health-based issues.

Eating Disorder Prevention Practices and the Three-Tier Service Delivery Model. Using mental health prevention terminology, primary universal prevention efforts are thought to focus on the promotion and maintenance of healthy development and the prevention of eating-disordered attitudes and behaviors (i.e., before symptoms begin). This is consistent with the Tier 1 service are delivery approach, in which universal, schoolwide prevention services available for all students (National Joint Committee on Learning Disabilities, 2005). Targeted, or selected, prevention efforts are intended to prevent the onset of eating-disordered attitudes and target behaviors in the early stages, before full clinical disorders manifest (Cook-Cottone & Phelps, 2006). Such efforts are more consistent with the Tier 2 levels of service delivery. That is, Tier 2 prevention efforts are specifically designed for, and delivered to, at-risk students identified by risk indicators such as psychological and/or behavioral vulnerability or inclusion in a high-risk subgroup of the population (e.g., late middle school to high school–aged females or high-risk sports participants). For some, universal and targeted interventions may not prove effective, and referral and/or more comprehensive assessment is indicated and intervention provided as needed; that is Tier 3 service delivery.

Universal Prevention. Traditional universal prevention programs may be most effective in the lower elementary years, before the crystallization of the preoccupation with body shape and weight within the construct of self (Piran, 2001). For many years, prevention efforts have been aimed at later middle school and high school students, because it was believed that eating-disordered behaviors and beliefs were rare among prepubertal children (Thelen, Powell, Lawrence, & Kulnert, 1992). However, eating-disordered behavior and the risk factors associated with its development may emerge as early as fourth grade (Thelen et al.). In older students, there is an increasing likelihood of (a) internalization of the thin-ideal, (b) dieting, and (c) experimentation with eating-disordered behaviors.

Targeted Prevention. For an effective prevention program, combining universal (Tier 1) and targeted prevention (Tier 2) efforts is recommended

(Piran, 2001). To illustrate, a yoga and wellness group run as part of the school's wellness program is open to all interested students (Tier 1, universal prevention). However, teachers, staff, parents, and administrators are also encouraged to refer students about whom they are concerned (Tier 2, targeted prevention). In such a case, group curriculum would be consistent with whole-school prevention goals and provide a more intensive review of content and skills. Curriculum includes skills to address risk factors. These empirically supported topics would include fortification of self-care (yoga/relaxation), enhancement of life skills (assertiveness and problem solving), development of emotional regulation skills, and improvement of community/culture-based skills (media literacy and critical thinking). For example, schoolwide goals would support the integration of social-emotional, classroom-based lessons that included emotional regulation curriculum covering topics such as making healthy behavioral choices while struggling with difficult emotions. Although emotional regulation is a common adolescent challenge (Tier 1, helping all), it is also a specific skill deficit believed to be connected to those at risk for symptomatic expression (Tier 2). Accordingly, the more intensive prevention group would provide further training and practice with these skills.

Identify At-Risk Individuals. The earlier an eating disorder is detected and treated, the better the prognosis. A strong behavioral indicator of risk is dieting (Thomas, Ricciardelli, & Williams, 2000). Dieting behaviors are not limited to adolescents and adults; they have occurred in children as young as 8 years old (Thomas et al.). Some of the other risk signs include excessive exercising; losing weight; eating only certain foods; obsessing over food, body, weight, or dieting; adopting odd eating rituals; lying or making excuses about eating; hiding weight loss with loose clothing; refusing to eat in front of others; frequenting the bathroom after meals; and exhibiting moodiness and withdrawal.

Make Referrals/Be Aware of Resources. To facilitate a timely referral process, every school should have a resource person to handle eating disorder concerns (Smolak, Harris, Levine, & Shisslak, 2001). Responsibilities include being knowledgeable about how to approach individuals at risk for an eating disorder, communicating with parents, and making referrals to an appropriate professional source (Smolak et al.). It is essential that the resource person be prepared with information about community resources.

Intervention Overview

If symptomatology reaches clinical levels, then comprehensive and multifaceted care is required (American Academy of Pediatrics [AAP], 2003). Treatment may be conducted either on an inpatient or outpatient basis, depending on the level of symptoms and the patient's health status. Current best practice in treatment recommends a multidisciplinary team to attend to health status and medication issues, nutrition and meal planning, and psychosocial treatment (APA Work Group on Eating Disorders, 2000).

EDs have many potential medical complications. Medical complications consistent with caloric restriction/starvation in AN include moderate to severe cardiovascular complications, gastrointestinal problems (e.g., constipation, bloating, liver malfunction), renal difficulties, anemia, endocrine problems, and neurological irregularities (AAP, 2003). In regard to BN, medical complications include electrolyte imbalance and depletion of key nutrients, irreversible myocardial damage with use of ipecac (used to induce vomiting), esophageal damage, dental erosion, gastric rupture, metabolic acidosis, chronic dehydration, menstrual irregularities, and amenorrhea (AAP).

IMPLICATIONS FOR EDUCATORS

Adequate support in the school setting can be a critical part of the treatment and recovery process (Manley, Rickson, & Standeven, 2000). This can be most effectively done within the context of a prevention-oriented school atmosphere already promoting zero tolerance of in-school advertising, body teasing, harassment, and gender-biased discourse and encouraging healthy nutritional behaviors and opportunities for positive physical and expressive experiences (e.g., soccer, yoga, track, swimming, art, and music; Cook-Cottone et al., 2004). Whether the student is reintegrating to school, in ongoing treatment, or in recovery, the school contact or resource person should provide support (Cook-Cottone et al.). The needed support includes ongoing school contact with the treatment team; student advocacy; in-school counseling; and ongoing consultation with, and support from, school faculty, administration, and staff (Cook-Cottone et al.).

School Reintegration

If a student requires hospitalization or day treatment, then his or her re-entry to school is an important transition. Providing support for this transition is vital to recovery (Manley et al., 2000). School personnel should work with the treatment team to plan for reintegration and address the student's medical, psychological, and academic needs. Student needs may include supportive counseling, medical monitoring, release from physical education classes, meal monitoring, and communication with the treatment team and family. By working together, the family, treatment team members, and teachers can create a schedule that minimizes academic impact and stress.

Educators, coaches, dance instructors, and school administrators should encourage healthy athletic practices and school climate. School administrators can encourage the appropriate school personnel to evaluate school lunches to ensure inclusion of healthy options and schedule inservices to develop a schoolwide plan for dealing with concerns related to eating disorders. School mental health professionals can work with teachers to (a) include prevention information in the curriculum (e.g., media literacy, nutrition); (b) discipline students who discriminate or harass others based on size; (c) model healthy attitudes (e.g., eating and exercising with a goal of health rather than a goal of weight loss); (d) refer at-risk students for prevention programs, screening, and referral; (e) allow alternative assignments for class activities that may be triggers for those with eating disorders, such as weighing in, coeducation swimming classes, or a calorie-counting nutrition class; and (f) focus on an individualized approach to curricular goals that provides the flexibility needed by those struggling with eating disorders.

EDUCATIONAL STRATEGIES

- Eating disorders are prevalent, chronic, and sometimes treatment resistant.
- The cooperation of school personnel, families, and treatment team specialists plays a vital role in the prevention and treatment of eating disorders through school-based prevention and treatment support.
- The school's role includes active and developmentally appropriate prevention efforts, that is, the identification and specialized prevention for students at risk and assessment and/or referral of those with emerging to clinical disorders.
- The treatment team serves to support patients with clinical-level symptoms through provision of medical services, nutritional counseling, and psychological treatment.
- The role of the treatment team includes collaboration and consultation with school personnel to create and maintain a healthy and responsible environment that can support treatment and maintain recovery efforts.

DISCUSSION QUESTIONS

1. What are the major risk factors for eating disorders that educators may observe among students in the school?

2. How are anorexia and bulimia nervosa different, and how are they the same?

3. Using the action points in Megan's case, how can school personnel play a role in the prevention of eating disorders and treatment support?

4. What aspects of the school culture and athletics contributed to the onset of the eating disorder described in Megan's situation? How might your school protect your students from these risks?

RESEARCH SUMMARY

- Eating disorders are disruptive to normal development and academic engagement and involve substantial medical risk and comparably high mortality rates.
- Individual risk factors include self-regulation, dieting and set-point-related physiological disruptions, pubertal onset, the disordered development of self-concept, and participation in specific weight-sensitive athletic or social contexts.

- Media influence is considered an important risk factor. Body dissatisfaction and dieting are the two strongest predictors of eating-disordered behaviors.
- From 1953 to 1999, the mortality rate for those diagnosed with AN averaged around 5%, the worst of any clinical disorder.
- For those with AN, less than 50% recover, 33% improve but may not be considered recovered, and 20% remain chronically ill. For those with BN, up to 75% recover in 5 years.
- Associated neurological features and psychological difficulties of BN include impulsivity and attention deficits, panic disorder, dramatic-erratic personality disorders, alcohol and substance abuse and dependence, novelty seeking, impulsivity, and affect instability.
- Prevention and treatment programs that address risk factors and help develop coping strategies and functional life skills have shown positive effects.

RESOURCES

GirlsHealth.gov: This Web site developed by the Department of Health and Human Services provides health information and support for girls (ages 10–16).

Gürze Books LLC: www.gurze.com. This publishing company specializes in books on eating disorders.

Media Education Foundation: www.mediaed.org. This nonprofit organization is devoted to media research and the production of resources to aid educators and others in fostering analytical media literacy.

National Eating Disorders Association (NEDA): www.nationaleatingdisorders.org

Something Fishy: www.something-fishy.org. This Web site provides support and information for those struggling with eating issues, their friends and family, and others interested in the subject.

HANDOUT

PREVENTION OF AND INTERVENTIONS FOR EATING DISORDERS

Definitions

Eating disorders (EDs) are characterized by an intense preoccupation with body size and shape, pathological fear of gaining weight, and pursuit of thinness.

- **Anorexia nervosa (AN):** Individuals with AN pursue and/or maintain excessively low body weight through a reduction in food intake and, possibly, self-induced vomiting, misuse of laxatives or diuretics, and/or excessive exercise. Younger children may fail to make expected weight gains as they increase in age and height, fear gaining weight, and have a distorted body image. In older females, the disorder is marked by the absence of menstruation.
- **Bulimia nervosa (BN):** Individuals with BN also place an excessive emphasis on body shape and weight in their self-evaluations. Those with BN struggle with recurrent episodes of binge eating and use inappropriate compensatory behaviors to prevent associated weight gain (e.g., self-induced vomiting, misuse of laxatives, diuretics, enemas, fasting, or obligatory exercise).

Risk Factors and Warning Signs

Many risk factors are associated with eating disorders. Often a combination of factors leads to problematic behaviors. Females are at the highest risk, especially those who enter puberty early. However, both genders show increases in incidence in specific weight-sensitive athletic or social contexts (e.g., boxing, dancing, gymnastics). Media influence is considered an important factor. Those at risk may have a preoccupation with weight, food, and dieting; poor self-regulation and self-concept; low family attunement; and/or a history of physical and sexual abuse. Warning signs include excessively exercising, losing weight, eating only certain foods, adopting odd eating rituals, lying or making excuses about eating, hiding weight loss with loose clothing, refusing to eat in front of others, frequenting the bathroom after meals, and exhibiting moodiness and withdrawal.

13

Steroids in Adolescents*

The Cost of Achieving the Physical Ideal

Sarita Gober and Paul C. McCabe

During his freshman year, 14-year-old Travis was a good student with an average build and somewhat melancholy disposition. When he returned for his sophomore year, his friends noticed that he had bulked up by adding muscle and subsequently was acting with more confidence. Travis worked hard in the weight room and spent hours looking at his body in the mirror and talking about his physical appearance. Over time, however, Travis's behavior became more erratic and aggressive. He also developed excessive acne and slightly enlarged breasts. He became disrespectful in class and brazen with his peers. Travis's gym teacher cautioned him repeatedly about his behavior and ultimately notified the principal, the school psychologist, and Travis's parents.

Travis's parents, who also noticed increasing defiance and changes in his appearance and habits, agreed to meet with the school support team. After discussing parent and staff reports and classroom observations, the school psychologist suggested that Travis might be taking steroids. When confronted by his parents, Travis acknowledged that he was using steroids and other performance-enhancing substances. What he did not realize was that his actions were putting himself and others potentially at risk. Travis, like many adolescents, wanted to look like the young men pictured in sports magazines and on television. He learned about steroids from the media and had started buying them from an older student.

(Continued)

*Adapted from Gober, S., Klein, M., Berger, T., Vindigni, C., & McCabe, P. C. (2006). Steroids in adolescence: The cost of achieving the physical ideal. *Communiqué, 34*(7), 38–40. Copyright by the National Association of School Psychologists, Bethesda, MD. Use is by permission of the publisher. www.nasponline.org

(Continued)

The school psychologist worked with Travis to build his self-esteem and self-confidence independent of body building. In addition, Travis began consulting with a nutritionist, who helped him maintain a balanced diet and exercise regimen. The school staff was provided training on how to encourage class discussions with students regarding self-image and self-esteem issues, as well as how to recognize signs of steroid use.

INTRODUCTION

Adolescent use of anabolic androgenic steroids continues, despite the potentially harrowing physiological and psychological side effects and despite the health warnings and campaigns designed to prevent steroid use (Johnson, 1990; Johnston, O'Malley, Bachman, & Schulenberg, 2009). Public campaigns designed to prevent steroid use have been ineffective, in part, because they have not addressed the various motivations underlying steroid use. The tripartite typology model presents three distinct motivational profiles of adolescent steroid users as a means to identify current and potential users and direct assistance toward the appropriate intervention and prevention program (Gober, Klein, & McCabe, 2009).

BACKGROUND

Dr. Nora D. Volkow (2005), then-director of the National Institute of Drug Abuse (NIDA), stated in her testimony to Congress:

> Steroids are available legally only by prescription, to treat conditions that occur when the body produces abnormally low amounts of testosterone, such as delayed puberty and some types of impotence. They are also used to treat body wasting in patients with AIDS and other diseases that cause a loss of lean muscle mass. (¶ 3)

The most commonly used steroids include testosterone, nandrolone, methenolone, stanozolol, and methandrostenolone. These drugs are typically smuggled from other countries or manufactured in illegal laboratories (Sharma, 2005). When used in combination with exercise, training, and high-protein diets, steroids can promote increased size and strength of muscles, improve endurance, and decrease recovery time between workouts.

Performance-enhancing drugs have become increasingly popular, as they are a legal alternative to steroids. They provide similar muscle-building effects; however, their effects are mostly unknown and rarely studied. The limited research that does exist indicates adverse physiological effects, including renal problems (Bell, Dorsch, McCreary, & Hovey, 2004). Adolescent lifetime use of creatine has been reported to be as high as 7.7% in males and 2.2% in females, and the pro-hormone androsterone is reportedly used by 1.7% of males with no reported use in females (Bell et al.). Furthermore, the ability to obtain these drugs legally legitimizes their use and implies they are safe, which is not the case (Field et al., 2005).

Steroid Use and Effects

Gender-Specific Health Risks. Among men, steroids cause decreased sperm count, atrophied testicles, and impotence. Although sperm count usually returns to normal after cessation of drug use, testicular atrophy often is irreversible. When testosterone from steroids is converted to estrogen, male users may suffer from gynecomastia, or excessive growth of breast tissue (Millman & Ross, 2003).

In the female body, anabolic steroids cause masculine effects, such as hirsutism (abnormal hair growth), deepening of voice, clitoral hypertrophy (enlarged clitoris), and male pattern baldness, and these may be irreversible (NIDA, 2000, 2009). Acne, increased libido, and menstrual irregularities also may be observed (Millman & Ross, 2003).

Although some physiological effects may be reversible for adults, this may not be the case for the maturing adolescent, as steroids may affect growth and maturation. Naturally rising levels of testosterone and other sex hormones normally trigger the growth spurt that occurs during adolescence. As the growth hormones reach certain levels in the normally developing teenager, they trigger a signal to the bones to stop growing. When a child or adolescent takes steroids, the artificially increased level of sex hormones can signal the bones to stop growing prematurely (NIDA, 2000, 2009).

Physiological Health Risks. Steroids have serious physiological side effects and the extent of the physiological damage depends on which steroid is administered, the amount and frequency of the dose, and the age and general health of the user (Johnson, 1990). Steroid abuse is associated with cardiovascular disease, including heart attack and stroke, even in athletes younger than 30 (NIDA, 2000). Continued use may lead to elevation in certain liver enzymes, which in turn can bring about cholestatic jaundice, a serious and potentially fatal condition (Millman & Ross, 2003). Continued use is also associated with liver tumors and a rare condition called peliosis hepatis, in which blood-filled cysts form in the liver. Both the tumors and the cysts sometimes rupture, causing internal bleeding (NIDA). Problems have also arisen from unsterile needle sharing, a practice that can spread viral infection (Durant, Rickert, Ashworth, Newman, & Slavens, 1993; NIDA). In addition, teenagers who engage in needle sharing are more likely to endorse the taking of multiple drugs and risk-taking behaviors.

Psychological and Behavioral Risks and Effects. Anabolic steroids have also been reported to cause other behavioral changes, including euphoria, increased energy, sexual arousal, mood swings, distractibility, forgetfulness, and confusion. Some studies of steroid usage have reported that a minority of participants develop behavioral symptoms that were so extreme that the symptoms disrupted their ability to function at work or in social settings or they presented as a threat to themselves and others (NIDA, 2000). Other symptoms described among AAS users included increased risk-taking behavior, extreme egocentrism, cognitive rigidity, altered physical identity, increased feelings of superiority, and extreme mood changes (Gonzalez, McLachlan, & Keaney, 2001). High doses of steroids can increase aggression, and they have been implicated in numerous instances of violence and aggression by athletes and body builders (Trenton & Currier, 2005). Although steroids can trigger negative reactions in any age group, it is during the teenage years that aggressive inhibitors are being developed. Steroids, such as testosterone, can interfere with brain development and may alter long-term capacity for aggressive inhibition (Benson, 2002).

Other studies examining the psychiatric effects of anabolic steroids have found that they cause or intensify psychiatric symptoms. In their review of published literature regarding steroid use and its ramifications, Trenton and Currier (2005) found several adverse psychological effects associated with steroid use, including mood changes occurring within days of initiating use of the drug.

Withdrawal. Often, the cessation of steroid use can result in adverse psychological effects. Depression is a common consequence of steroid withdrawal (Trenton & Currier, 2005). Similarly, severe depression can occur during withdrawal and, if not treated properly, may lead to suicide (NIDA, 2000, 2009). Although suicide has been associated with steroid use, the direct relationship is not yet clear. In many cases, the suicides completed while the individual was actively using steroids occurred in conjunction with manic behavior and were more impulsive in nature. However, suicides completed during withdrawal were often premeditated and associated with severe depression. In either circumstance, anabolic steroids may have been one of the factors contributing to the completion of suicide (Trenton & Currier).

Little research has focused on the treatment of steroid dependence. However, given the similarities that exist between steroid and other drug use, effective treatment intervention plans may be similar (Brower, 1992). Steroid dependence treatment consists of, but is not limited to, offering the patient relief of the withdrawal symptoms while providing the necessary medical and psychological support needed during this time.

Prevalence of Steroid Use

According to the 2008 Monitoring the Future survey, an annual national survey that assesses drug use among 8th, 10th, and 12th graders, prevalence rates reported of lifetime use were 1.4%, 1.4%, and 2.2%, respectively (Johnston et al., 2009). Although there has been an overall decline in steroid usage in recent years, there is still a high percentage of abusers (Johnston et al.).

Reasons for Steroid Use

Research suggests that several factors motivate the adolescent to use steroids. We developed the following tripartite typology model as a means to organize and elucidate three motivational profiles that explain why adolescents choose to use steroids (Gober et al., 2009).

Typology 1: Sports and Physical Performance Improvement. The most commonly cited motivation is the possibility of improved athletic performance and muscle strength. The athletic adolescent turns to steroids to achieve a higher level of performance. Because of the high stakes that are placed on school athletic performance and the competitive nature of sports, adolescents who participate in school athletic programs are more likely to use steroids than those adolescents who are not involved in sports. Athletes who do strength training, such as that involved in football, wrestling, and track and field, have more reported users than athletes in other sports (Bahrke, Yesalis, Kopstein, & Stephen, 2000). These users are often unaware of the consequences of steroid use (Volkow, 2005) and take steroids because of the short-term benefits. In addition, adolescents are significantly influenced by professional athletes who have used steroids to improve their athletic performance. The fact that these role models seem to obtain desired results while using these substances can greatly influence the impressionable teenager to turn to steroids.

Typology 2: Appearance. Another motivation for steroid use has been to improve one's appearance (Field et al., 2005; Nilsson, Allebeck, Marklund, Baigi, & Fridlund, 2004). The idealized male physique is depicted in media and fashion as increasingly muscular with little body fat. This ideal promotes a body type that is often physically unattainable except through steroid usage, dehydration, and other unhealthy practices (Stout & Frame, 2004). The media is influential in perpetuating this idealized and unachievable body type, and the glamorization of this build may cause many adolescents to view their bodies negatively (Denham, 2006). When one is unable to achieve these glamorized ideals, negative self-image contributes to feelings of body dissatisfaction, low self-worth, and psychological distress. Ricciardelli and McCabe (2003) found that low self-esteem predicted body dissatisfaction among adolescent boys and girls, a trait that is correlated with steroid use. However, it has also been suggested that steroid use improves body image, since it may provide individuals with the idealized body they are trying to achieve. Body dissatisfaction has historically been viewed as a concern among females, yet there is increasing prevalence of body dissatisfaction among males (Cohane & Pope, 2001). An extreme form of body dissatisfaction often seen in males is muscle dysmorphia. Muscle dysmorphia, a subtype of body dysmorphic disorder, occurs when an individual becomes preoccupied with muscularity; although the individual is well built, he views himself as being undersized and inadequate (Stout & Frame, 2004).

Typology 3: Illicit Drug Use and Other Risky, Sensation-Seeking Behaviors. The final typology of steroid users are those who take these drugs in combination with other illegal substances and in conjunction with other risky and sensation-seeking behaviors. Research has shown a correlation among adolescent steroid use, problem behaviors, and use of other drugs, including cigarettes, marijuana, alcohol, cocaine, and injected drugs (Durant & Escobedo, 1995). Steroid use is also linked to adolescents performing risky behaviors, including not wearing a seat belt or motorcycle helmet, driving while intoxicated, carrying a weapon, and attempting suicide (Middleman, Faulkner, & Anne, 1995).

Recent evidence suggests an overlap among the typologies described above such that steroid users may fit more than one typology. For example, some steroid users participate in school athletic programs, abuse illicit drugs, and engage in risky behaviors.

IMPLICATIONS FOR EDUCATORS

In general, the motivations that cause adolescents to turn to steroids are common issues among many adolescents. Schools need to implement prevention programs that are appropriate to their student bodies to thwart steroid use. Many teens are unaware of the adverse effects of steroids; education is the first step in helping adolescents understand that these drugs have negative side effects. Programs that go beyond presenting facts about steroids and also focus on strengthening self-esteem and promoting individual and interpersonal communication skills have been shown to be effective.

The more educators are aware of the physical and behavioral manifestations associated with adolescent steroid use, the more likely users will be identified and targeted for intervention. In addition, because adolescents may take steroids for several reasons, it is important that educators are aware of these varied motivations. Interventions need to be tailored to match the user's motivation. For example, gearing interventions only to adolescent athletes will not address the motivations of adolescent users who are not athletes and have little interest in improving physical prowess. In addition, school districts need to enforce and communicate clearly strict policies and penalties for steroid use among students, athletes and nonathletes alike, similar to current drug policies.

For students who take steroids to improve athletic performance, ATLAS (Athletes Training & Learning to Avoid Steroids) is a widely recognized program that targets student athletes. This school-based steroid prevention program, which has been implemented in many high schools, aims to teach student athletes to build muscle strength and employ weight-training alternatives while peers educate the athletes on proper nutrition and the harmful effects of steroid use.

The adolescent who is motivated to use steroids to improve appearance requires an intervention that creates awareness about the media's unrealistic and largely unattainable body ideal and societal pressures to conform to this ideal (Nilsson et al., 2004). Programs should also focus on body image and self-esteem. Adolescents who wish to improve their appearance should be encouraged by family and school members to eat and exercise in a healthy manner.

Drug testing is a popular option among administrators looking to discourage illicit drug use, including steroids. Although expensive and involving other issues, such as privacy, it has been adopted by several states. Drug prevention programs are useful in targeting those adolescents who are at risk for all types of illicit drug use (Durant & Escobedo, 1995). Teaching risk avoidance skills to those who engage in risk-taking activities (including illicit substance use) is also recommended (Durant et al., 1993).

EDUCATIONAL STRATEGIES

- Educate teachers, coaches, parents, and students about the adverse effects of anabolic steroid use and about the physical and behavioral signs that indicate when an adolescent is taking steroids.
- Implement schoolwide or student-specific programs to prevent or intervene when adolescents are using steroids, performance-enhancing

drugs, or dietary supplements. Programs may overlap with other illicit and licit drug prevention programs.

- Identify and intervene with students who may be suffering from depression and self-image problems and are, thus, more likely to take steroids.

- Implement rules and regulations that clearly publicize the penalties for steroid and performance-enhancing drug use. It is important to delineate what constitutes steroids and performance-enhancing drugs versus dietary supplements, a distinction that may be confusing to some students.

- Establish clear rules about what kind of advice coaches and trainers can give to students who wish to enhance their bodies and athletic performance. Coaches and trainers may benefit from advanced training in healthy ways to improve fitness, strength, and nutrition.

- Gym classes and sports teams should foster an atmosphere of openness, team cooperation, and ethical responsibility in sporting activities, rather than cutthroat competition that may lead some students to desperate means of staying competitive.

- Identify appropriate referral sources for families of steroid users.

DISCUSSION QUESTIONS

1. How can educators and other school support staff work more effectively and proactively with students who are at risk or are already taking steroids?

2. How can educators and other school support staff help adolescents cope with the glamorization of unattainable body images presented to students by the media, professional athletes, and other sources?

3. How can parents and educators better collaborate to prevent steroid use?

4. To what extent should educators discuss healthy physical ideals with students and promote lifestyle changes to obtain these ideals? Should this type of education be limited to coaches, gym teachers, and parents?

5. If school personnel discover that a parent has encouraged his or her child to take steroids to improve athletic performance, what, if anything, should be done?

RESEARCH SUMMARY

- The use of anabolic steroids and performance-enhancing drugs among adolescents shows increases with age, from 1.5% of 8th graders and 1.8% of 10th graders to 2.2% of 12th graders.

- Steroids have legal medical uses when prescribed as part of a disease-fighting regimen but are illegal when used without a prescription to build muscle mass and strength. When steroids are taken in combination with a program of muscle-building exercise and diet, they may contribute to increases in body weight and muscular strength.

- There are dangerous and potentially irreversible physiological and psychological side effects from taking steroids in addition to effects specific to the growing teenager.
- The tripartite typology model explains adolescent motivation to take steroids:

    o Desire to improve athletic ability and strength
    o Desire to improve physical appearance
    o Desire to engage in illicit drug use and/or risky behaviors

Prevention and intervention programs need to be geared toward the specific reasons and motivation for steroid use.

RESOURCES

National Institute on Drug Abuse (NIDA): www.drugabuse.gov/ Infofacts/Steroids.html. This is a useful fact sheet about steroid use.

U.S. Department of Justice: www.deadiversion.usdoj.gov/pubs/ brochures/steroids/index.html

ATLAS (Athletes Training & Learning to Avoid Steroids): www.ohsu .edu/hpsm/atlas.cfm. ATLAS is a scientifically proven education program for male athletes.

Drug-Rehabs: www.drug-rehabs.com. This Web site includes search tools to help find appropriate drug rehabilitation programs, whether on an outpatient or inpatient basis.

HANDOUT

ANABOLIC STEROID USE AMONG ADOLESCENTS

Many adolescents continue to use steroids despite the physical, psychological, and psychiatric short- and long-term harm steroids cause. Steroids are man-made illegal substances that, when taken with a high-calorie and high-protein diet and an intensive exercise regimen, can build muscle mass and strength. However, the side effects of their use are significant, even life threatening.

Several physical and behavioral signs may become apparent when an adolescent is taking steroids:

- Increased muscle mass and strength
- Feelings of invincibility, which can lead to impaired judgment
- Mood swings (including manic-like symptoms that can lead to violence)
- Extreme irritability
- Hostility and aggression
- Nervousness or agitation
- Depression and suicidal ideation
- Premature termination of the adolescent growth spurt (teens may be shorter than had they not taken steroids)
- Acne (especially concentrated on the chest, back, neck, and arms)
- Heart, liver, and kidney complications

Some physiological side effects are gender-specific. Females may develop more masculine characteristics, including decreased body fat and breast size, deepening of the voice, excessive growth of body hair, and loss of scalp hair. Males may experience baldness and/or gynecomastia (irreversible breast enlargement).

It is also important to understand the reasons why adolescents may decide to take steroids, as this will help identify the appropriate intervention for each teen.

- **Desire to improve athletic ability and strength.** This is the most commonly stated reason for adolescent steroid use. The decision to use steroids has been influenced by the increasingly high-stakes and competitive nature of school-sponsored sports. Professional athletes who have used performance-enhancing drugs and steroids have also contributed to teenager use. Some parents encourage their children to use steroids.
- **Desire to improve physical appearance.** Another reason an adolescent might turn to steroids is to improve physical appearance because of negative body image. This is often influenced by the media's portrayal of an "ideal" physique that consists of well-defined muscles and low body fat, an ideal often unattainable by many adolescents.
- **Desire to engage in illicit drug use and/or other risky behaviors.** Many adolescents use steroids in conjunction with illicit and licit drugs, including cigarettes, marijuana, alcohol, cocaine, and injected drugs. In these cases, steroids are one of several substances they are using to self-medicate.

The appropriate intervention depends on why the adolescent is motivated to use steroids. For the athletic teenager, there are educational programs (e.g., ATLAS; www.ohsu.edu/ohsuedu/academic/som/medicine/hpsm/atlas.cfm) that teach strength-training practices and improved nutrition as an alternative to steroids. Programs that focus on self-esteem and body image would be appropriate for the adolescent who turns to steroids to change physical appearance. Rehabilitation programs that are geared toward assisting those with drug abuse and addiction issues have also been shown to help steroid users.

Glossary

Chapter 2

Agonist—A drug or other chemical that mimics a naturally occurring neurotransmitter and facilitates increased transmission of a naturally occurring neurochemical pathway, such as dopamine

Antagonist—Opposite of an agonist, an antagonist is a drug that interferes with transmission from one neuron to another by means of blocking its nerve receptor or reducing the amount of the neurotransmitter available to aid the transmission.

Cerebral Cortex—Outer layer of gray matter of the brain largely responsible for higher brain functions, including sensation, voluntary muscle movement, thought, reasoning, and memory

Comorbid—Diseases or disorders that occur at the same time. They may or may not be related to one another.

Complex Motor Tic—Sudden movement of longer duration than a simple motor tic

Complex Phonic Tic—Syllables, words, or phrases, as well as odd patterns of speech, in which there are sudden changes in rate, volume, and/or rhythm

Coprolalia—Type of tic that involves involuntary uttering of obscenities or socially inappropriate phrases

Copropraxia—A sudden, ticlike vulgar, sexual, or obscene gesture

Dopamine—One of the neurotransmitters involved in transmission of responses from one nerve cell to another that has been implicated in neuromotor pathways

Echolalia—Complex phonic tic that involves repeating the last heard sound, word, or phrase

Echopraxia—Complex motor tic that involves imitation of someone else's movements

Neurotransmitters—Chemicals that the cells of the nervous system (i.e., neurons) use to communicate with one another

Palilalia—Complex phonic tic that involves repeating one's own sounds or words

Premonitory Urges—Sensations perceived by individuals immediately preceding an involuntary movement or vocalization

Receptor—A protein on the surface of a neuron (or any other cell) that recognizes and binds with a molecule or chemical (such as dopamine), creating an electrochemical signal, which then causes the receiving neuron to act on that signal

Chapter 3

Antipsychotics—A class of psychotropic medication often used to treat bipolar disorder

Hypersexuality—The exhibition of developmentally inappropriate sexual behaviors

Mania—A severe condition characterized by extremely elevated mood, energy, and unusual thought patterns that interfere with daily functioning

Mood—A state of mind and emotional feeling that normally fluctuates for all individuals. Two mood disorders exist (depressive disorder and bipolar disorder) wherein mood is impaired to the degree that life activities are disrupted.

OHI—This stands for Other Health Impaired. It refers to a special education program allowing access to an IEP. Pediatric bipolar disorder is a medical condition that can fall under this program's supports if adverse affects on the child's learning are documented.

Chapter 4

Agoraphobia—An anxiety disorder characterized by anxiety about, or avoidance of, open spaces or situations from which escape might be difficult (or embarrassing) or in which help may not be available in the event of having a panic attack or paniclike symptoms

Environmental-Situational Phobia—A subtype of a specific phobia in which the fear is cued by a specific environmental situation

Flooding—A therapy technique that places the client in the presence of an aversive stimulus without escape so that the client eventually accommodates to the stimulus

Generalized Anxiety Disorder—An anxiety disorder characterized by excessive, uncontrollable worry and associated feelings of tension or restlessness

Social Phobia—An anxiety disorder characterized by excessive and disabling fear of social or evaluative situations

Chapter 5

Bipolar Disorder—Bipolar disorder (manic-depressive illness) is a mood disorder involving episodes of both significant mania and depression. The person's mood swings from excessively "high" (excited, irritable, flight of ideas) to sad and hopeless.

Cyclothymia—A mild bipolar disorder characterized by instability of mood and a tendency to swing between mild euphorias and depressions

Dopaminergic—Relating to, involved in, or initiated by the neurotransmitter activity of dopamine or related neurotransmitters

Dysthymia—A chronic mood disorder characterized by mild depression, or despondency or a tendency to be despondent, over a long period

Euphoria—A feeling of happiness, confidence, or well-being sometimes inflated in pathological states as mania

Hyperthymia—An abnormal decrease in the intensity with which emotions are experienced, such as flatness of affect

Hypomania—A mild state of mania, especially as a phase of a manic-depressive cycle

Mesolimbic—A central portion of the limbic system of the brain, including the ventral tegmental area, with high concentrations of dopaminergic neurons and innervations to the amygdala, nucleus accumbens, and olfactory tubercle mesolimbic system. The system plays a primary role in the control of memory and emotion.

Chapter 6

Atypical Antipsychotic Medications—Second-generation antipsychotics used to treat schizophrenia and other thought disorders. They have recently been used for children with developmental disabilities and behavior problems. They include these chemical classes: dibenzoxazepine (e.g., Clozapine), thienobenzodiazepine (e.g., Olanzapine), and benzisoxazole (e.g., Risperidone).

Autonomic Dysfunction—A disorder of the autonomic nervous system, which controls heart rate, blood pressure, digestive functions, and responses to stress

Dopamine—A hormone and neurotransmitter that has many functions in the brain, including important roles in behavior and cognition, motor activity, motivation and reward, and learning

Dopamine (DA) Receptors—An important component of the central nervous system associated with the processing of dopamine. Disorders of the DA receptors are associated with ADHD, depression, and schizophrenia. DA receptors are a target of antipsychotic medications.

Extrapyramidal Symptoms (EPS)—Neurological side effects of antipsychotic medications. EPS can cause a variety of symptoms, including involuntary movements, tremors and rigidity, body restlessness, muscle contractions, and changes in breathing and heart rate.

Limbic System—Subcortical brain structures that support a variety of functions, including emotion, long-term memory, and aggression

Off-Label Use—The practice of prescribing drugs for a purpose outside the scope of the drug's approved label, most often concerning the drug's indication

Serotonin—A hormone and neurotransmitter. Changes in the serotonin levels in the brain can alter mood. For example, medications that affect the action of serotonin are used to treat depression.

Striatum—A subcortical structure that is rich in DA receptors. The striatum is associated with impulse control and aggression.

Tardive Dyskinesia—Repetitive, involuntary, purposeless movements. Features of the disorder may include grimacing, tongue protrusion, lip smacking, puckering and pursing of the lips, and rapid eye blinking.

Typical Antipsychotic Medications—Typical antipsychotics (sometimes referred to as first-generation antipsychotics, conventional antipsychotics, classical neuroleptics, or major tranquilizers) are a class of antipsychotic drugs first developed in the 1950s and used to treat psychosis (in particular, schizophrenia). Commonly prescribed typical antipsychotics include chloropromazine and haloperidol. They are generally being replaced by atypical antipsychotic drugs.

Chapter 7

Akathisia—An unpleasant sensation of inner restlessness. The patient may display an inability to sit still or remain motionless.

Athetoid Movements—Slow, sinuous, and continual movements of the tongue, jaw, or extremities.

Atypical Antipsychotics—A class of medication first used in the 1970s to treat mental illness. Because they are thought to have less serious side effects, they are being used to replace typical antipsychotics.

Choreiform Movements—Rapid, jerky, and nonrepetitive movements of the tongue, jaw, or extremities

Dopamine—A hormone and neurotransmitter that has many functions in the brain. It is implicated in motor activity, cognition, attention, motivation, mood, and sleep, among other functions.

Dystonia—Sustained muscle contractions causing twisting and repetitive movements or abnormal postures. The involuntary movements may affect a single muscle, a group of muscles, or the entire body.

Neuroleptic Medication—Medication used to treat psychosis, often having a tranquilizing effect

Rhythmic Movements—Stereotypical movements of the tongue, jaw, or extremities

Stereotypic Movements Disorder—Condition in which a person engages in repetitive, often rhythmic, but purposeless movements such as rocking, hand shaking or waving, and mouthing of objects

Chapter 8

Amphetamine-Based Stimulants—Drugs (amphetamines) that influence the levels of dopamine and norepinephrine in the brain and have been used to treat ADHD, narcolepsy, and other central nervous system dysfunction. Brand names include Dexedrine and Desoxyn.

Attention Deficit/Hyperactive Disorder—A neurodevelopmental disorder with symptoms of inattention, hyperactivity, and impulsivity leading to impairment in functioning across multiple settings. This neurodevelopmental disorder is highly heritable.

Dopamine (DA) Receptors—An important component of the central nervous system associated with the processing of dopamine. Disorders of the DA receptors are associated with ADHD, depression, and schizophrenia. DA receptors are a target of stimulant medications.

Immediate-Release Stimulants—These medications are short-acting (3 to 4 hours) medicines that require multiple doses (2 or 3) throughout the day to see desired benefits.

Long-Acting Stimulants—Referred to as extended-release (ER or XR), sustained-release (SR), or continuous delivery (CD). Found to be as efficacious in treating ADHD as short-acting or immediate release medications. Long-acting stimulants offer convenience via single daily dosing.

Methylphenidate-Based Stimulants—Drugs (methylphenidate [MPH]) that influence the levels of dopamine and norepinephrine in the brain and have been used to treat ADHD, narcolepsy, and other central nervous system dysfunction. Brand names include Ritalin, Metadate, Focalin, and Concerta.

Mixed Amphetamine Salts—Include medications such as Adderall or Adderall XR. Targets dopamine and norepinephrine levels within the brain synapses.

Norepinephrine—Neurotransmitter implicated in depression, anxiety, and ADHD

Prodrug—A drug that when administered is inactive or partially inactive until it becomes metabolized in the body. An example is lisdexamfetamine (brand name Vyvanse), which is considered an extended-release version of dextroamphetamine and has Food and Drug Administration (FDA) approval to treat ADHD.

Selective Norepinephrine Reuptake Inhibitors (SNRIs)—Class of medicines including the drug Strattera, which is FDA approved for treating ADHD in children and adults

Stimulant—Sympathomimetic drug that increases the synaptic catecholamines (primarily dopamine) by inhibiting the presynaptic reuptake mechanism and releasing presynaptic catecholamines

Titration—Process of gradually adjusting a medication dose to achieve the desired result

Chapter 9

Adjunctive Polypharmacy—The use of one medication to alleviate the side effects or secondary symptoms caused by another medication from a different medication class (e.g., clonidine to treat sleep problems in children being treated with a psychostimulant).

Augmentation—The use of a medication at a lower dose than is typically prescribed in combination with another medication that is prescribed at a typical therapeutic dose for similar symptoms (e.g., the addition of fluoxetine to a partial response to fluvoxamine or the use of atomoxetine with a partial response to a psychostimulant)

Combined Pharmacotherapy—The use of more than one medication to treat one disorder

Concomitant Psychotropic Medication Therapy—The simultaneous use of two or more psychotropic medications for the same or different target symptoms/behaviors

Contra-Therapeutic Polypharmacy—Unexpected or unintended negative outcomes that are associated with the use of two or more medications. This results in an evidence base against the use of those medications in combination. Sometimes referred to as "irrational polypharmacy."

Copharmacy—The use of two or medications to treat different disorders

Monotherapy—The use of one drug or intervention to treat one or more conditions

Multiclass Polypharmacy—The use of more than one medication from different medication classes for the same group of symptoms (e.g., the use of methylphenidate and atomoxetine for the treatment of hyperactivity and inattention)

Off-Label Prescription Practices—The use of medications for conditions or with populations in which they have not been approved or thoroughly investigated

Polypharmacy—The use of two or more medications for one or more conditions

SAIL (Simple, Adverse Effects, Indication, List)—A mnemonic strategy used by physicians when making decisions regarding the appropriateness of drug therapy. Keep it simple and avoid complex drug regimens (**S**). Understand the adverse effects associated with each drug, individually and when used in combination with other drugs (**A**). Each drug should have a clear indication and a well-defined goal for improving the targeted symptom (**I**). Record and list the name and dose of any drug prescribed, as keeping accurate notes and logs is essential for close progress monitoring (**L**).

Same-Class Polypharmacy—The use of more than one medication from the same class of medicines to treat a patient's symptoms. For example, both fluvoxamine and sertraline (two selective serotonin reuptake inhibitors) may be prescribed to target symptoms associated with obsessive-compulsive disorder.

Therapeutic Polypharmacy—Use of multiple drugs to treat a disease based on evidence or research support (i.e., Food and Drug Administration approval). Within childhood mental health conditions, this has yet to be clearly established for any combination of drugs.

Total Polypharmacy—The total count of medications used within a patient. This is also referred to as "drug load." It includes all forms of biological treatments, including prescribed medicines, over-the-counter medicines, alternative medication approaches, and illicit drugs.

Chapter 10

Analgesic—Any of a diverse group of medications used to relieve pain

Anticonvulsant—A drug used to control seizures, sometimes used to treat migraine headaches

Antipyretic—Medication used to reduce fever

Corticosteroid—A prescription steroid drug frequently used to treat inflammation

Multisymptom Formula—Nonprescription medication that contains several different drugs to control a number of different symptoms

NSAIDs—Nonsteroidal anti-inflammatory drugs, including ibuprofen, naproxen sodium, and related drugs

Over-the-Counter (OTC)—Describes medicines sold to customers without a prescription

Physician's Desk Reference **(PDR)**—A comprehensive list of all drugs available in the United States with description of use, dosage, interactions, and side effects

Psychomotor Speed—The ability to perform fine motor tasks (such as writing or copying) quickly

Side Effect—Effect that occurs beyond or in addition to the desired therapeutic effect of the drug

Chapter 11

Asperger Syndrome—One of the autism spectrum disorders characterized by impaired social interaction and restricted, stereotyped patterns of behavior, interests, and activities. Children display typical language and cognitive development.

Autism—A disorder appearing by age 3 that is characterized by lack of communication, lack of social skills, stereotyped and/or repetitive interests and activities, withdrawal, and developmental delays

Casein—A protein in milk

Gluten—A protein found in wheat, rye, barley, and oats

Opiod-Excess Hypothesis—Hypothesis on which the gluten-free casein-free diet is based. States that when gluten and casein are not completely broken down during the digestive process, peptides remain in the digestive tract and are absorbed into the bloodstream. These peptides are hypothesized to become biologically active and be treated as neuropeptides by the brain. As neuropeptides, they stimulate an opiate-like effect on the brain and potentially cause and/or contribute to behaviors associated with autism spectrum disorders.

Peptides—Short chains of amino acids that remain in the digestive tract

Placebo Effect—A favorable response to an intervention, regardless of whether it is a true intervention or a placebo. The favorable response is attributed to the expectation of the intervention.

Chapter 12

Anorexia Nervosa (AN)—Individuals with AN pursue and/or maintain excessively low body weight (i.e., 85% of normal weight or a body mass index [BMI] of 17.5 kg/m^2) through a reduction in food intake and, possibly, self-induced vomiting, misuse of laxatives or diuretics, and/or excessive exercise.

Binge Eating—A *binge* is defined by the *DSM-IV-TR* as eating a large amount of food in a discrete period of time (i.e., definitely a larger amount than most individuals would eat within about 2 hours).

Binge-Eating/Purging Type—This subtype of AN involves regularly binge eating, purging, or both. Notably, some individuals in this subtype do not binge eat. Rather, they regularly purge after consumption of small amounts of food.

Body Image Distortion—Body image distortion involves a distorted experience of body weight and shape. This includes feelings of being globally overweight, as well as over-focus on and distortion regarding particular parts of the body (e.g., abdomen, buttocks, and thighs).

Body Mass Index—Body mass index (BMI) is a measure of body fat based on weight and height typically used for adult men and women. Per the National Institutes of Health, the BMI categories include (a) underweight, <18.5; (b) normal weight, 18.5–24.9; (c) overweight, 25.0–29.9; and (d) obesity, ≥ 30.

Body Mass Index-for-Age Percentile—A BMI-for-age percentile is considered the most appropriate weight comparison method for children. Per the Centers for Disease Control and Prevention, it is calculated by using the child's weight, height, age, and gender to compare to growth charts that demonstrate age-appropriate growth expectations.

Bulimia Nervosa (BN)—Individuals with BN place an excessive emphasis on body shape and weight in their self-evaluations. There are two subtypes: purging type (regular engagement in the use of vomiting, laxatives, diuretics, or enemas) and nonpurging type (use of other compensatory behaviors, such as fasting or exercise).

Compulsory Exercise (or Obligatory Exercise)—Compulsive exercise is the qualitative measure of exercise. Exercise is considered compulsive when it is marked by maintenance of a rigid exercise schedule, detailed record keeping, and priority over other daily life activities, as well as feelings of anxiety and guilt associated with missed sessions.

Nonpurging Type—This subtype of BN presents with alternative, inappropriate compensatory behaviors (e.g., fasting and excessive exercise) without engagement in typical purging behaviors (e.g., self-indicted vomiting or misuse of laxatives, diuretics, and enemas).

Purging—Purging behaviors include self-induced vomiting or the misuse of laxative or diuretics.

Chapter 13

Anabolic Androgenic Steroids—Manufactured substances related to male sex hormones, such as testosterone. *Anabolic* refers to muscle-building and growth properties, and *androgenic* refers to the increase in male sexual characteristics.

Diagnostic and Statistical Manual of Mental Disorders, fourth edition, text revision (DSM-IV-TR)—A manual published by the American Psychiatric Association that lists mental disorders and criteria for proper diagnosis of these disorders

Muscle Dysmorphia—A disorder where individuals become preoccupied with their muscularity and, even if they are well built, view themselves as being undersized and inadequate. It is a specific subtype of body dysmorphic disorder.

Performance-Enhancing Drugs—FDA-approved legal substances that have many of the same properties as steroids, such as creatine

Testosterone—A sex hormone that is essential to maturation and sex differentiation. When derived from the ingestion of steroids, however, testosterone also contributes to the building of lean muscle mass.

References

Chapter 1

Bachmann, M., Bachmann, C., Rief, W., & Mattejat, F. (2008). Efficacy of psychiatric and psychotherapeutic interventions in children and adolescents with psychiatric disorders—a systematic evaluation of meta-analyses and reviews. Part I: Anxiety disorders and depressive disorders. *Zeitschrift für Kinder- und Jugendpsychiatrie und Psychotherapie, 36,* 309–320.

Boylan, K., Romero, S., & Birmaher, B. (2007). Psychopharmacologic treatment of pediatric major depressive disorder. *Psychopharmacology, 191,* 27–38.

Breuer, M. E., Chan, J. S., Oosting, R. S., Groenink, L., Korte, S. M., Campbell, U., et al. (2008). The triple monoaminergic reuptake inhibitor DOV 216,303 has antidepressant effects in the rat olfactory bulbectomy model and lacks sexual side effects. *European Neuropsychopharmacology: The Journal of the European College of Neuropsychopharmacology, 18,* 908–916.

David, D., Szentagotai, A., Lupu, V., & Cosman, D. (2008). Rational emotive behavior therapy, cognitive therapy, and medication in the treatment of major depressive disorder: A randomized clinical trial, posttreatment outcomes, and six-month follow-up. *Journal of Clinical Psychology, 64,* 728–746.

Fasano, C., DesGroseillers, L., & Trudeau, L. E. (2008). Chronic activation of the D2 dopamine autoreceptor inhibits synaptogenesis in mesencephalic dopaminergic neurons in vitro. *European Journal of Neuroscience, 28,* 1480–1490.

Findling, R. L., Robb, A., Nyilas, M., Forbes, R. A., Jin, N., Ivanova, S., et al. (2008). A multiple-center, randomized, double-blind, placebo-controlled study of oral aripiprazole for treatment of adolescents with schizophrenia. *American Journal of Psychiatry, 165,* 1432–1441.

Flament, M. F., Geller, D., Irak, M., & Blier, P. (2007). Specificities of treatment in pediatric obsessive-compulsive disorder. *CNS Spectrums, 12,* 43–58.

François, B. L., Czesak, M., Steubl, D., & Albert, P. R. (2008). Transcriptional regulation at a HTR1A polymorphism associated with mental illness. *Neuropharmacology, 55,* 977–985.

Imel, Z. E., Malterer, M. B., McKay, K. M., & Wampold, B. E. (2008). A meta-analysis of psychotherapy and medication in unipolar depression and dysthymia. *Journal of Affective Disorders, 110,* 197–206.

Ipser, J. C., Sander, C., & Stein, D. J. (2009, January 21). Pharmacotherapy and psychotherapy for body dysmorphic disorder. *Cochrane Database of Systematic Reviews,* No. 1. Retrieved October 22, 2009, from http://mrw.interscience.wiley.com/cochrane/clsysrev/articles/CD005332/frame.html

Kirsch, I., Deacon, B. J., Huedo-Medina, T. B., Scoboria, A., Moore, T. J., & Johnson, B. T. (2008). Initial severity and antidepressant benefits: A meta-analysis of data submitted to the Food and Drug Administration. *PLoS Medicine, 5,* 260–268.

Koelch, M., Schnoor, K., & Fegert, J. M. (2008). Ethical issues in psychopharmacology of children and adolescents. *Current Opinion in Psychiatry, 21,* 598–605.

Mojtabai, R., & Olfson, M. (2008). National trends in psychotherapy by office-based psychiatrists. *Archives of General Psychiatry, 65,* 962–970.

National Institute of Mental Health (NIMH). (2008). *Mental health medications* (NIH Publication No. 02–3929). Bethesda, MD: National Institute of Mental Health, National Institutes of Health, U.S. Department of Health and Human Services. Retrieved October 22, 2009, from http://www.nimh.nih.gov/health/publications/medications/complete-publication.shtml

Northoff, G. (2008). Neuropsychiatry: An old discipline in a new gestalt bridging biological psychiatry, neuropsychology, and cognitive neurology. *European Archives of Psychiatry and Clinical Neuroscience, 258,* 226–238.

Ögren, S. E., Eriksson, T. M., Elvander-Tottie, E., D'Addarioa, C., Ekström, J. C., Svenningsson, P., et al. (2008). The role of 5-HT$_{1A}$ receptors in learning and memory. *Behavioural Brain Research, 195,* 54–77.

Paz, R. D., Tardito, S., Atzori, M., & Tseng, K. Y. (2008). Glutamatergic dysfunction in schizophrenia: From basic neuroscience to clinical psychopharmacology. *European Neuropsychopharmacology, 18,* 773–786.

Scharf, M. A., & Williams, T. P. (2006). Psychopharmacology in adolescent medicine. *Adolescent Medicine Clinics, 17,* 165–181.

Tallman, J. F., & Dahl, S. G. (2002). New drug design in psychopharmacology: The impact of molecular biology. In F. E. Bloom & D. J. Kupfer (Eds.), *Psychopharmacology: The fourth generation of progress.* Philadelphia: Lippincott Williams & Wilkins.

Tan, J. O., & Koelch, M. (2008). The ethics of psychopharmacological research in legal minors. *Child and Adolescent Psychiatry and Mental Health, 2,* 39–53.

Tizzano, J. P., Stribling, D. S., Perez-Tilve, D., Strack, A., Frassetto, A., Chen, R. Z., et al. (2008). The triple uptake inhibitor (1R,5S)-(+)-1-(3,4-dichlorophenyl)-3-azabicyclo[3.1.0] hexane hydrochloride (DOV 21947) reduces body weight and plasma triglycerides in rodent models of diet-induced obesity. *The Journal of Pharmacology and Experimental Therapeutics 324,* 1111–1126.

Vitiello, B. (2003). Ethical considerations in psychopharmacological research involving children and adolescents. *Psychopharmacology, 171,* 86–91.

Chapter 2

Albin, R. L. (2006). Neurobiology of basal ganglia and Tourette syndrome: Striatal and dopamine function. *Advances in Neurology, 99,* 99–106.

American Psychiatric Association (APA). (2000). *Diagnostic and statistical manual of mental disorders* (4th ed., text revision). Washington, DC: Author.

Bloch, M. H., Peterson, B. S., Scahill, L., Otka, J., Katsovich, L., Zhang, H., et al. (2006). Adulthood outcome of tic and obsessive-compulsive symptom severity in children with Tourette syndrome. *Archives of Pediatrics & Adolescent Medicine, 160,* 65–69.

Chevalier, G., & Deniau, J. M. (1990). Disinhibition as a basic process in the expression of striatal functions. *Trends in Neurosciences, 13,* 277–280.

Coffey, B. J., & Biederman, J. (2000). Anxiety disorders and tic severity in juveniles with Tourette disorder. *Journal of the American Academy of Child and Adolescent Psychology, 39,* 562–568.

Fonagy, P., Target, M., Cottrell, D., Phillips, J., & Kurtz, Z. (2002). *What works for whom: A critical review of treatments for children and adolescents.* New York: Guilford Press.

Freeman, R. D. (2007). Tic disorders and ADHD: Answers from a world-wide clinical dataset on Tourette syndrome. *European Child & Adolescent Psychiatry, 16,* 15–23.

Freeman, R. D., Fast, D. K., Burd, L., Kerbeshian, J., Robertson, M. M., & Sandor, P. (2000). An international perspective on Tourette syndrome: Selected findings from 3,500 individuals in 22 countries. *Developmental Medicine and Child Neurology, 42,* 436–437.

Gaze, C., Kepley, H. O., & Walkup, J. T. (2006). Co-occurring psychiatric disorders in children and adolescents with Tourette syndrome. *Journal of Child Neurology, 21,* 657–664.

Hendren, G. (2002). Tourette syndrome: A new look at an old condition. *Journal of Rehabilitation, 68,* 22–27.

Hounie, A. G., Rosario-Campos, M. C., Diniz, J. B., Shavitt, R. G., Ferrao, Y. A., Lopes, A. C., et al. (2006). Obsessive-compulsive disorder in Tourette syndrome. *Advances in Neurology, 99,* 22–38.

Individuals with Disabilities Education Improvement Act of 2004 (IDEIA), 20 U.S.C. § 401 *et seq.* (2004).

Kienast, T., & Heinz, A. (2006). Dopamine and the diseased brain. *CNS & Neurological Disorders Drug Targets, 5,* 109–131.

Leckman, J. F. (2002). Tourette syndrome. *Lancet, 360,* 1577–1586.

Leckman, J. F., Zhang, H., Vitale, A., Lahnin, F., Lynch, K., Bondi, C., et al. (1998). Course of tic severity in Tourette syndrome: The first two decades. *Pediatrics, 102,* 14–19.

Marcks, B. A., Berlin, K. S., Woods, D. W., & Davies, W. H. (2007). Impact of Tourette syndrome: A preliminary investigation of the effects of disclosure on peer perceptions and social functioning. *Psychiatry, 70,* 59–67.

Murray, J. B. (1997). Psychophysiological aspects of Tourette syndrome. *Journal of Psychology, 131,* 615–626.

Pappert, E. J., Goetz, C. G., Louis, E. D., Blasucci, L., & Leurgans, S. (2003). Objective assessments of longitudinal outcome in Gilles de la Tourette's syndrome. *Neurology, 61,* 936–940.

Prestin, K. (2003). Tourette syndrome: Characteristics and interventions. *Intervention in School and Clinic, 39,* 67–71.

Robertson, M. M. (1994). Annotation: Gilles de la Tourette syndrome—An update. *Journal of Child Psychology and Psychiatry, and Allied Disciplines, 35,* 597–611.

Roberston, M. M. (2006). Mood disorders and Gilles de la Tourette's syndrome: An update on prevalence, etiology, comorbidity, clinical associations, and implications. *Journal of Psychosomatic Research, 61,* 349–358.

Robertson, M. M., Banerjee, S., Hiley, P. J., & Tannock, C. (1997). Personality disorder and psychopathology in Tourette's syndrome: A controlled study. *The British Journal of Psychiatry: The Journal of Mental Science, 171,* 283–286.

Robertson, M. M., & Orth, M. (2006). Behavioral and affective disorders in Tourette syndrome. *Advances in Neurology, 99,* 39–60.

Schultz, R. T., Carter, A. S., Gladstone, M., Scahill, L., Leckman, J. F., Peterson, B. S., et al. (1998). Visual-motor integration functioning in children with Tourette syndrome. *Neuropsychology, 12,* 134–145.

Stefanoff, P., & Mazurek, J. (2003). Epidemiological methods used in studies in the prevalence of Tourette syndrome. *Psychiatria Polska, 37,* 97–107.

Tourette Syndrome Association. (2009). *Facts about Tourette syndrome.* Retrieved October 22, 2009, from http://www.tsa-usa.org/imaganw/Fact_Sheet.pdf

Chapter 3

American Psychiatric Association (APA). (2000). *Diagnostic and statistical manual of mental disorders* (4th ed., text revision). Washington, DC: Author.

Biederman, J., Faraone, S. V., Wozniak, J., Mick, E., Kwon, A., & Aleardi, M. (2004). Further evidence of unique developmental phenotypic correlates of pediatric bipolar disorder: Findings from a large sample of clinically referred preadolescent children assessed over the last 7 years. *Journal of Affective Disorders, 82S,* S45–S58.

Biederman, J., Mick, E., & Faraone, S. V. (2004). A prospective follow-up study of pediatric bipolar disorder in boys with attention-deficit/hyperactivity disorder. *Journal of Affective Disorders, 82S*, S17–S23.

Biederman, J., Mick, E., Spencer, T. J., Wilens, T. E., & Faraone, S. V. (2000). Therapeutic dilemmas in the pharmacotherapy of bipolar depression in the young. *Journal of Child and Adolescent Psychopharmacology, 10*, 185–192.

Danielson, C. K., Feeny, N. C., Findling, R. L., & Youngstrom, E. A. (2004). Psychosocial treatment of bipolar disorder in adolescents: A proposed cognitive-behavioral intervention. *Cognitive and Behavioral Practice, 11*, 283–297.

Duffy, A. (2007). Does bipolar disorder exist in children? A selected review. *The Canadian Journal of Psychiatry, 52*, 409–417.

Fristad, M. A. (2006). Psychoeducational treatment for school aged children with bipolar disorder. *Development and Psychopathology, 18*, 1289–1306.

Fristad, M. A., & Goldberg-Arnold, J. S. (2003). Family interventions for early-onset bipolar disorder. In B. Geller & M. P. DelBello (Eds.), *Bipolar disorder in childhood and early adolescence* (pp. 295–313). New York: Guilford Press.

Fristad, M. A., & Goldberg-Arnold, J. S. (2004). *Raising a moody child: How to cope with depression and bipolar disorder.* New York: Guilford Press.

Geller, B., & DelBello, M. P. (2003). *Bipolar disorder in childhood and early adolescence.* New York: Guilford.

Geller, B., & DelBello, M. P. (2008). *Treatment of bipolar disorder in children and adolescents.* New York: Guilford.

Geller, B., Zimmerman, B., Williams, M., DelBello, M. P., Bolhofner, K., Craney, J. L., et al. (2002). *DSM-IV* mania symptoms in a prepubertal and early adolescent bipolar phenotype compared to attention-deficit hyperactive and normal controls. *Journal of Child and Adolescent Psychopharmacology, 12*, 11–25.

Giedd, J. N. (2000). Bipolar disorder and attention-deficit/hyperactivity disorder in children and adolescents. *Journal of Clinical Psychiatry, 61*, 31–34.

Kowatch, R. A., Fristad, M., Birmaher, B., Wagner, K. D., Findling, R. L., & Hellander, M. (2005). Treatment guidelines for children and adolescents with bipolar disorder: Child psychiatric workgroup on bipolar disorder. *Journal of American Academy of Children and Adolescent Psychiatry, 4*, 213–235.

Lewinsohn, P. M., Seeley, J. R., & Klein, D. N. (2003). Bipolar disorder in adolescents: Epidemiology and suicidal behavior. In B. Geller & M.P. DelBello (Eds.), *Bipolar disorder in childhood and early adolescence* (pp. 7–24). New York: Guilford Press.

Masi, G., Perugi, G., Toni, C., Millepiedi, S., Mucci, M., Bertini, N., et al. (2004). Obsessive-compulsive bipolar comorbidity: Focus on children and adolescents. *Journal of Affective Disorders, 78*, 175–183.

McClure, E. B., Treland, J. E., Dickstein, D. P., Towbin, K. E., Charney, D. S., Pine, D. S., et al. (2005). Memory and learning in pediatric bipolar disorder. *Journal of the American Academy of Child and Adolescent Psychiatry, 44*, 461–469.

Miklowitz, D. J., George, E. L., Axelson, D. A., Kim, E. Y., Birmaher, B., Schneck, C., et al. (2004). Family-focused treatment for adolescents with bipolar disorder. *Journal of Affective Disorders, 82S*, S113–128.

Papolos, D. F. (2003). Bipolar disorder and comorbid disorders: The case for a dimensional nosology. In B. Geller & M. P. DelBello (Eds.), *Bipolar disorder in childhood and early adolescence* (pp. 76–106). New York: Guilford Press.

Pavuluri, M. N., Grayczyk, P., Carbray, J., Heidenreich, J., Henry, D., & Miklowitz, D. (2004). Child and family focused cognitive behavior therapy in pediatric bipolar disorder. *Journal of American Academy of Child and Adolescent Psychiatry, 43*, 528–537.

Pavuluri, M. N., Naylor, M. W., & Janicak, P. G. (2002). Recognition and treatment of pediatric bipolar disorder. *Contemporary Psychiatry, 1*, 1–9.

Post, R. M., & Kowatch, R. A. (2006). The health care crisis of childhood-onset bipolar illness: Some recommendations for its amelioration. *Journal of Clinical Psychiatry, 67,* 115–125.

Schapiro, N. A. (2005). Bipolar disorders in children and adolescents. *Journal of Pediatric Health Care, 19,* 131–141.

Smith, D. (2007). Controversies in childhood bipolar disorders. *The Canadian Journal of Psychiatry, 52,* 407–408.

Tillman, R., & Geller, B. (2003). Definitions of rapid, ultrarapid, and ultradian cycling and of episode duration in pediatric and adult bipolar disorders: A proposal to distinguish episodes from cycles. *Journal of Child and Adolescent Psychopharmacology, 13,* 267–271.

Weller, E. B., Calvert, S. M., & Weller, R. A. (2003). Bipolar disorder in children and adolescents: Diagnosis and treatment. *Current Opinion in Psychiatry, 16,* 383–388.

Wolf, D. V., & Wagner, K. D. (2003). Bipolar disorder in children and adolescents. *CNS Spectrum, 8,* 954–959.

Young, M. E., & Fristad, M. A. (2007). Evidence based treatments for bipolar disorder in children and adolescents. *Journal of Contemporary Psychotherapy, 37,* 157–164.

Chapter 4

American Psychiatric Association (APA). (2000). *Diagnostic and statistical manual of mental disorders* (4th ed., text revision). Washington, DC: Author.

Ballash, N., Leyfer, O., Buckley, A. F., & Woodruff-Borden, J. (2006). Parental control in the etiology of anxiety. *Clinical Child and Family Psychology Review, 9,* 113–133.

Bayer, J. K., Sanson, A. V., & Hemphill, S. A. (2006). Parent influences on early childhood internalizing difficulties. *Journal of Applied Developmental Psychology, 27,* 542–559.

Brinkmeyer, M. Y., & Eyberg, S. M. (2003). Parent-child interaction therapy for oppositional children. In A. E. Kazdin (Ed.), *Evidence-based psychotherapies for children and adolescents* (pp. 204–223). New York: Guilford Press.

Capps, L., Sigman, M., Sena, R., Henker, B., & Whalen, C. (1996). Fear, anxiety and perceived control in children of agoraphobic parents. *Journal of Child Psychology and Psychiatry, 37,* 445–452.

Chao, R. K. (2001). Extending research on the consequences of parenting styles for Chinese Americans and European Americans. *Child Development, 72,* 1832–1843.

Chorpita, B. F., & Barlow, D. H. (1998). The development of anxiety: The role of control in the early environment. *Psychological Bulletin, 124,* 3–21.

Colder, C. R., Lochman, J. E., & Wells, K. C. (2006). The moderating effects of children's fear and activity level on relations between parenting practices and childhood symptomatology. *Journal of Abnormal Child Psychology, 25,* 251–263.

DiBartolo, P. M., & Helt, M. (2007). Theoretical models of affectionate versus affectionless control in anxious families: A critical examination based on observations of parent-child interactions. *Clinical Child and Family Psychology, 10,* 253–274.

Dumas, J. E., LaFreniere, P. J., & Serketich, W. J. (1995). "Balance of power": A transactional analysis of control in mother-child dyads involving socially competent, aggressive and anxious children. *Journal of Abnormal Psychology, 104,* 104–113.

Dwairy, M., Achoui, M., Abouserie, R., & Farah, A. (2006). Parenting styles, individuation, and mental health of Arab adolescents. *Journal of Cross-Cultural Psychology, 37,* 262–272.

Elizabeth, J., King, N., Ollendick, T. H., Gullone, E., Tonge, B., Watson S., et al. (2006). Social anxiety disorder in children and youth: A research update on aetiological factors. *Counselling Psychology Quarterly, 19,* 151–163.

Grolnick W. S., & Slowiaczek, M. L. (1994). Parents' involvement in children's schooling: A multidimensional conceptualization and motivational model. *Child Development, 65,* 237–252.

Harrington, D. M., Block, J. H., & Block, J. (1978). Intolerance of ambiguity in preschool children: Psychometric considerations, behavioral manifestations, and parental correlates. *Developmental Psychology, 14,* 242–256.

Kearney, C. A., Sims, K. E., Pursell, C. R., & Tillotson, C. A. (2003). Separation anxiety disorder in young children: A longitudinal and family analysis. *Journal of Clinical Child and Adolescent Psychology, 32,* 593–598.

Kim, A., & Yeary, J. (2008). Making long-term separations easier for children and families. *Young Children, 63,* 32–36.

Klein, R. (1995). Is panic disorder associated with childhood separation anxiety disorder? *Clinical Neuropharmacology, 18,* S7–S14.

Lauchlan, F. (2003). Responding to chronic non-attendance: A review of intervention approaches. *Educational Psychology in Practice, 19,* 133–149.

Muris, P., & Merckelbach, H. (1998). Perceived parental rearing behaviour and anxiety disorders symptoms in normal children. *Personality and Individual Differences, 25,* 1999–1206.

Pincus, D. B., Eyberg, S. M., & Choate, M. L. (2005). Adapting parent-child interaction therapy for young children with separation anxiety disorder. *Education and Treatment of Children, 28,* 163–181.

Putnam, S. P., Sanson, A.V., & Rothbart, M. K. (2002). Child temperament and parenting. In M. Bornstein (Ed.), *Handbook of parenting: Vol. 1. Children and parenting* (2nd ed., pp. 255–277). Ipswitch, MA: Lawrence Erlbaum Associates.

Randolph, S. M. (1995). African American children in single-mother families. In B. J. Dickerson (Ed.), *African American single mothers: Understanding their lives and families* (pp. 117–145). Thousand Oaks, CA: Sage.

Rubin, K. H., Cheah, C. S., & Fox, N. A. (2001). Emotion regulation, parenting and the display of social reticence in preschoolers. *Early Education and Development, 12,* 97–115.

Steinberg, L., Lamborn, S. D., Dornbusch, S. M., & Darling, N. (1994). Impact of parenting practices on adolescent achievement: Authoritative parenting, school involvement and encouragement to succeed. *Child Development, 63,* 1266–1281.

Turner, S. M., Biedel, D. C., & Epstein, L. H. (1991). Vulnerability and risk for anxiety disorders. *Journal of Anxiety Disorders, 5,* 151–166.

Whaley, S. E., Pinto, A., & Sigman, M. (1999). Characterizing interactions between anxious mothers and their children. *Journal of Consulting and Clinical Psychology, 67,* 826–836.

Wood, J. J. (2006). Parental intrusiveness and children's separation anxiety in a clinical sample. *Child Psychiatry Human Development, 37,* 73–87.

Chapter 5

Andreasen, N. C. (1987). Creativity and mental illness: Prevalence rates in writers and their first-degree relatives. *American Journal of Psychiatry, 144,* 1288–1292.

Brand, A. G. (1989). *The psychology of writing: The affective experience.* New York: Greenwood.

Haselton, M. G., & Miller, G. F. (2006). Women's fertility across the life cycle increases the short-term attractiveness of creative intelligence. *Human Nature, 17,* 50–73.

Jamison, K. R. (1989). Mood disorder and patterns of creativity in British writers and artists. *Psychiatry, 52,* 125–134.

Jamison, K. R. (1993). *Touched with fire*. New York: Simon & Schuster.

McDermott, J. F. (2001). Emily Dickinson revisited: A study of periodicity in her work. *The American Journal of Psychiatry, 158*, 686–690.

Nettle, D. (2006a). The evolution of personality variation in humans and other animals. *American Psychologist, 61*, 622–631.

Nettle, D. (2006b). Schizotypy and mental health amongst poets, artists and mathematicians. *Journal of Research in Personality, 40*, 876–890.

Nettle, D., & Clegg, H. (2006). Schizotypy, creativity and mating success in humans. *Proceedings of the Royal Society of London, Series B: Biological Sciences, 273*, 611–615.

Ramey, C. H., & Weisberg, R. W. (2004). The poetic activity of Emily Dickinson: A further test of the hypothesis that affective disorders foster creativity. *Creativity Research Journal, 16*, 173–185.

Rawlings, D., & Locarnini, A. (2008). Dimensional schizotypy, autism, and unusual word associations in artists and scientists. *Journal of Research in Personality, 42*, 465–471.

Richards, R. L. (1997). Conclusions: When illness yields creativity. In M. Runco & R. Richards, *Eminent creativity, everyday creativity and health* (pp. 485–540). Greenwich, CT: Ablex.

Rybakowski, J., Klonowska, P., Patrza, A., & Jaracz, J. (2006). Psychopathology and creativity. *Psychiatria polska, 40*, 1033–1049.

Santosa, C. M., Strong, C. M., Nowakowska, C., Wang, P. O., Rennicke, C. M., & Ketter, T. A. (2007). Enhanced creativity in bipolar disorder patients: A controlled study. *Journal of Affective Disorders, 100*, 31–39.

Schuldberg, D. (1990). Schizotypal and hypomanic traits, creativity and psychological health. *Creativity Research Journal, 3*, 218–230.

Shapiro, P. J., & Weisberg, R. W. (1991). *Daily affect in creative writers: The relationship between mood and creative process*. Unpublished manuscript.

Strong, C. M., Nowakowska, C., Santosa, C. M., Wang, P. O., Kraemer, H. C., & Ketter, T. A. (2007). Temperament-creativity relationships in mood disorder patients, healthy controls and highly creative individuals. *Journal of Affective Disorders, 100*, 41–48.

Wilson, D. (1992). Evolutionary epidemiology. *Acta Biotheoretica, 47*, 87–90.

Chapter 6

Aman, M. G., Buitelaar, J., De Smedt, G., Wapenaar, R., & Binder, C. (2005). Pharmacotherapy of disruptive behavior and item changes on a standardized rating scale: Pooled analysis of risperidone effects in children with subaverage IQ. *Journal of Child and Adolescent Psychopharmacology, 15*, 220–232.

Aman, M. G., & Langworthy, K. S. (2000). Pharmacotherapy for hyperactivity in children with autism and other pervasive developmental disorders. *Journal of Autism and Developmental Disorders, 30*, 451–459.

Aman, M. G., & Madrid, A. (1999). Atypical antipsychotics in persons with developmental disabilities. *Mental Retardation and Developmental Disabilities Research Reviews, 5*, 253–263.

Carey, B. (2006, June 5). Antipsychotic drug use is climbing, study finds. *The New York Times*. Retrieved October 22, 2009, from http://www.nytimes.com/2006/06/05/health/05cnd-psych.html

Chavez, B., Chavez-Brown, M., & Rey, J. A. (2006). Role of risperidone in children with autism spectrum disorder. *The Annals of Pharmacotherapy, 40*, 909–916.

Cheng-Shannon, J., McGrough, J. J., Pataki, C., & McCracken, J. T. (2004). Second-generation antipsychotic medications in children and adolescents. *Journal of Child and Adolescent Psychopharmacology, 14*, 372–394.

Correll, C. U. (2008). Antipsychotic use in children and adolscents. *Journal of the American Academy of Child and Adolescent Psychiatry, 47*, 9–20.

Curtis, L. H., Masselink, L. E., Ostbye, T., Hutchinson, S., Dans, P. E., Wright, A., et al. (2005). Prevalence of atypical antipsychotic drug use among commercially insured youths in the United States. *Archives of Pediatric Medicine, 159,* 362–366.

Dinca, O., Paul, M., & Spencer, N. J. (2005). Systematic review of randomized controlled trials of atypical antipsychotics and selective serotonin reuptake inhibitors for behavioural problems associated with pervasive developmental disorders. *Journal of Psychopharmocology, 19,* 521–532.

DuBois, D. (2005). Toxicology and overdose of atypical antipsychotics in children: Does newer mean safer? *Current Opinions in Pediatrics, 17,* 227–233.

Fedorowicz, V. J., & Fombonne, E. (2005). Metabolic side effects of antipsychotics in children: A literature review. *Journal of Psychopharmocology, 19,* 533–550.

Hellings, J. A., Zarcone, R. J., Valdovinos, M. G., Reese, R. M., Gaughan, B. A., & Schroeder, S. R. (2005). Risperidone-induced prolactin elevation in a prospective study of children, adolescents, and adults with mental retardation and pervasive developmental disorders. *Journal of Child and Adolescent Psychopharmacology, 15,* 888–892.

Isbister, G. K., Balit, C. R., & Kilham, H. A. (2005). Antipsychotic poisoning in young children: A systematic review. *Drug Safety, 28,* 1029–1044.

Martin, A., Koenig, K., Scahill, L., & Bregman, J. (1999). Open-label quetiapine in the treatment of children and adolescents with autistic disorder. *Journal of Child and Adolescent Psychopharmacology, 9,* 99–107.

Matson, J. L., & Dempsey, T. (2008). Autism spectrum disorders: Pharmacotherapy for challenging behaviors. *Journal of Developmental and Physical Disabilities, 20,* 175–191.

McDougle, C. J., Kem, D. L., & Posey, D. J. (2002). Case series: Use of ziprasidone for maladaptive symptoms in youths with autism. *Journal of the American Academy of Children & Adolescent Psychiatry, 41,* 921–927.

Patel, N. C., Crismon, L., Hoagwood, K., Johnsrud, M. T., Rascati, K. L., Wilson, J. P., et al. (2005). Trends in the use of typical and atypical antipsychotics in children and adolescents. *Journal of the American Academy of Child & Adolescent Psychiatry, 44,* 548–556.

Perry, R., Pataki, C., Munoz-Silva, D. M., Armenteros, J., & Silva, R. R. (1997). Risperidone in children and adolescents with pervasive developmental disorder: Pilot trial and follow-up. *Journal or Child and Adolescent Psychopharmacology, 7,* 167–179.

Potenza, M. N., Holmes, J. P., Kanes, S. J., & McDougle, C. J. (1999). Olanzapine treatment of children, adolescents, and adults with pervasive developmental disorders: An open-label pilot study. *Journal of Clinical Psychopharmacology, 19,* 37–44.

Purdon, S. K., Jones, B. D., & Labelle, A. (1994). Risperidone in the treatment of pervasive developmental disorders: An open-label pilot study. *Canadian Journal of Psychiatry, 39,* 400–405.

Selengut Brooke, N., Wiersgalla, M., & Salzman, C. (2005). Atypical uses of atypical antipsychotics. *The Harvard Review of Psychiatry, 13,* 317–339.

Snyder, R., Turguy, A., Aman, M., Binder, C., Fisman, S., Carroll, A., & The Risperidone Conduct Study Group. (2002). Effects of risperidone on conduct and disruptive behavior disorders in children with subaverage IQs. *Journal of the American Academy of Child & Adolescent Psychiatry, 41,* 1026–1036.

Toren, P., Ratner, S., Laor, N., & Weitzman, A. (2004). Benefit-risk assessment of atypical antipsychotics in the treatment of schizophrenia and comorbid disorders in children and adolescents. *Drug Safety, 27,* 1135–1156.

Zuddas, A., Ledda, M. G., Fratta, A., Muglia, P., & Cianchetti, C. (1996). Clinical effects of clozapine on autistic disorder. *The American Journal of Psychiatry, 153,* 738.

Chapter 7

American Psychiatric Association (APA). (2000). *Diagnostic and statistical manual of mental disorders* (4th ed., text revision). Washington, DC: Author.

Chaplin, R., & Potter, M. (1996). Tardive dyskinesia: Screening and risk disclosure. *Pediatric Bulletin, 20,* 714–716.

Conner, D., Fletcher, K., & Wood, J. (2001). Neuroleptic-related dyskinesias in children and adolescents. *Journal of Clinical Psychiatry, 62,* 967–974.

Cooper, W., Arbogast P., Ding, H., Hickson, G., Fuchs, C., & Ray, W. (2006). Trends in prescribing of antipsychotic medications for US children. *Ambulatory Pediatrics, 6,* 79–83.

Doey, T., Handelman, K., Seabrook, J., & Steele, M. (2007). Survey of atypical antipsychotic prescribing by Canadian child psychiatrists and developmental pediatricians for patients aged under 18 years. *Canadian Journal of Psychiatry, 52,* 363–368.

Gebhardt, S., Hartling, F., Hanke, M., Mittendorf, M., Theisen, F., Wolf-Ostermann, K., et al. (2006). Prevalence of movement disorders in adolescent patients with schizophrenia and in relationship to predominantly atypical antipsychotic treatment. *European Child & Adolescent Psychiatry, 15,* 371–382.

Guy, W. (1976). *ECDEU assessment manual for psychopharmacology* (Rev. ed.). Washington, DC: U.S. Department of Health, Education and Welfare.

Jenson, P., Bhatara, V., & Vitiello, B. (1999). Psychoactive medication prescribing practices for U.S. children: Gaps between research and clinical practice. *Journal of the American Academy of Child and Adolescent Psychiatry, 38,* 557–565.

Kumra, S., Jacobsen, L., Lenane, M., Smith, A., Lee, P., Malanga, C. J., et al. (1998).Case series: Spectrum of neuroleptic-induced movement disorders and extrapyramidal side effects in childhood-onset schizophrenia. *Journal of the American Academy of Child and Adolescent Psychiatry, 37,* 221–227.

Lalonde, P. (2003). Evaluating antipsychotic medications: Predictors of clinical effectiveness. *Canadian Journal of Psychiatry, 48,* 3S–12S.

Malone, R., Maislin, G., Choudhury, M., Gifford, C., & Delaney, M. (2002). Risperidone treatment in children and adolescents with autism: Short- and long-term safety and effectiveness. *Journal of the American Academy of Child and Adolescent Psychiatry, 41,* 140–147.

Margolese, H., Chouinard, G., Kolivakis, T., Beauclair, L., & Miller, R. (2007). Tardive dyskinesia in the era of typical and atypical anti-psychotics. Part 1: Pathophysiology and mechanisms of induction. *Canadian Journal of Psychiatry, 50,* 541–547.

Margolese, H., Chouinard, G., Kolivakis, T., Beauclair, L., Miller, R., & Annable, L. (2007). Tardive dyskinesia in the era of typical and atypical anti-psychotics. Part 2: Incidence and management strategies in patients with schizophrenia. *Canadian Journal of Psychiatry, 50,* 703–714.

Rani, F., Murray, M. L., Byrne, P. J., & Wong, I. C. (2008). Epidemiologic features of antipsychotic prescribing to children and adolescents in primary care in the United Kingdom. *Pediatrics, 121,* 1002–1009.

Rodnitzky, R. (2003). Drug induced movement disorders in children. *Seminars in Pediatric Neurology, 10,* 80–87.

Sachdev, P. (2000). The current status of tardive dyskinesia. *Australian and New Zealand Journal of Psychiatry, 34,* 355–369.

Schachter, D., & Kleinman, I. (2004). Psychiatrists' attitudes about and informed consent practices for antipsychotics and tardive dyskinesia. *Psychiatric Services, 55,* 714–717.

Seeman, P. (2002). Atypical antipsychotics: Mechanism of action. *Canadian Journal of Psychiatry, 47,* 27–39.

Shirzadi, A., & Ghaemi, N. (2006). Side effects of atypical antipsychotics: Extrapyramidal symptoms and the metabolic syndrome. *Harvard Review of Psychiatry, 14,* 152–163.

Silva, R., Matzner, F., Diaz, J., Singh, S., & Dummit, S. (1999). Bipolar disorders in children and adolescents: A guide to diagnosis and treatment. *CNS Drugs, 12,* 437–450.

Vitiello, B., & Jenson, P. (1995). Developmental perspectives in pediatric psychopharmacology. *Psychopharmacology Bulletin, 31,* 75–81.

Chapter 8

American Psychological Association (APA). (2007). *Working group on psychoactive medications for children and adolescents: Psychopharmacological, psychosocial, and combined interventions for childhood disorders; Evidence base, contextual factors, and future directions.* Washington, DC: Author.

Amiri, S., Mohammadi, M. R., Mohammadi, M., Nouroozinejad, G. H., Kahbazi, M., & Akhondzadeh, S. (2008). Modafinil as a treatment for ADHD in children and adolescents: A double-blind randomized clinical trial. *Progress in Neuropsychopharmacology and Biological Psychiatry, 32,* 145–149.

Barton, J. (2005). Atomoxetine: A new pharmacotherapeutic approach in the management of attention deficit/hyperactivity disorder. *Archives of Disease in Childhood, 90,* 26–29.

Biederman, J., Melmed, R. D., Patel, A., McBurnett, K., Konow, J., Lyne, A., et al. (2008). A randomized, double-blind, placebo-controlled study of guanfacine extended release in children and adolescents with attention-deficit/hyperactivity disorder. *Pediatrics, 15,* 476–495.

Biederman, J., & Spencer, T. J. (2008). Psychopharmacological interventions. *Child and Adolescent Psychiatric Clinics of North America, 17,* 439–458.

Carlson, J. S., Kruer, J., Ogg, J. A., Mathiason, J., & Magen, J. (2007). Methylphenidate, atomoxetine, and caffeine: A primer for school psychologists. *Journal of Applied School Psychology, 24,* 127–146.

Findling, R. L., Buckstein, O. G., Melmed, R. D., Lopez, F. A., Sallee, F. R., Arnold, L. E., et al. (2008). A randomized double-blind, placebo controlled, parallel-group study of methylphenidate transdermal system in pediatric patients with attention-deficit/hyperactivity disorder. *Journal of Clinical Psychiatry, 69,* 149–159.

Findling, R. L., McNamara, N. K., Stransbrey, R. J., Maxhimer, R., Periclou, A., Mann, A., et al. (2007). A pilot evaluation of the safety, tolerability, pharmacokinetics, and effectiveness of memantine in pediatric patients with attention-deficit/hyperactivity disorder combined type. *Journal of Child and Adolescent Psychopharmacology, 17,* 19–33.

Kollins, S. H., & March, J. S. (2007). Advances in the pharmacotherapy of attention-deficit/hyperactivity disorder. *Biological Psychiatry, 62,* 951–953.

Lerner, M., & Wigal, T. (2008). Long-term safety of stimulant medications used to treat children with ADHD. *Psychiatric Annals, 38,* 43–51.

Madaan, V., Daughton, J., Lubberstedt, B., Mattai, A., Vaughn, B. S., & Kratochvil, C. J. (2008). Assessing the efficacy of treatments for ADHD: Overview of methodological issues. *CNS Drugs, 22,* 275–290.

Palumbo, D. R., Sallee, F. R., Pelham, W. E., Bukstein, O. G., Daviss, W. B., McDermott, M. P., et al. (2008). Clonidine for attention-deficit/hyperactivity disorder: I. Efficacy and tolerability outcomes. *Journal of the American Academy of Child and Adolescent Psychiatry, 47,* 180–188.

Rappley, M. D. (2005). Attention deficit-hyperactivity disorder. *New England Journal of Medicine, 352,* 165–173.

Silva, R. R., Muniz, R., Pestreich, L., Brams, M., Mao, A. R., Childress, A., et al. (2008). Dexmethylphenidate extended-release capsules in children with attention-deficit/hyperactivity disorder. *Journal of the American Academy of Child and Adolescent Psychiatry, 47,* 199–208.

Tehrani-Doost, M., Moallemi, S., & Shahrivar, Z. (2008). An open-label trial of reboxetine in children and adolescents with attention-deficit/hyperactivity disorder. *Journal of Child and Adolescent Psychopharmacology, 18,* 179–184.

Weber, W., Vanderstoep, A., McCarty, R. L., Weiss, N. S., Biederman, J., & McClellan, J. (2008). Hypericum perforatum (St. John's wort) for attention-deficit/hyperactivity disorder in children and adolescents: A randomized controlled trial. *Journal of the American Medical Association, 299,* 2685–2686.

Wilens, T. E. (2008). *Straight talk about psychiatric medications for kids* (3rd ed.). New York: Guilford Press.

Wilens, T. E., Kratochvil, C., Newcorn, J. H., & Gao, H. (2006). Do children and adolescents with ADHD respond differently to atomoxetine? *Journal of the American Academy of Child and Adolescent Psychiatry, 45,* 149–157.

Chapter 9

American Academy of Child and Adolescent Psychiatry (AACAP). (2001). Prescribing psychoactive medication for children and adolescents. Retrieved October 22, 2009, from http://www.aacap.org/cs/root/policy_statements/prescribing_psychoactive_medication_for_children_and_adolescents

Aras, S., Varol Tas, F., & Unlu, G. (2007). Medication prescribing practices in a child and adolescent psychiatry outpatient clinic. *Child Care, Health and Development, 33,* 482–490.

Bhatara, V. S., Feil, M., Hoagwood, K., Vitiello, B., & Zima, B. (2002). Trends in combined pharmacotherapy with stimulants for children. *Psychiatric Services, 53,* 244.

Breland-Noble, A. M., Elbogen, E. B., Farmer, E. M. Z., Dubs, M. S., Wagner, H. R., & Burns, B. J. (2004). Use of psychotropic medications by youths in therapeutic foster care and group homes. *Psychiatric Services, 55,* 706–708.

Carlson, J. S. (2008). Best practices in assessing the effects of psychotropic medications on student performance. In A. Thomas & J. Grimes (Eds.), *Best practices in school psychology* (pp. 1377–1388). Washington, DC: National Association of School Psychologists.

Connor, D. F., Ozbayrak, K. R., Kusiak, K. A., Caponi, A. B., & Melloni, R. H. (1997). Combined pharmacotherapy in children and adolescents in a residential treatment center. *Journal of the American Academy of Child and Adolescent Psychiatry, 36,* 248–254.

dosReis, S., Zito, J. M., Safer, D. J., Gardner, J. F., Puccia, K. B., & Owens, P. L. (2005). Multiple psychotropic medication use for youths: A two-state comparison. *Journal of Child and Adolescent Psychopharmacology, 15,* 68–77.

Lekhwani, M., Nair, C., Nikhinson, I., & Ambrosini, P. J. (2004). Psychotropic prescription practices in child psychiatric inpatients 9 years old and younger. *Journal of Child and Adolescent Psychopharmacology, 14,* 95–103.

Martin, A., Van Hoof, T., Stubbe, D., Sherwin, T., & Scahill, L. (2003). Multiple psychotropic pharmacotherapy among child and adolescent enrollees in Connecticut Medicaid managed care. *Psychiatric Services, 54,* 72–77.

Najjar, F. N., Welch, C., Grapetine, W. L., Sachs, H., Siniscalchi, J., & Price, L. H. (2004). Trends in psychotropic drug use in a child psychiatric hospital from 1991–1998. *Journal of Child and Adolescent Psychopharmacology, 14,* 87–93.

National Association of State Mental Health Directors (NASMHPD). (2001). NASMHPD medical directors' technical report on psychiatric polypharmacy. Alexandria, VA: Author. Retrieved October 22, 2009, from http://www.nasmhpd.org/general_files/publications/med_directors_pubs/polypharmacy.pdf

Olfson, M., Marcus, S., Weissman, M., & Jensen, P. (2002). National trends in the use of psychotropic medications by children. *Journal of the American Academy of Child and Adolescent Psychiatry, 41*, 514–521.

Preskorn, S. H., & Lacey, R. L. (2007). Polypharmacy: When is it rational? *Journal of Psychiatric Practice, 13*, 97–105.

Pruitt, D. B., & Kiser, L. J. (2004). Psychiatric polypharmacy and children: Examining pediatric multipsychotropic regimens. *Behavioral Health Management, 24*, S1–S4.

Russell, P. S., George, C., & Mammen, P. (2006). Predictive factors for polypharmacy among child and adolescent psychiatry inpatients. *Clinical Practice and Epidemiology in Mental Health, 2*, 25–28.

Safer, D. J., Zito, J. M., & dosReis, S. (2003). Concomitant psychotropic medication for youths. *American Journal of Psychiatry, 160*, 438–449.

Sourander, A. (2004). Combined psychopharmacological treatment among children and adolescent inpatients in Finland. *European Child & Adolescent Psychiatry, 13*, 179–184.

U.S. Department of Health and Human Services (HHS). (1999). *Mental health: A report of the Surgeon General*. Rockville, MD: Author. Retrieved October 22, 2009, from http://www.surgeongeneral.gov/library/mentalhealth/home.html

Zakriski, A. L., Wheeler, E., Burda, J., & Shields, A. (2005). Justifiable psychopharmacology or overzealous prescription? Examining parental reports of lifetime prescription histories of psychiatrically hospitalized children. *Child and Adolescent Mental Health, 10*, 16–22.

Zamvil, L., & Cannon, J. (2002). Polypharmacy in children and adolescents. In S. N. Ghamei (Ed.), *Polypharmacy in psychiatry* (pp. 231–244). New York: Informa Health Care.

Zito, J. M., Safer, D. J., de Jong-van den Berg, L. T. W., Janhsen, K., Fegert, J. M., Gardner, J. F., et al. (2008). A three-country comparison of psychotropic medication prevalence in youth. *Child and Adolescent Psychiatry and Mental Health, 2*, 26–33.

Zito, J. M., Safer, D. J., Sai, D., Gardner, J. F., Thomas, D., Coombes, P., et al. (2008). Psychotropic medication patterns among youth in foster care. *Pediatrics, 121*, e157–e163.

Zonfrillo, M. R., Penn, J. V., & Leonard, H. L. (2005). Pediatric psychotropic polypharmacy. *Psychiatry, 2*, 14–19.

Chapter 10

Amann, R., & Peskar, B. A. (2002). Anti-inflammatory effects of aspirin and sodium salicylate. *European Journal of Pharmacology, 447*, 1–9.

Brown, M. B. (2008). Best practices in designing and developing training programs. In A. Thomas & J. Grimes (Eds.), *Best practices in school psychology V* (pp. 2029–2040). Washington, DC: National Association of School Psychologists.

Brown, R. T., & Sawyer, M. G. (1998). *Medications for school-age children: Effects on learning and behavior*. New York: Guilford Press.

Celano, M. P., & Geller, R. J. (1993). Learning, school performance, and children with asthma: How much at risk? *Journal of Learning Disabilities, 26*, 23–32.

Charles, J., Pan, Y., & Britt, H. (2004). Trends in childhood illness and treatment in Australian general practice, 1971–2001. *The Medical Journal of Australia, 180*(5), 216–219.

Conner, D. F., & Meltzer, B. M. (2006). *Pediatric psychopharmacology: Fast facts*. New York: W. W. Norton.

Consumer Healthcare Products Association. (2007). *Testimony before the Food and Drug Administration*. Washington, DC: American Association of Poison Control Centers.

Drotar, D. (2006). *Psychological interventions in childhood chronic illness.* Washington, DC: American Psychological Association.

DuPaul, G. J., Coniglio, J. M., & Nebrig, M. R. (2004). Pharmacological approaches. In R. T. Brown (Ed.), *Handbook of pediatric psychology in the schools* (pp. 579–598). Mahwah, NJ: Lawrence Erlbaum Associates.

Eick, A. P., Blumer, J. L., & Reed, M. D. (2001). Safety of antihistamines in children. *Drug Safety, 24,* 119–147.

Eiland, L. S. (2007). Anticonvulsant use for prophylaxis of the pediatric migraine. *Journal of Pediatric Healthcare, 21,* 392–395.

Eiland, L. S., Jenkins, L. S., & Durham, S. H. (2007). Pediatric migraine: Pharmacological agents for prophylaxis. *Annals of Pharmacotherapy, 41,* 1181–1190.

Geist, R., Grdisa, V., & Otley, A. (2003). Psychosocial issues in the child with chronic conditions. *Best Practice & Research in Clinical Gastroenterology, 17,* 141–152.

Kratochwill, T. R., Cowell, E., Feeney, K., & Sannetti, L. H. (2004). Behavioral approaches to intervention in educational settings. In R. T. Brown (Ed.), *Handbook of pediatric psychology in the schools* (pp. 551–554). Mahwah, NJ: Lawrence Erlbaum Associates.

Loring, D. W., & Meador, K. J. (2004). Cognitive side effects of antiepileptic drugs in children. *Neurology, 62,* 872–877.

Martin, A., Scahill, L., Charney, D. S., & Leckman, J. F. (2003). *Pediatric psychopharmacology: Principles and practice.* New York: Oxford University Press.

Murray, S., & Brewerton, T. (1993). Abuse of over-the-counter dextromethorphan by teenagers. *Southern Medical Journal, 86,* 1151–1153.

Naude, H., & Pretorius, E. (2003). Investigating the effects of asthma medication on the cognitive and psychosocial functioning of primary school children with asthma. *Early Child Development and Care, 173,* 699–709.

Newacheck, P.W., & Halfon, N. (1998). Prevalence and impact of disabling chronic conditions in childhood. *American Journal of Public Health, 88,* 610–617.

PDR concise drug guide for pediatrics (2nd ed.). (2008). New York: Thompson Healthcare.

Shiu, S. (2001). Issues in the education of students with chronic illness. *International Journal of Disability, Development and Education, 48,* 269–281.

Spirito, A., & Kazak, A. E. (2006). *Effective and emerging treatments in pediatric psychology.* New York: Oxford University Press.

Theis, K. M. (1999). Identifying the educational implications of chronic illness in school children. *Journal of School Health, 69,* 392–397.

Thompson, R. J., & Gustafson, K. E. (1996). *Adaptation to chronic childhood illness.* Washington, DC: American Psychological Association Press.

Woo, T. (2008). Pharmacology of cough and cold medicines. *Journal of Pediatric Health Care, 22*(2), 73–79.

Chapter 11

Cade, R., Privette, M., Fregly, M., Rowland, N., Sun, Z., Zele, V., et al. (1999). Autism and schizophrenia: Intestinal disorders. *Nutritional Neuroscience 2,* 57–72.

DePinna, C., & McCabe, P. C. (2008). Food allergies and autism: The gluten-free/casein-free hypothesis. *Communiqué, 36,* 10–11.

Elder, J., Shankar, M., Shuster, J., Theriaque, D., Burns, S., & Sherrill, L. (2006). The gluten-free, casein-free diet in autism: Results of a preliminary double blind clinical trial. *Journal of Autism and Developmental Disorders, 36,* 413–420.

Gidding, S., Dennison, B., Birch, L., Daniels, S., Gilman, M., Lichtenstein, A., et al. (2006). Dietary recommendations for children and adolescents: A guide for practitioners. *Pediatrics, 117*(2), 544–559.

Klaveness, J., & Bigam, J. (2002). GFCF kids diet survey. In *13th International Durham Conference on Autism: Building bridges* (pp. 77–84). Sunderland, England: Autism Research Unit, University of Sunderland & Autism North.

Knivsberg, A. M., Reichelt, K. L., Hoien, T., & Nodland, M. (2002). A randomized, controlled study of dietary intervention in autistic syndromes. *Nutritional Neuroscience, 5,* 251–261.

Knivsberg, A. M., Reichelt, K. L., Nodland, M., & Hoien, T. (1995). Autistic syndromes and diet: A follow-up study. *Scandinavian Journal of Educational Research, 39,* 223–236.

Knivsberg, A. M., Wiig, K., Lind, G., Nodland, M., & Reichelt, K. L. (1990). Dietary intervention in autistic syndromes. *Brain Dysfunction, 3,* 315–327.

McCabe, P. C., & DePinna, C. (2008). The exigency of immediateness: Reconciling the lack of empirically validated intervention when immediate action is sought. *Communiqué, 36,* 5.

Reichelt, K. L., Ekrem, J., & Scott, H. (1990). Gluten, milk proteins and autism: Dietary intervention effects on behavior and peptide secretion. *Journal of Applied Nutrition, 42,* 1, 1–11.

Reichelt, K. L., Sælid, G., Lindback, T., & Boler, J. B. (1986). Childhood autism: A complex disorder. *Biological Psychiatry, 21,* 1279–1290.

Rimland, B. (2000). Parent ratings of behavioral effects of drugs, nutrients, and diets. *Autism Research Review International, 14,* 4.

Seung, H., Rogalski, Y., Shankar, M., & Elder, J. (2007). The gluten- and casein-free diet and autism: Communication outcomes from a preliminary double-blind clinical trial. *Journal of Medical Speech Language Pathology, 15,* 337–345.

Shattock, R. (1995). Can dietary intervention be used successfully as a therapy in autism? In *6th International Durham Conference on Autism: Psychological perspectives in autism* (pp. 203–208). Sunderland, England: Autism Research Unit, University of Sunderland.

Shattock, P., & Whiteley, P. (2002). Biochemical aspects in autism spectrum disorders: Updating the opioid-excess theory and presenting new opportunities for biomedical intervention. *Expert Opinion on Therapeutic Targets, 6,* 175–183.

Sun, Z., & Cade, J. R. (1999). A peptide found in schizophrenia and autism causes behavioral changes in rats. *Autism, 3,* 85–95.

Sun, Z., Cade, J. R., Fregly, M. J., & Privette, R. M. (1999). β-Casomorphin induces Fos-like immunoreactivity in discrete brain regions relevant to schizophrenia and autism. *Autism, 3,* 67–83.

Wakefield, A. J., Puleston, J. M., Montgomerty, S. M., Anothonly, A., O'Leary, J. J., & Murch, S. H. (2002). Review article: The concept of entero-colonic encephalopathy, autism and opioid receptor ligands. *Alimentary Pharmacology and Therapeutics, 16,* 663–674.

Whiteley, P., Rodgers, J., Savery, D., & Shattock, P. (1999). A gluten-free diet as an intervention for autism and associated spectrum disorders: Preliminary findings. *Autism, 3,* 45–65.

Chapter 12

American Academy of Pediatrics (AAP). (2003). Identifying and treating eating disorders: Policy statement by the Committee on Adolescence. *Pediatrics, 111,* 204–211.

American Psychiatric Association (APA). (2000). *The diagnostic and statistical manual of mental disorders* (4th ed., text revision). Washington, DC: Author.

American Psychiatric Association (APA) Work Group on Eating Disorders. (2000). Practice guideline for the treatment of patients with eating disorders (revision). *American Journal of Psychiatry, 157,* 1–39.

Becker, A. E., Burwell, R. A., Gilman, S. E., Herzog, D. B., & Hamburg, P. (2002). Eating behaviors and attitudes following prolonged exposure to television among ethnic Fijian adolescent girls. *British Journal of Psychiatry, 180,* 509–514.

Ben-Tovim, D. I. (2003). Eating disorders: Outcome, prevention and treatment of eating disorders. *Current Opinion in Psychiatry, 16,* 65–69.

Cook-Cottone, C. P. (2009). The neuropsychology of eating disorders in women. In E. Fletcher-Janzen (Ed.), *Neuropsychology of women* (175–207). New York: Springer.

Cook-Cottone, C. P., Kane, L., Scime, M., & Beck, M. (2004). *Group prevention and treatment of eating disorders: A constructivist integration of mind and body strategies.* Paper presented at the annual meeting of the New York Association for Specialists in Group Work, Buffalo, NY.

Cook-Cottone, C. P., & Phelps, L. (2006). Adolescent eating disorders. In G. G. Bear & K. M. Minke (Eds.), *Children's Needs III* (pp. 977–988). Bethesda, MD: NASP.

Duchesne, M., Mattos, P., Fontenelle, L., Veiga, H., Rizo, L., & Appolinario, J. C. (2004). Neuropsychology of eating disorders: A systematic review of the literature. *Review of Brazilian Psychiatry, 26,* 107–117.

Herzog, D. B., & Eddy, K. T. (2007). Diagnosis, epidemiology, and clinical course of eating disorders. In J. Yager & P. S. Powers (Eds.), *Clinical manual of eating disorders* (pp. 1–29). Washington, DC: American Psychiatric Association.

Hoek, H. W., & van Hoeken, D. (2003). Review of the prevalence and incidence of eating disorders. *International Journal of Eating Disorders, 24,* 383–396.

Jacobi, C., Paul, T., deZwaan, M., Nutzinger, D. O., & Dahme, B. (2004). Specificity of self-concept disturbances in eating disorders. *International Journal of Eating Disorders, 35,* 204–210.

Manley, R. S., Rickson, H., & Standeven, B. (2000). Children and adolescents with eating disorders: Strategies for teachers and school counselors. *Intervention in School & Clinic, 35,* 228–231.

Myers, T. C., Wonderlich, S., Norton, M., & Crosby, R. D. (2004). An integrative cognitive therapy approach to the treatment of multi-impulsive bulimia nervosa. In J. L. Levitt, R. A. Sansone, & L. Cohn (Eds.), *Self-harm behavior and eating disorders* (pp. 163–174). New York: Brunner-Routledge.

National Joint Committee on Learning Disabilities. (2005). *Responsiveness to intervention and learning disabilities.* Author.

Patel, D. P., Greydanus, D. E., Pratt, H. D., & Phillips, E. L. (2003). Eating disorders in adolescent athletes. *Journal of Adolescent Research, 18,* 280–296.

Pearson, J., Goldklang, D., & Striegel-Moore, R. H. (2002). Prevention of eating disorders: Challenges and opportunities. *International Journal of Eating Disorder, 31,* 233–239.

Piran, N. (2001). The body logic program: Discussions and reflections. *Cognitive and Behavioral Practice, 8,* 259–264.

Smolak, L., Harris, B., Levine, M. P., & Shisslak, C. M. (2001). Teachers: The forgotten influence on the success of prevention programs. *Eating Disorders: The Journal of Treatment & Prevention, 9,* 261–265.

Steiger, H., & Bruce, K. R. (2007). Phenotypes, endophenotypes, and genotypes in bulimia spectrum eating disorders. *La revue canadienne de psyciatrie, 52,* 220–227.

Steinhausen, H. C. (2002). The outcome of anorexia nervosa in the 20th century. *American Journal of Psychiatry, 159,* 1284–1293.

Tchanturia, K., Campbell, I. C., Morris, R., & Treasure, J. (2005). Neuropsychological studies in anorexia nervosa. *International Journal of Eating Disorders, 37,* S72–S76.

Thelen, M. H., Powell, A. L., Lawrence, C., & Kuhnert, M. E. (1992). Eating and body image concern among children. *Journal of Clinical Child & Adolescent Psychology, 21,* 41–46.

Thomas, K., Ricciardelli, L. A., & Williams, R. J. (2000). Gender traits and self-concept as indicators of problem eating and body dissatisfaction among children. *Sex Roles, 43,* 441–458.

Wisniewski, L., & Kelly, E. (2003). The application of dialectic behavior therapy to the treatment of eating disorders. *Cognitive and Behavioral Practice, 10,* 131–138.

Wonderlich, S. A., Crosby, R. D., Mitchell, J. E., Roberts, J. A., Haseltine, B., DeMuth, G., et al. (2000). Relationship of childhood sexual abuse and eating disturbance in children. *Journal of the American Academy of Child & Adolescent Psychiatry, 39,* 1277–1283.

Chapter 13

Bahrke, M. S., Yesalis, C. E., Kopstein, A. N., & Stephen, J. A. (2000). Risk factors associated with anabolic-androgenic steroid use among adolescents. *Sports Medicine, 29,* 395–405.

Bell, A., Dorsch, K. D., McCreary, D. R., & Hovey, R. (2004). A look at nutritional supplement use in adolescents. *Journal of Adolescent Health, 34,* 508–516.

Benson, E. (2002). More male than male. *APA Monitor, 33,* 49–52.

Brower, K. J. (1992). Clinical assessment and treatment of anabolic steroid users. *Psychiatric Annals, 22,* 35–40.

Cohane, G. H., & Pope, H. G. (2001). Body image in boys: A review of the literature. *International Journal Eating Disorders, 29,* 373–379.

Denham, B. E. (2006). Effects of mass communication on attitudes toward anabolic steroids: An analysis of high school seniors. *Journal of Drug Issues, 36,* 809–829.

Durant, R. H., & Escobedo, L. G. (1995). Anabolic-steroid use, strength training, and multiple drug use among adolescents in the United States. *Pediatrics, 96,* 23–28.

Durant, R. H., Rickert, V. I., Ashworth, C. S., Newman, C., & Slavens, G. (1993). Use of multiple drugs among adolescents who use anabolic steroids. *New England Journal of Medicine, 13,* 922–926.

Field, A. E., Austin, S. B., Camargo, C. A., Jr., Taylor, C. B., Striegel-Moore, R. H., Loud, K. J., et al. (2005). Exposure to the mass media, body shape concerns, and use of supplements to improve weight and shape among male and female adolescents. *Pediatrics, 116,* 214–220.

Gober, S., Klein, M., & McCabe, P. (2009). *A tripartite model to explain adolescent steroid use: A guide for assessment and intervention.* Unpublished manuscript.

Gonzalez, A., McLachlan, S., & Keaney, F. (2001). Anabolic steroid misuse: How much should we know? *International Journal of Psychiatry in Clinical Practice, 5,* 159–167.

Johnson, M. D. (1990). Anabolic steroid use in adolescent athletes. *Pediatric Clinics of North America, 37,* 1111–1123.

Johnston, L. D., O'Malley, P. M., Bachman, J. G., & Schulenberg, J. E. (2009). *Monitoring the Future national survey results on drug use, 1975–2008: Volume I. Secondary school students* (NIH Publication No. 09-7402). Bethesda, MD: National Institute on Drug Abuse. Retrieved October 22, 2009, from http://www.monitoringthefuture.org/pubs/monographs/vol1_2008.pdf

Middleman, A. B., Faulkner, A. H., & Anne, H. (1995). High-risk behaviors among high school students in Massachusetts who use anabolic steroids. *Pediatrics, 96,* 268–272.

Millman, B., & Ross, E. (2003). Steroid and nutritional supplement use in professional athletes. *American Journal on Additions, 12,* 48–54.

National Institute on Drug Abuse (NIDA). (2000). *Anabolic steroid abuse* (NIH Pub. No. 00-3721). Retrieved October 22, 2009, from http://www.drugabuse.gov/pdf/rrsteroi.pdf

National Institute on Drug Abuse (NIDA). (2009). *NIDA InfoFacts: Steroids (anabolic-androgenic).* Retrieved October 22, 2009, from http://www.nida.nih.gov/PDF/Infofacts/Steroids09.pdf

Nilsson, S., Allebeck, P., Marklund, B., Baigi, A. & Fridlund, B. (2004). Evaluation of a health promotion programme to prevent the misuse of androgenic anabolic steroids among Swedish adolescents. *Health Promotion International, 19,* 61–67.

Ricciardelli, L. A., & McCabe, M. P. (2003). Sociocultural and individual influences on muscle gain and weight loss strategies among adolescent boys and girls. *Psychology in the Schools, 40,* 209–224.

Sharma, M. (2005). Anabolic steroids and other performance enhancing drugs. [Review of the book *Anabolic steroids and other performance enhancing drugs* by P. L. London]. *Journal of Alcohol and Drug Education, 49,* 89–90.

Stout, E. J., & Frame, M. W. (2004). Body image disorder in adolescent males: Strategies for school counselors. *Professional School Counseling, 8,* 176–181.

Trenton, A. J., & Currier, G. W. (2005). Behavioural manifestations of anabolic steroid use. *CNS Drugs, 19,* 571–595.

Volkow, N. D. (2005, March 17). *Consequences of the abuse of anabolic steroids—Before the Committee on Government Reform—United States House of Representatives. National Institute on Drug Abuse.* Retrieved October 22, 2009, from http://www.nida.nih.gov/Testimony/3–17–05Testimony.html

Index

CORWIN

A SAGE Company

The Corwin logo—a raven striding across an open book—represents the union of courage and learning. Corwin is committed to improving education for all learners by publishing books and other professional development resources for those serving the field of PreK–12 education. By providing practical, hands-on materials, Corwin continues to carry out the promise of its motto: **"Helping Educators Do Their Work Better."**

**NATIONAL
ASSOCIATION OF
SCHOOL
PSYCHOLOGISTS**

The National Association of School Psychologists represents school psychology and supports school psychologists to enhance the learning and mental health of all children and youth.